ACADEMIA LUNARE
Call For Papers 2020

Worlds Apart
Worldbuilding in Fantasy and Science Fiction

Edited By
Francesca T Barbini

Editor Introduction © Francesca T Barbini 2021
Articles © is with each individual author 2021
Cover Design © Francesca T Barbini 2021
Cover Image "Winter Landscape" Keisai Eisen, Japan, Edo period (1615–1868)

First published by Luna Press Publishing, Edinburgh, 2021

Worlds Apart. Worldbuilding in Fantasy and Science Fiction © 2021. All rights reserved. No part of this publication may be reproduced, stored in a retrieval system, or transmitted in any form or by any means, electronic, mechanical, photocopy, recording or otherwise, without prior written permission of the copyright owners. Nor can it be circulated in any form of binding or cover other than that in which it is published and without similar condition including this condition being imposed on a subsequent purchaser.

www.lunapresspublishing.com

ISBN-13: 978-1-913387-74-7

Academia Lunare CfPs Series

Gender Identity and Sexuality in Fantasy and Science Fiction (2017)
Winner of the British Fantasy Society Awards
1 Article Shortlisted for the BSFA Awards
2 Article Nominated for the BSFA Awards

The Evolution of African Fantasy and Science Fiction (2018)
Shortlisted for the British Fantasy Society Awards
2 Article Nominated for the BSFA Awards

A Shadow Within: Evil in Fantasy and Science Fiction (2019)
Nominated for the BSFA Awards

Ties that Bind: Love in Fantasy and Science Fiction (2020)
Shortlisted for the BSFA Awards

Contents

Introduction
Francesca T Barbini vi

No elf is an island. Understanding worldbuilding through system thinking
Ricardo Victoria-Uribe and *Martha Elba González-Alcaraz* 1

Fragmented Worlds: Glimpse Morsels for the Imagination
Allen Stroud 19

Relationships with the Land in Fantasy and Science Fiction: Landscape as Identity, Mentor, or Antagonist
Sarah McPherson 41

Freedom Is Slavery: The sociopolitical implications of worldbuilding in speculative fiction
Sébastien Doubinsky 59

Worldbuilding with Sex and Gender
Cheryl Morgan 74

Town Planning in Viriconium: M John Harrison and Worldbuilding
Peter Garrett 89

Worldbuilding in Ngũgĩ wa Thiong'o's *The Perfect Nine: The Epic of Gĩkũyũ and Mũmbi*
Eugen Bacon 114

Environmental Change as Catalyst for Worldbuilding in Ursula K. Le Guin's *Always Coming Home*
Octavia Cade — 127

Tolkien: When worlds are built within dreams
Enrico Spadaro — 142

Patrick McGrath's Ghastly New York: The Perfect Decaying Cityscape for Restless Minds
Tatiana Fajardo — 163

The Book of Copper and the Anvil of Death: William Blake's Gothic Creation Myth
Claire Burgess — 183

Canada's Fantasy Worlds: Exploring Worldbuilding in Urban Fantasy
Ellen Forget — 208

Above the Level of the Everyday: The Estranging and Familiar Worlds of Simon Stålenhag
Kevin Cooney — 226

The Nordic Countries in Worldbuilding: *Frozen* and *Frozen II*
Jyrki Korpua — 237

Criminal Cityscapes: Christopher Nolan's Gotham
Rachel Jones — 254

Contributors by Paper — 276

Introduction

What do we mean by worldbuilding?

A world is more than just a scenic backdrop; it's more than a map. A world is made up of land, weather systems and cityscapes, flora and fauna, the people who inhabit it and all that comes with them: politics, culture, art, belief systems, etc. Characters' actions are a response to the world that has been built for them, a world that changes around, with, and because of them.

With or without rules, opposite to the known world or uncanny to it, a secondary world is where we stand while reading the story. We contribute, as readers, to its creation, by filling in the blanks and adding our own interpretations of it. Interestingly, the concept of the 'uncanny', the 'familiar become strange', seems to have made an appearance in the majority of these papers. While the call was out, we produced two hybrid books of essays and short stories on this: *Uncanny Bodies* (Goldschmidt, et al., 2020) and *The Flicker Against the Light and Writing the Contemporary Uncanny* (Alexander, 2021). It seems that, as a concept, the uncanny continues to be present in our collective consciousness, confirming perhaps its reality and validity in human perception.

The fifteen papers in this year's edition are, as always with this series, varied, as we invited authors to tackle the topic from different angles to create an array of paths for leading the reader to the focussed theme. I have divided the papers into three sections. The first one deals with the more technical aspects of worldbuilding, from methodology (Victoria-Uribe and González-Alcarez; Stroud), to the use of broader themes such as land and politics (McPherson; Doubinsky), and finishing with fresh approaches to worldbuilding through the eyes of Nature (Morgan).

In the second section, we take a closer look at specific authors, their methodology, and the issues raised by their works: M. John Harrison (Garrett), Ngũgĩ wa Thiong'o (Bacon), Ursula K. Le Guin (Cade), J.R.R. Tolkien (Spadaro), Patrick McGrath (Domench-Fajardo), and William Blake (Burgess). Concluding this section is a paper on how the real world can inform worldbuilding, using works belonging to a specific sub-genre—urban fantasy—and location—Canada (Forget).

Finally, we further expand on the topic by crossing into different mediums: the art of Simon Stålenhag (Cooney), the Nordic countries as represented in the *Frozen* franchise (Korpua), and the criminal cityscapes of Christopher Nolan's iteration of Gotham (Jones).

Francesca T Barbini

No elf is an island. Understanding worldbuilding through system thinking

Ricardo Victoria-Uribe
and
Martha Elba González-Alcaraz

Abstract

Worldbuilding, the act of creating a world for fictional characters to live in and narratives to take place, comes as the result of interconnecting a series of elements – such as food, weather, history, geography, folklore, and even fashion. This helps to inform the reader through subtle cues and detailed explanations of the kind of world where the story, the characters, and the setting exist, while also providing a sense of tangibility. When done properly, worldbuilding can elicit on the audience an attachment to the work in question, generating discussions about how those elements play into the narrative created by the author(s) of a given work. It can be argued that this is because worldbuilding is reminiscent of our reality, in the sense that several interconnected elements and subsystems form the structure of the world surrounding us. System thinking, a discipline born from biology and mathematics, allows us to identify and understand the patterns that conform to our world, in order to find solutions to complex problems or situations. It also helps us to understand how the context of a given situation, might affect its outcome.

Thus, system thinking can be a powerful tool to examine existing works of science fiction and fantasy (SFF) as well as to develop the skills needed by an author to create an engaging, coherent work of fiction. This paper aims to explain what system thinking is and how it can be used to gain a better understanding of worldbuilding as an activity, both as a reader or as a creator of an SFF work.

Introduction

Science Fiction and Fantasy (SFF) narratives, by nature, seek to tell stories within worlds that feel expansive (Phillips, 2019), not unlike our complex history within planet Earth, where hundreds of cultures intermingle, creating traditions, folklore, economies, familiar relationships and so on, that feed into each other, evolve and change with time. A prime example of this is the work of J. R. R. Tolkien (Phillips, 2019), who created a world with a level of detail rarely seen before the publication of his novels. The level of detail is such, that the languages he created for the inhabitants of Middle-earth can be studied as if they had been spoken by real people. This, coupled with the myths, and the passing references to historical events within the story he is telling, give the reader a sense that they are part of something larger (Phillips, 2019), of an actual, tangible world, part of a system, such as the ones that surround us.

It could be argued that a narrative – be it a short story, a novel, or a whole series – is a system, a conjunction of interconnected elements arranged to achieve a purpose. The elements are the characters, the setting, the individual plot arcs, the backstory, the overall plot, the underlying message, and even the MacGuffin[1] that allow the plot to move forward. The interconnections are laid upon the story as it progresses, some pay off and some do not. A narrative can have different purposes: convey a message about a specific topic, showcase the progression of a determined character under a particular plotline, or simply offer the audience a good time.

Story arcs can be structured like systems, beyond the

---

[1]. McGuffin, a term coined first by Alfred Hitchcock, is an object, event, or character whose purpose in a narrative is to keep the plot in motion, regardless of its ultimate importance (Merriam-Webster, n.d.).

elements that participate in them. In this regard, Dan Harmon's circle theory can be used to explain how this system works. Dan Harmon, the creator of *Community* and *Rick and Morty*, codified the storytelling process to plot his stories, do the worldbuilding for them and even plan the gags that would pay off episodes or even seasons later. Said code or scheme consists of eight steps (Raferty, 2011):

1. A character is in a zone of comfort
2. But they want something
3. They enter an unfamiliar situation
4. Adapt to it
5. Get what they wanted
6. Pay a heavy price for it
7. Then return to their familiar situation
8. Having changed

Under this scheme, it is possible to understand how a story becomes a system unto itself, yielding a result and where each step is an element of said system. While the plot in itself is interesting as the hook that attracts the audience, the fictional world where the narrative takes place can become more attractive (Phillips, 2019). This can be said of pretty much every story that has become a staple of current pop culture, from the Wizarding World of *Harry Potter* to the Far Far Away Galaxy of Star Wars, passing by the Alpha Quadrant of *Star Trek*, or paying a visit Westeros from *A Song of Ice and Fire*, and so on. The stories are engaging, but it is the world that seals the deal. That is the main objective of properly done worldbuilding: to offer a solid place for escapism within the minds of the audience, where they can be transported to live their own adventures and enjoy themselves.

Despite its importance in making a narrative attractive to the audience, worldbuilding has been often derided as unnecessary or cumbersome, given that it is usually presented in info dumps that slow the pacing of the narrative or lack internal coherence. However, when the worldbuilding is well done and intertwined in the narrative through subtle hints, comments, and observations by the characters themselves, or through descriptions of the world from their point of view, then it becomes engaging. Thus, instead of seeing the worldbuilding as a haphazard collection of elements that are thrown together randomly to differentiate the setting from the real world to provide the characters with a stage on which to carry out the narrative, worldbuilding should be seen as a series of interconnected, nested systems, not unlike our world.

Using system thinking on worldbuilding generates three main characteristics to understand it:

- Everything has a source
- Everything has an impact
- Everything exists next to something else

In the following sections, it will be explained what is a system, what is system thinking, and how it applies to worldbuilding, in order to provide a different perspective to analyze it and perhaps use it as a new approach or methodology to create a successful world in SFF stories.

What is system thinking, and how does it help to understand worldbuilding?

New perspectives to understand reality are needed as the real world keeps changing at a fast pace, and the elements that compose it become more and more complicated. This is where system thinking enters. But first, it is necessary to explain what a system is.

A system can be defined as a set of elements – be it living beings, cells, geographical aspects, steps of an industrial process – that are interconnected among them in a way that generates patterns of behavior as the time goes (Meadows, 2009). More importantly, any system must accomplish something or have a purpose. In this regard, for a conjunction of elements to be a system, it has to be confirmed by three things: elements, interconnections between said elements, and a purpose, product or function (Meadows, 2009).

A system can be as simple as a cup of coffee, or the water pipes of a house, or as complex as the weather, or a multiple-book spanning saga. A narrative can have as many moving parts as the author desires. System thinking is used to better understand and analyze these systems, and how they can be delimited, activated, or driven by internal or external forces, how they behave, etc.

System thinking is a way to understand and analyze how systems work. But it does not focus on the system itself as a unit to be observed. Rather, it focuses on the interconnections between the diverse elements that conform it, and the feedback loops that coexist inside said connections. In a simpler analogy, it is seeing the forest and the tree at the same time, by focusing on how each tree relates to the others, to the animals living inside said forest and to external forces, such as fires. Or in more storytelling terms, how the different Avengers members interact with each other, and how their individual stories join into a wider narrative with an Endgame in mind.

System thinking identifies patterns to study why a system yields a particular result. System thinking helps to recognize the circular nature of the world we live in (Goodman, 1997). And, since an author writes about what they know, more often than not, stories tend to reflect the patterns and the circular nature of their world. This is particularly more notorious in SFF narratives, where the setting in which the story takes place is often as complex – sometimes, even more than – as the plot itself. And, as it can be seen in the sections below, both authors and audience tend to think in systems when it comes to their stories, whether they notice it or not, since identifying patterns is a natural tendency of the human mind. This applies in particular to the process of worldbuilding.

Interconnected systems within SFF as the backbone for a narrative – Organic growth Vs. fanservice

Worldbuilding, which can be defined as "the process of constructing an imaginary world, sometimes associated with a whole fictional universe" (Hamilton, 2009), is a staple of the SFF genres. It could be argued that it is one of its main attractions, at times overshadowing the story itself and becoming the reason of why a particular narrative can resonate with its audience. While there are many guides to explain how to do worldbuilding – which is not the purpose of this paper – all come to the same purpose, which is to create a coherent setting with geography, weather, an ecology, a history, laws, customs, folklore, legends, religions, and even rules for physics and magic. All come to the same point: these settings are systems. When a specific setting is well planned, or at least has been given consideration for the internal coherence of the interplay between its different elements, the world resonates with the reader, who is even capable of finding connections that the author might not be aware of – at least consciously.

When it doesn't, the lack of coherence becomes a plot hole that could affect the story itself. For example: in a setting where magic and technology co-exist – as is the case of the Marvel Cinematic Universe, anime such as *Full Metal Alchemist*, or videogames such as *Final Fantasy VI* or *VII* – the existence of magic has an impact on the development of technology. Magic becomes a power source or a competing paradigm. It could be quantified and studied. Or at least acknowledged by the wider public within that world or by the secret cabals that work to keep it hidden from the rest of the world. An example of worldbuilding that failed is the *Divergent* series, where the setting is so dependent on the people being divided in specific traits, that the story is unable to hold itself with the plot twists that come along, leaving many disappointed fans in the end.

Civilizations are often influenced by the geography of their location, such as Egypt with the Nile, which became a deity, or a representation of one of them, or the North in Westeros, where the culture is defined by the cruel winters in the region. Notice how the Northmen see as a sacred duty the 'guest rights'[2] and breaking them is akin to Kinslaying. In a region where winters are harsh and crops are scarce, survival often comes from forming communities to share resources and might have started during or after the Long Night[3]. Guest rights then becomes a result of ecology, weather, history, myth, and even the economy.

Now, here is the main dilemma when it comes to worldbuilding. By nature, a setting from a fictional story is an artificial construct, created by the designs of the ultimate deity

---

2. 'Guest right' is a law of hospitality. When a guest eats and drinks off a host's table, it is invoked, and when that happens neither guest nor host can harm the other.

3. The Long Night is a period of darknesswhich fell across Westeros, lasting for years and bringing famine and terror.

of that world: the author. As an external observer, the author can go back and forth in time, adding and subtracting elements to the system – that is, the world where their story takes place –, and alter how said elements interact and give feedback loops to each other. A story can be constructed linearly or through seemingly random spurs. That's possible because the author is outside the world. In real life, this is not possible. Living beings exist within the world. Thus, the worldbuilding of our reality grows organically, and while new narratives can be created to explain events from the past, regardless of how factual they are – think conspiracy theories or revisionist history –, the events in the past, from wars to a simple rain, take place and can't be removed. In that regard, an author has the advantage of being able to alter the worldbuilding of their setting to better fit the plot they are seeking to narrate.

However, doing so without consideration of how each element of the system affects the others, has a major impact on the story. When the worldbuilding feels organic, the payoff from little details can be meaningful making complete sense in the mind of the audience. However, when the author adds details upon details without reason, or to justify post facto things that were left out or are inconsequential to the larger plot, they feel like add-ons, patches to the story, in detriment to its organic growth, as has happened to the Wizarding World by J.K. Rowling in recent years. Then the worldbuilding doesn't work in conjunction with the story, but rather becomes fan service and can collapse the system, making the plot holes in the original story more evident.

This is not to say that authors should have everything plotted from day one when it comes to worldbuilding. Rather, that they should be mindful of how each new element is introduced into their setting, be it through the main story or side narratives, and it has to have an impact, as consequences into the larger tales being told. That way, the story feels organic and more immersive. This requires awareness by the author and is where understanding the basics of system thinking can help to see the wider picture while focusing on the details and their interconnections. Thus, system thinking can be used as an alternative approach to worldbuilding, one that helps authors to create worlds organically and with internal coherence, while helping avid members of the audience to have a better understanding of the narrative they are following.

In the following sections, it will be discussed which is the most notorious system and how it works for a particular narrative, in order to provide the reader with an insight of how system thinking has shaped the worlds where said stories take place and how they can be studied for a better experience, either as the author or as the audience. These sections will be structured as proposed in the introduction of this paper.

Everything has a source: the case of the MCU and the value of interconnected little details to world build

""I am Iron Man". You think you're the only superhero in the world? Mr. Stark, you've become part of a bigger universe, you just don't know it yet."
Nick Fury. (Iron Man, 2008)

With this phrase, Nick Fury (portrayed by Samuel L. Jackson) welcomes both Tony Stark (portrayed by Robert Downey Jr.) and the audience to the franchise-building experiment of ten years that is the Marvel Cinematic Universe (MCU). When the phrase is said, at the stinger of *Iron Man*, Marvel Studios wasn't sure there would be a second *Iron Man* film, even less an expansive cinematic universe. However, following the lead of its source material, comic books, the movie was peppered with small nods, mentions, and Easter eggs that at first, seemed addressed to the fans of said comics. However, as the franchise grew, adding new entries and characters, with intertwined plots culminating in *Avengers: Endgame*, these details became the connective tissue used for the worldbuilding of the MCU. Case in point, the Infinity Stones that appear in at least six different films, serve as the objects of ultimate power that link the stories of *Captain America*, *Guardians of the Galaxy*, *Thor*, *Doctor Strange* and the *Avengers* in general, serving as well as the cause of origin, or source of power for a handful of characters – Scarlet Witch, Ultron, Doctor Strange. And origin is the lesson that system thinking draws from the MUC: everything comes from somewhere.

Worlds are, by nature, closed systems. This means that what's inside of them is all that exists. Everything has a source, an origin that in turn has a source that gives them a place. Nothing appears out of the thin air. It could be argued that, in fantasy, this rule wouldn't apply – in a world where magic and deities exist, things can and have appeared from thin air. But even then, someone within that world, wished that object to exist, thus becoming the source. These tiny details, these objects, help to interconnect the world, giving it a sense of tangibility, by relating to other objects, characters, or locations where they could hail from. Whether these related items appear in the narrative or are just mentioned, their purpose when it comes to worldbuilding is to provide the audience with details on how that world is composed, be it in terms of regions, of natural resources, of industrial processes or magical rituals, that while they are not germane to the main plot, play a role to provide context.

A good example is Captain America's shield. By tracing

the origin of a major character's iconic equipment, a series of relationships and systems reveals itself, connecting with other stories. The first time its existence is hinted at was in *Iron Man 2*, where a prototype replica was seen at Stark's workshop, as he is working on a new version of his armor's power source. Then it appears in earnest in *Captain America: First Avenger*. When this happens, it is mentioned that it is made from vibranium, an element of unknown origin and strange properties. Vibranium's characteristics are briefly hinted at during *Captain America: Winter Soldier*, and expanded further in *Avengers: Age of Ultron*, as a super durable material that could be bonded through nanotechnology with other materials or processes, into complex structures such as humanoid bodies to host artificial intelligences (Ultron, Jarvis/Vision), and its location of origin is mentioned for the first time: Wakanda. This fictional African country is seen in full by the audience in *Black Panther*. It is in *Black Panther*, where the properties or vibranium are further expanded into medical development, futuristic science, weapons, and hi-tech suits composed of nanobots. Those nanobots suits reappear in Avengers: Infinity War, with Iron Man's latest armor iteration. Two more connections develop from within this system: Wakanda is first glimpsed in a map during Iron Man 2, and the core of Vision's existence is the Infinity Stone of the Mind, which appeared first in Avenger's, embedded in Loki's staff, and is connected to the main structure of the MCU's narrative with the rest of the Infinity Stones.

As can be seen, the small detail of an object appearing for a few seconds in a movie filmed in 2010 interconnected a series of nested systems related to technology, culture, urban legends, and so on, giving the MCU a sense of internal coherence that grew organically with each movie. And part of said coherence comes not only from every detail or aspect having a source – even if is not known by the audience –, but from the impact said details have in the main narrative.

Everything has an impact: the case of *ASOIAF*, and the value of historical parallels, myths, and side stories within the worldbuilding

It could be argued that between official and unofficial sources, there are more words written or spoken about *A Song of Ice and Fire* (*ASOIAF*) and the TV series that emanated from it – *Game of Thrones* – than in the main books themselves. While this might sound counterintuitive, the passionate fandom of the book series has taken to analyze every single detail of the books, seeking clues that could predict how the story will end. This is in part because the author, George R.R. Martin, is a history fan, and has used events from world history as inspiration for his epic saga, most notably, the War of the Roses. (Flood, 2018). In this regard, it's worth noting that the setting for *ASOIAF*, the continents of Westeros and Essos, has as many locations, local customs, traditions, and historical events as our real world. Podcasts such as *Radio Westeros* and *History of Westeros* have analysed these elements of worldbuilding, drawing from the information mentioned in the main books themselves, as well as the ancillary books published over the years: *A World of Ice and Fire* (Martin, et al., 2014), *Fire & Blood* (Martin, 2018) and *A Knight of the Seven Kingdoms* (Martin, 2015). The first two books are written from the perspective of people from inside the world, with all the unreliable narrators' quirks that come with it. The third book is a collection of novellas taking place approximately a century before the main books. Through these books, Martin has worked his worldbuilding through three tools: myths, historical parallels, and side stories. This has allowed him to create a detailed backstory for his main story, from which to draw parallels and explain bits that couldn't fit in the main series but have a considerable impact on it and how the setting developed.

The first tool, myths, was mentioned before with the example of the Northern culture – in particular, the guest right – as a result of the Long Night. Specifically, this myth within the story is one of the main and most discussed plots as readers try to find parallels on how the incoming second Long Night will be solved, how individual arcs of certain characters – such as Jon Snow – will evolve, and even smaller aspects as to how, through fleeting mentions in the Empire of Dawn, the dragons and the Valyrian Freehold came to be, came to fall (Martin, et al., 2014) and how that might affect both magic and the future of the saga. This is tied to the second tool: historical parallels. *Fire & Blood* and *World of Ice & Fire* are examples of how certain themes of the main series took place in previous events. For example, the ill disposition towards bastards, stemming from the impact the legalization of the Great Bastards by Aegon the Unworthy had on the Seven Kingdoms (Martin, et al., 2014), even to the present day of the current main narrative.

The third tool is side stories, which in the case of *ASOIAF* came mostly in the form of the Dunk & Egg novellas. Through them, from the peculiar perspective of a hedge knight and his squire – secretly a member of the royal family – the author explores the situation of the Seven Kingdoms from the eyes of someone low in the social ladder, which gives a different perspective on aspects such as human rights, economy, social and political relationships, and the ever-present threat of rebellion, from that of the nobility, commonly viewed by the main cast in the main series. Side stories, be it prequels, sequels, or parallel narratives, are a good way to expand upon worldbuilding elements that are mentioned in passing at the main series. One of the authors of this chapter even uses this tool to develop their worldbuilding. By listening to passing comments, such as the mention of Bloodraven, an important – yet secondary character for the overall plot – and exploring this through the eyes of other characters on a side story, it becomes possible to further explore elements such as the magic used in the setting, the political tensions of lesser players that inform the situation on the main series (e.g., Bracken vs. Blackwood as an example of the frailty of the Riverlands as a political entity). As well, this tool follows the new trend in worldbuilding about creating 'franchises' that can be explored in offerings to the audience.

As can be seen, systems are not only composed of physical elements but also by a succession of historical or pseudohistorical events within the setting that can inform the current plot and conception of the world by the characters. Even a passing reference to a particular historical figure within the setting can be a trove of treasures for worldbuilding. And this can be applied as well to locations not seen in the narrative, but mentioned in it, as it will be explained in the next section.

Everything exists next to something else: the case of *The Wheel of Time* and interconnected details that hint at a larger world outside the location of the narrative

In a system, places that are not mentioned – or relevant for the main story – can also be affected by the actions from the main plot or characters. The world of *The Wheel of Time*, created by Robert Jordan and concluded by Brandon Sanderson after the passing of the former, is complex and full of details of places and characters. The story follows the journey of six youngsters from a secluded town while they travel across one continent, learn about magic, and fight against the forces of evil to seal back The Dark One, which is awakening after over 3,000 years being locked away (Jordan & Sanderson, 2014).

During the first part of the story, a severe heatwave and drought seem to be following the lead characters. Later, it's shown that the heatwave affects not only where the action is happening, but the whole continent. As the story progresses, the drought has repercussions: by the time the ending is near, although the drought has subsided, the continent has been left almost to the point of starvation. This creates a sense of desperation in the people from the places where the characters pass through, as well as complications when everyone is preparing for the final war. For the audience, repercussions of what is happening in one place and how these affect others demonstrate that the story is not just happening around the characters, but it is affecting the world.

At some point in the story, magic goes haywire for a while. This fact has two different repercussions in the world: it causes distortions in the One Power in a specific location, which ends causing great difficulties during an important battle. Also, this fact leads a whole civilization into panic and suicide further on in the narrative, leading the Sea Folk to accept that the final battle is near. The impending doom in both situations contributes to the tension within the story, and the need for resolution before the constraints of the world's reality are broken.

Throughout the story, manifestations of the evil being awakened – known as bubbles of evil – occur in the world. We see them first at the beginning of book three, affecting only the main characters and anyone around them. By the end of the books, these bubbles are reported to appear randomly anywhere in the world, not just around the main characters. These bubbles might do anything from causing objects to move and attack people, to create phantom villages that drag living people underground, or turning entire quarters of a city into dust. The fear coming from the people in this world is transmitted to the audience. This, along with the near-starvation already in place, gives a sense of urgency and desperation, pressing the main characters to end the conflict before the situation becomes unbearable.

Showing in the narration how the places are affected, even those far away from where the actual story is happening, can give the audience a feel for the world and the people in it, not only for the characters. It can also help to build the mood for the kind of ending the author is preparing, and allows the audience to better understand how the actions from characters in the story can have repercussions in other places.

Conclusions

System thinking is a useful tool to consider for worldbuilding. By considering the interconnections of the different elements present in the world, an author can enrich the story and help their audience to feel more at ease within the world.

The three principles shown in this chapter: everything has a source, everything has an impact, and everything exists next to something else, allow having different approaches to what is needed for the world to feel organic and believable for the audience. Placing different elements throughout the narration allows the audience to find out how said elements are interconnected, by appealing at the innate human need for identifying patterns. These elements, being sources of objects, actions that have repercussions or effects of the plot on different regions, help the audience to understand how the setting is conformed. As well, it confers the setting a sense of dynamism, change and evolution, just like the real world. Finally, these elements allow the author to provide their work with internal coherence. The systems approach thus become very relevant to both the author when is worldbuilding, and to the audience when is enjoying the final work. Understanding how it can be applied to the creation of fictional worlds can become a helpful tool in future works.

References

Flood, A., 2018. *George RR Martin: 'When I began A Game of Thrones I thought it might be a short story'*. [online] Available at: <https://www.theguardian.com/books/2018/nov/10/books-interview-george-rr-martin> [Accessed 28 February 2021].

Goodman, M., 1997. *The Systems Thinker - Systems thinking: what, why, when, where, and how?*. [pdf] Available at: <https://thesystemsthinker.com/wp-content/uploads/pdfs/080202pk.pdf> [Accessed 25 April 2020].

Hamilton, J., 2009. *You Write It: Science Fiction*. s.l.:ABDO.

Iron Man. 2008. [Film] Directed by Jon Favreau. s.l.: Marvel Studios.

Jordan, R. & Sanderson, B., 2014. *The Complete Wheel of Time*. s.l.:Tor Books.

Martin, G. R., 2015. *A Knight of the Seven Kingdoms*. s.l.:Bantam.
—, 2018. *Fire & Blood*. s.l.:Bantam.

Martin, G. R., García Jr , E. M. & Antonsson , L., 2014. *The World of Ice & Fire: The Untold History of Westeros and the Game of Thrones.* s.l.:Bantam.

Meadows, D. H., 2009. *Thinking in Systems. A primer*. 1 ed. London: Earthscan.

Merriam-Webster, n.d. *MacGuffin*. [online] Available at: <https://www.merriam-webster.com/dictionary/MacGuffin> [Accessed 11 May 2020].

Phillips, M., 2019. *The Narrative Experiment That Is the Marvel Cinematic Universe*. [online] Available at: <https://www.newyorker.com/culture/culture-desk/the-narrative-experiment-that-is-the-marvel-cinematic-universe> [Accessed 28 February 2021].

Raferty, B., 2011. How Dan Harmon Drives Himself Crazy Making Community. *Wired*, Issue 9.

Fragmented Worlds: Glimpse Morsels for the Imagination

Allen Stroud

Abstract

Much of the writing process of worldbuilding focuses on research, rules and creation. However, the process of engaging and experiencing a text is a partnership between the reader and the writer.

This paper will explore the methodology of mythmaking as part of the worldbuilding process and seeks to explain the ways in which a writer can make room for the reader's creativity within their story, acknowledging the way in which a reader's imagination has a place in the reading experience and looking at ways in which this can be activated and encouraged.

This paper draws on the work of Roland Barthes, whose essay *The Death of the Author* provides a starting point for this study. Barthes indicates that critics should read and analyse a text for itself. This paper will indicate how and why a critic can also analyse the absence of things within a text – using a mythic frame and noting the uses of imperfection, fragments and partiality to invoke the reader's speculative engagement with the story. The argument outlined will also make use of Aristotle's *Poetics*, Baudrillard's *Simulacra and Simulation* and Christine Brooke-Rose's *A Rhetoric of the Unreal: Studies in Narrative and Structure, Especially of the Fantastic*. Most notably her theories on the megatext, which provide a framework for the writer to assume a shared understanding of key concepts with the reader.

This paper will use examples from genre fiction that demonstrate the qualities of mythmaking as part of the worldbuilding of the narrative and the story context.

Introduction

When beginning to read a fantasy novel, the much-celebrated author, Diana Wynne Jones, writing in her *Tough Guide to Fantasyland* (1996), urges the reader to first "find the map". Her comment is humorously made and meant. The *Tough Guide* is a catalogue of archetypes, tropes and repetitive analogues that characterise a particular type of fantasy writing. Indeed, the publication of maps, of timelines, appendices and additional explanatory exposition has become something of a genre defining quality for fantasy fiction in the "Tolkien tradition".

Wynne Jones had some experience of Tolkien as a tutor at Oxford. Her gentle poke at the tradition that has followed his work is not an attack on him or any author in particular, but it does hold a mirror up to fantasy writing, particularly the writing of a quest narrative based on a re-imagination of European medieval society – the type that has been published for the last seventy years and remains popular with readers. The second world, sub creations that so many writers have escaped to at times in their lives, quietly forging them into a newly imagined world that they see as being different to all the others that readers purchase and escape to when life becomes difficult.

In reality, for the most part, these worlds are not overly different. The timelines, the rationalisations of magic, the systemic construction of simplified worlds where good and evil are defined and able to triumph, or be defeated are in part, reactions to the powerlessness of individuals – writers and readers to have the same power in their own lives. Our experience of our world is generally one where we have a limited ability to influence the direction of society, of culture or at times of our immediate context. This experience is common, as is the desire to imagine escapist realities where our actions, or the actions of protagonists who we can identify with, are more definitive, in terms of their effect. These realities draw from our experiences, knowledge, and imagination, with many elements woven into new contexts that fit the narrative we are trying to shape.

The shared experience of readers and writers has been identified as a subconscious source – the megatext, a term coined by Christine Brooke-Rose in her work *Rhetoric of the Unreal* (1981). Brooke-Rose develops the ideas of Roland Barthes' cultural code (Barthes, 1969) and applies her concept to Tolkien, delivering a scathing condemnation of his excessive exposition and the readers who are dazzled by it.

> Clearly LR is overcoded in this way, since the megatext, being wholly invented and unfamiliar, has to be constantly explained. Apart from the 'hypertrophic' redundancy in the text itself, the recapitulations and repetitions , there are long appendices, not only on the history and genealogy but on the language of elves, dwarves, wizard and other powers, together with their philological development, appendices which, though ostensibly given to create belief in the 'reality' of these societies, in fact and even frankly, playfully reflect the author's professional interest in this particular slice of knowledge, rather than narrative necessity, since all of the examples of runic and other messages inside the narrative are both given in their 'original' and 'translated'. Nor are the histories and genealogies in the least necessary to the narrative, but they have given much infantile happiness to the Tolkien clubs and societies, whose members apparently write to each other in Elvish.
> (Brooke-Rose, 1981, p.247)

Brooke-Rose's identification of an over emphasis on lore within Tolkien's work is easy to recognise. *The Lord of the Rings* came from a world built over decades to contain his vision of an alternative mythology. The writing is exposition heavy, with layered explanations of the unfamiliar aspects of Middle-earth, coupled with what writer Michael Moorcock describes as Epic Pooh – soothing fairytale-like prose that evokes memories of childhood.

> The sort of prose most often identified with "high" fantasy is the prose of the nursery room. It is a lullaby, it is meant to soothe and console. It is mouth-music. It is frequently enjoyed not for its tensions but for its lack of tensions. It coddles, it makes friends with you; it tells you comforting lies. It is soft. (Moorcock, 2004, p.123)

However, the concept of the megatext as defined by Brooke-Rose is that it is based on the familiar. Brooke-Rose identifies Tolkien's megatext as being unfamiliar and solely applicable to its own world, but leaden with exposition to reduce that unfamiliarity or 'Exoticism' into familiar themes. This analysis ignores some of the other intentions of the writer and denies the curiosity the text generates in its readers. The intention is to build the sense of a world beyond the narrative through this variety of expositions and to intrigue the reader without drawing them out of the story. This desire can be sated after the tale of the trilogy has concluded, with the inclusion of Appendices and Tolkien's subsequent publication of *The Silmarillion* (1983).

There is a conflation in Brooke-Rose' analysis. A conflation between the subconscious experiential relationship a reader shares with the writer; in this context, 1) their interest in the familiar strangeness of fantasy inspired by the past – Europe's Roman period, its Dark Ages and Feudal times and the Medieval and 2) the specific world of Tolkien's text, as outlined in his expositional passages. These two ideas are connected, but they are also separate constructs, performing different functions that interrelate.

Brooke-Rose describes Tolkien's work as being "hitched to a megatext" (Brooke-Rose, 1981, p.243), which highlights her dual application of the term she invented – the subconscious familiar cultural code and the unfamiliar canon of Middle-earth.

Another way of looking at this is to use different terms. If the megatext is the subconscious 'anonymous book', then a macrotext can be the specific world back story. The opus written as research in this case to set the context of the stories of Middle-earth in their own world and history, right from the beginning – the moment of creation.

It is this element of Tolkien's work that has become a blueprint for many fantasy writers. However, not all of us are internationally renowned Oxford scholars and professors of Anglo-Saxon. The use of timelines, character biographies, languages, maps and more have become a familiar set of tools. These are often published as part of the text, in an emulation of Tolkien's work. Such elements do satisfy the need of a reader to learn more about the locations being described, if the text has provoked such a need.

Where these elements have a greater practical use is in a collaborative project. By establishing a timeline and a context leading up to the point of departure – the moment a story begins, the writer can be confident in creating their introduction. If there are multiple texts to be made, then a shared source document (macrotext or world bible) provides a way in which storytellers can become familiar with the fictional world in which their story will be set. By having source material like this, artists, filmmakers, game creators, novelists and short story writers will have a briefing to inform them before they begin creating their work.

But this is a different process to the work of an individual writer.

Design and Inspiration

When we consider worldbuilding as a construction project, then this separation of terms becomes much plainer and easier to understand. The construction of the macrotext – the world bible of the fantasy – is a discreet process, requiring research and time for the writer to establish a catalogue of all things that might be a part of the story they want to tell. This worldbuilding – the way it is done and the different research and devices used by writers to manage it – has become a popular topic of panels, interviews, blog articles and more as individuals who have created stories, reveal their construction processes, often demonstrating another similarity; that the detail of making their world involves techniques that are much the same as other writers and that they are often meticulous about that detail.

This design process can be likened to Nietzsche's definitions of art. In *The Birth of Tragedy* (1993), Nietzsche writes about two types of art – the Apollonian and the Dionysian. The former is designed art, the constructed and created through labour and intention, the latter is inspirational art, the unplanned for reaction or moment, or ignorant brilliance that often finds itself embedded in creations that we consider to be works of unparalleled genius.

However, according to Nietzsche, despite our best intentions in the construction of such work, there is always an element of the unexpected and uncontrolled. Within the writing of fiction, that aspect manifests in the shape of the audience – the reader, the viewer, the participator, etc, depending on the form in which your fiction takes.

It is here that the work of Brenda Laurel becomes important to our discourse. Laurel's signature work, *Computers as Theatre* (2013) defines the displayed desktop – the graphical user interface – as a stage. Her contextualisation of what we see on the screen as being similar to what a theatre audience would be asked to focus on between the curtains as the actors perform, with the concerns of lighting cues, sound effects, costume changes and all other 'off-stage' matters being the same as the continual processes that a computer's operating system runs in the background, provides significant insight which we can adapt further. Laurel's identification of the performance in this medium can be applied to the writing of a story. The story itself, within the book, is the performance, whilst the worldbuilding, the macrotext, the research and everything going on to assist in ensuring the story is as good as it might be, are off-stage functions or system files running in the background. Occasionally they are relied upon and important, but for the most part, they achieve their function by not drawing undue attention to themselves.

Laurel draws on Aristotle to establish her premise, applying Aristotelian concepts to the context of computers. But we can also draw on Roland Barthes to inform her ideas. Barthes' 1967 critical paper, *The Death of the Author*, contends that critics (of the time) were too concerned with perceived authorial intention and legacy. Barthes argues that criticism of a text should concern the text itself, prioritising this above all other considerations that relate to how the work fits into a larger catalogue. If we apply this concern to Laurel's idea that the screen is the stage, then when we consider storytelling, the research, labelled in popular terms as worldbuilding, should be subservient to the requirements of the story, and only emerge in glimpses, when such elements are necessary requirements to inform the reader of the context around the events that are being dramatized.

If we take Laurel's sense of a story as a performance, the Apollonian and mostly unobtrusive quality of worldbuilding, and the unpredictable but experientially connected Dionysian aspect of the encounter with the text's audience, then we are starting to create a framework that gives a sense of what is happening in the process of creating and sharing the fiction we have made. It is from this framework and perspective that we can start to examine the impact and use of worldbuilding.

The Tapestry

In *Building Imaginary Worlds: The Theory and History of Subcreation* (2012), Mark Wolf develops the idea of multiple narratives, introducing the concepts of narrative objects and complexities to describe the way in which story elements can exist and interrelate.

Narrative Unit	An event
Narrative Thread	A series of events which are casually connected. These may revolve around a character, place or object.
Narrative Braid	Multiple narrative threads that run concurrently with events that happen simultaneously in multiple threads.
Narrative Fabric	The entire depicted narrative of a created fiction with multiple texts.

When we consider the concept of worldbuilding within a text, framing the essential elements in the context of the narrative gives us a better idea of the importance of these elements in the experience of the story. We can think in Aristotelian terms, utilising multiplicity of character, of viewpoint and location to create a greater sense of size and importance. Aristotle describes these qualities as essential to the creation of an epic story.

> Epic has an important distinctive resource for extending its length. In tragedy, it is not possible to imitate many parts of the action being carried on simultaneously, but only the one on stage involving the actors. But in epic, because it is narrative, it is possible to treat many parts as being carried on simultaneously and these (provided they are germane) make the poem more impressive.
> (Aristotle, 1996, pp.39-40).

The tapestry as described by Wolf indicates the relationship between these elements. Narrative is progress – developing themes that run through the story as characters shape events or are changed by them.

It is in part, this tapestry that creates the world in the mind of the reader and the interrelationship that is so essential to giving the impression of it being something more than the sum of its parts. Each thread is indicated to continue, even when the reader is not present to see it. In a way, a writer can use the multiplicity of narrative elements to turn the viewpoint of a work into a lens that brings focus onto what is shown (the character who it might be focused on) and what it doesn't (other characters acting in another location). A clever practitioner of the craft knows how to make the hidden events meaningful, even perhaps as meaningful as what we do see.

Myths, Mythology and Mythmaking

Another aspect of this use of partiality is the practice of mythmaking in fiction.

A myth is a thing that can or has been believed, but by being labelled a myth, is considered to be false in some particular way.

Within popular parlance, the meaning applied to mythology usually involves an historical perspective on the deities of an ancient culture, but we have started to see it applied to current themes in contemporary society, where a community or an ideological group cling to a specific perception of the world in the face of substantive evidence against their position.

Myths and mythology in literature are a constant rich source of connective tissue between stories. The megatext thrives in such ground, allowing writers to develop and continue narrative threads from the loose ends of others, or embellish further, deepening a mystery, by plugging their new story into the weft and weave of what went before.

Marina Warner's *Managing Monsters* (1994) and *From the Beast to the Blonde* (2000) both identify the way in which myths can be played with and become more meaningful as they are returned to. Warner identifies unconscious reinforcement in her Reith Lecture paper, *Monstrous Mothers* (1994) and highlights the effect of intention in her investigation of the *Grotta della Sibilla*, where a court legend was the alleged reason for a papal excommunication being levied on anyone who might visit a cave in the Umbrian mountains.

For a writer, the intentional use of myth, whether in connecting a story to history or works by other writers, or by connecting it to elements of their own, is an opportunity to project depth into a story and demonstrates the true craft of worldbuilding. Whilst there is insight to be found in learning of the research techniques different writers employ in the development of their novels, the worlds they make are imagined in the minds of their readers. So, the use of myth and the making of myths, provides an opportunity for this. Offering the reader a glimpse into the wider context in which a story might be set.

This is the real process of worldbuilding, the way in which a writer creates the world of the story in the mind of the reader. Much of this about partiality – the acceptance of only having partial control over the construction of images within the narrative. Even the most exact and precise writer must acknowledge that the reader is the one experiencing the text and, within a written work without visuals, imagining the setting, objects, characters and events that are described.

A good example of this comes from Tolkien. The scene in *The Fellowship of the Ring* (1997), when a partial account of Balin's expedition to Moria is found.

> At last Gandalf looked up. 'It seems to be a record of the fortunes of Balin's folk,' he said. 'I guess that it began with their coming to Dimrill Dale nigh on thirty years ago: the pages seem to have numbers referring to the years after their arrival…'
> (Tolkien, 1997, p.313)

To use another phrase from Wolf, the narrative resolution of this account is not as high as it might be. We have characters reading the journal of the expedition, reporting events that occurred some time before. The function of this is to build tension into the eventual confrontation between the Fellowship and the denizens of Moria. To do otherwise, and dramatize the events of Balin's expedition, would mean the focus on Frodo's quest might be lost and the account would not serve its purpose. As it stands, the fragmented journal gives the reader clues and hints of what was, providing foreshadowing of what might be to come.

> '...*The Watcher in the Water took Oin. We cannot get out. The end comes*, and then *drums, drums in the deep*. I wonder what that means. The last thing written in in a scrawl of elf-letters: *they are coming*. There is nothing more.' Gandalf paused and stood in silent thought.
> (Tolkien, 1997, p.314)

The trail of fragments here is plain to follow. The Fellowship have already encountered the Watcher in the Water and immediately after this, they hear drums. They are motivated to run and chance an escape, rather than be trapped as Balin and his people were.

The partiality of this extract is essential. This is mythmaking within the text, the scene activates the reader's imagination, to fill in the gaps, wondering at the events being described and the parts that remain untold. This builds the world in the mind of the reader, offering enough structure for the speculative mind to fill in details, particularly when the book is closed for the night, letting the imagination loose to dream of the Dwarves and their tragic expedition.

Tolkien's presentation of the trilogy offers some additional fragments. The appendices of the third volume, *The Return of the King* (1997) offer additional context, providing more of the background about the dwarves and their relationship with Khazad-dûm, the region that came to be known as Moria. But again, we do not have the complete story. Only hints of what happened before that may have motivated Balin and his expedition.

It is here that we see a practical application of Nietzsche's definitions. Using fragments and partiality, the writer acknowledges and relinquishes control. The Dionysian aspect of the moment, the inspirational and current is always going to come from the mind of the reader, as the writer has long since completed their work. The written words cannot be changed, but a glimpse of a story's depth, a fragment of history, of legend or otherwise directs the activity of the audience toward their own visualisation to fill in the detail and complete this narrative thread. There is artifice here, intention to involve the reader and acknowledge the partnership. It is through this acknowledgement and transference of ownership that the writer is able to transcend the words on the page and become something far more personal and meaningful to each individual who reads their work.

It is this element which many writers seem to struggle with. It is difficult to let go in this way, particularly on a project that is so meaningful and requires such self-determined focus, but the reader is always going to be an active part of the experience of a text. Even if we define their role as being passive – not making active choices in determining the direction of the narrative – they remain creators. Within the experience of a written text without accompanying images, they are within the immediate experience and can shape the images of the narrative to suit themselves, as they experience it. If we consider Laurel's framing of that experience as being a stage performance, then the writer should prioritise this experience in the focus of their work, above any background considerations beyond those that go so far as to inform and influence the matter at hand.

Beyond the Books

> Telling a story transmedia-style involves one of two processes, actually. Either you take a single story and you splinter it across multiple media, or you start with one story and you keep adding pieces on to it, *ad infinitum*.
> (Phillips, 2012, p.15)

Andrea Phillips defines Transmedia Storytelling as being presented in two specific structures. The fragmented story makes use of the different platforms, presenting sections of narrative across each of these in such a way as to encourage the consumer's curiosity so they would choose to hunt them down. The layered narrative adds detail with each new text, but the majority of these narratives are self-contained enough that they do not require the additional material for the other texts to be complete standalone story experiences on their own.

The vast sprawling transmedia franchises like *Star Wars* and Marvel's Cinematic Universe develop their worlds in a different way. Here, the contributions come from such a variety of sources, so those that are given the opportunity to create something do so within a series of constraints designed to keep their work consistent with what went before and leaving room for what might come after.

It is in collaborative franchises, that the macrotext becomes a key document – a co-ordinating text that sits behind the published material and that is continually added to as new work is released. As more contributors add to the fiction, the macrotext has to incorporate the relevant elements that change the overall world narrative, informing new creators each time something new is conceived.

However, as the franchise becomes more diverse, the macrotext is also pushed back from the audience. There is less need for a 'Silmarillion' type explanatory text in most diversified fiction franchises as the different stories layer over one another, providing detailed treatments in high narrative resolution.

An exception that proves the rule in this regard is the Wachowski created Matrix fiction which began with the first film, *The Matrix* (1999) and was followed by *The Matrix Reloaded* (2003) and *The Matrix Revolutions* (2003).

The Animatrix (2003) was a follow up anthology of stories that added layers to the story of the trilogy. Much of the collection filled in character backstory or provided continuity between films, etc. However, the two-part animation, 'The Second Renaissance' is an animated documentary, chronicling the world's history from the moment of the films, filling in the gap between contemporary society and the beginning of the first film of the trilogy.

> Welcome to the Zion Archive. You have selected historical file number 12-1, The Second Renaissance.
> In the beginning, there was man, and for a time it was good.
> (Wachowski & Wachowski, 2003)

A lot of context is covered in these two short films, in a fairly low-resolution narrative led by a voiceover, with the animation acting as illustration of the moments being described. but the need is there, possibly because the trilogy of films embraced the complex mystery of its premise so clearly without diverging from the need to tell the Neo/Smith story being told.

The connection of this story to the real world, connecting our present and past into the narrative gives the fiction more depth. This is part of the attraction of Science Fiction narratives that deal with futures that are connected to our own experience.

The anchoring into our world makes the story believable and immediate – an imaginative connection for us to dream about what may come to pass after we are gone.

The franchise has other stories to tell, but these are ancillary to the central epic of Zion, the machines and humanity's battle to survive. Each are a lesser part to the Neo narrative, but 'The Second Renaissance' does come the closest in priority to all the other transmedia narratives presented in comics, games, films and writing as part of this franchise.

Another text that makes incredible use of what already exists in the minds of its audience is *Ready Player One* (2012). Here the interconnectedness of the new story with the real world is for the most part delivered through the incorporation of existing franchises and narratives within the world Ernest Kline, the writer, is describing. Again, the appear of these texts is short-cutted rather than wholly immersive, but the introduction of each is a cameo and a call out to the shared nostalgic experience of the reader with the writer. Perhaps some will be unknown, but others will be familiar and their existence within the world of *Ready Player One*, allows Kline's story to lean on them as required, creating in the conclusion, a dramatization of the kind of epic imaginative cross-world conflict a child might create for themselves in their own bedroom with all of their toys.

The World of the Game

In many ways, game design already embraces the idea of prioritising the experience of the consumer – in this case the player as opposed to the reader or viewer. In part this is because the method of interaction with the game text is much more varied. The interactive opportunities afforded in a game environment provide a means for the individual experiencing the text to shape the narrative, making choices that alter and change the direction of events. Whatever shape these controls take, they tend to provide the player with a closer connection to the text, as their ability to interact with it, offers the illusion or reality of their being able to personalise the story they are partaking in.

This control element, whether limited to a series of choices, a set of outcomes that emerge based on the completion of puzzles or tasks, or something else, have to be part of the design of the text. By incorporating them, the creator willingly relinquishes complete control of the narrative, understanding that the world being created for the player to experience the story in has to be learned about through that experience. This is particularly true when attempting to learn the parameters of the game world. Learning through doing – in a tutorial, is almost universally preferred to reading a manual – which might be compared to the low resolution narrative exposition we have mentioned before.

That said, by their very nature games do rely upon systems and mechanics, although some of the most successful and profound experiences created in games do their best to hide these elements, ensuring that the player remains uncertain by removing the numbers in their simulation of combat, or the representation of enemies and obstacles. *Alien Isolation* (2014) is perhaps an example of one of the most successful games that does this, using algorithms to create the illusion of 'learning' in the Xenomorph enemy. The game also makes use of the franchise it came from, anchoring the experience directly into the narrative of the films that have already established their own mythos. The duel between the alien and the player is intertextually connected to the stories in the films, putting the player in the same position as the principle characters in the franchise. The survival narrative of the game also activates the imagination in a similar way as the player tries to avoid the creature.

The Playground Between Wikis

As the layers of a transmedia narrative build up, so the means of learning about the world becomes a deeper and richer experience. The more content that is given a high-resolution treatment, the more of an experience the audience/reader/user has when they elect to immerse themselves in a particular fiction.

It is this experience that grants us the most in-depth exploration of the narrative, providing opportunities to follow different characters, different time periods and explore different locations. In a sense, a transmedia narrative constructed in this way follows Aristotle's guidance, with the multiplicity of viewpoints and locations contained in a multiplicity of texts.

The consumer has a choice to explore these texts as they wish. They might watch the *Star Wars* films in their fictional chronology, or they might watch them in the actual chronology of when they were made, or in some other order. Each experience deepens their knowledge of the material and, if they find themselves being one of the first to see a new text in the franchise, they might find themselves with privileged information amongst fans of a franchise.

Fandoms often organise themselves in hierarchies. These might be structured as pyramids of knowledge, with those at the apex being the loremasters – individuals who have absorbed everything they can of a particular fiction. This store of information, of knowledge about the world revealed by a sprawling story of multiply rich texts, can be used as a commodity, reinforcing the status of those who have knowledge over those who seek it out.

In many franchises, macrotexts exists to co-ordinate the development of new narratives, which are devoured by eager fans who construct wiki's that are essentially, macrotexts themselves. These reduce the high-resolution experiences of multiple media into low resolution exposition, reversing the process of those involved in creating the content in the first place.

This trend of audiences prioritising the accruement of knowledge over the experience of a text in the form in which it is published for them to engage with is a product of these sprawling transmedia franchises. The priority of writing narratives that generate mysteries and of activating the imaginations of readers through glimpses of a larger story and projecting back into a forgotten past kindles a need for answers and in contemporary society, where consumers are saturated by content, the prioritisation of obtaining those answers over taking the time to indulge in the full immersive opportunity that has been carefully crafted for them is a dilemma that is emerging for content creators working in these vast transmedia products.

With audiences for the largest of these franchises numbering millions, the impact of this kind of shortcutting to acquire the knowledge of a story's plot may not be felt economically. The demand for this knowledge is not necessarily matched by a willingness to devote the necessary time and concentration needed to best enjoy the experience. Narrative design may have to adapt to accommodate this alteration in the priority of audiences. Otherwise, if the experience of the text solely relies on the audience's desire to learn more of the world lore, then it can be bypassed when the answers are catalogued and reported on by others who are sharing their knowledge of the work.

Conclusions

There are many different interpretations of what constitutes worldbuilding as a process. Whilst we are driven to understand our own world, and to codify the science of its wonders and marvels, we are also driven to experience it as it happens. The systemisation of a world can reduce the wonder of that experience and ignore the reader's participation in that experience with the writer as they read the text.

Additionally, an emphasis on the systemification of how these invented worlds work can draw the writer away from using techniques that activate the imagination of the reader. Where the writer makes use of the cultural code and of partiality in their work, they provide opportunities for the reader's imagination to be activated and become a part of creating the story as it is read. This establishes a stronger connection between the reader and the writer.

The true magic of worldbuilding lies in gradually building up the narrative through layer after layer of storytelling. The threads, braids and fabric become a weave of texts, a tapestry of narratives that mimic the world we live in. Our concern as writers is most often about the experiences of human beings – this is how we experience our world. Therefore, the interconnected stories of individual humans within a fictional setting, devised by a writer who can prioritise the experience of the reader makes for the most immersive and inspiring world where readers can dream and imagine and perhaps become writers themselves.

References

Aristotle, 1996. *Poetics*. London: The Penguin Group.
—, 1992. *Politics*. London: The Penguin Group.

Barthes R., 1972. *Mythologies*. London: Paladin Books.
—, 1991. S/Z. London: Farrar, Straus & Giroux Inc.

Baudrillard J., 1991. *Simulacra and Simulation*. Michigan: University of Michigan Press.

Broderick D., 1995. *Reading by Starlight*. London: Routledge.

Brooke-Rose C., 1981. *A Rhetoric of the Unreal: Studies in Narrative and Structure Especially of the Fantastic*. Cambridge: Cambridge University Press.

Jenkins H., 2006. *Convergence Culture: Where Old and New Media Collide*. New York: New York University Press.

Klein, E., 2012. *Ready Player One*. London: Arrow.

Laurel, B., 2013. *Computers as Theatre 2nd Edition*. Boston: Addison-Wesley Professional.

Moorcock M., 2004. *Wizardry and Wild Romance*. London: Monkey Brain Books.

Nietzsche, F., 1993. *The Birth of Tragedy.* London: Penguin Classics.

Phillips, A., 2012. *A Creator's Guide to Transmedia Storytelling*. New York: Mcgraw-Hill.

Suvin D., 1979. *Metamorphoses of Science Fiction*. Yale: Yale University Press.

Tolkien J. R. R., 1975. *The Hobbit.* London: Unwin Paperbacks.
—, 1979. *The Silmarillion.* London: Unwin Paperbacks.
—, 2001. *Tree and Leaf*. London: Harpercollins publishers.
—,1993. *The Lord of the Rings*. Unabridged Paperback Edition London: Harpercollins Publishers London.

Warner M., 1994. *Managing Monsters: Six Myths of Our Time*. London: Vintage.
—, 1995. *From the Beast to the Blonde*. London: Vintage.
—, 2000. *No Go the Bogeyman*. London: Vintage.

Wolf, M. J. P., 2012. *Building Imaginary Worlds: The Theory and History of Subcreation*. New York: Routledge.

Wolfe G. K., 1979. *The Known and the Unknown: The Iconography of Science Fiction*. Ohio: Kent State University Press.
—, 2011. *Evaporating Genres: Essays on Fantastic Literature*. Middletown: Wesleyan University Press.

Wynne-Jones, D., 1996. *The Though Guide to Fantasyland*. London: Gollancz.

Games

Ansell T., 2014. *Alien: Isolation*. Horsham: Creative Assembly.

Relationships with the Land in Fantasy and Science Fiction: Landscape as Identity, Mentor, or Antagonist

Sarah McPherson

Abstract

Many fantasy and science fiction authors construct and utilise landscapes within their work in which the land itself is key to the story, not simply a setting but almost functioning as a character in its own right (although not necessarily sentient), and something that the protagonists have a relationship with throughout the book. This can be done effectively in both fictionalised versions of real landscapes and entirely new, imagined worlds. The landscape can aid the protagonists or work against them, and is often a key part of who the characters are, and how they construct their identities.

Well known authors from the fantasy tradition who use landscape effectively in this way include J. R. R. Tolkien (*The Hobbit* and *The Lord of the Rings*), Susan Cooper (*The Dark is Rising* Sequence), and Alan Garner (*The Weirdstone of Brisingamen* and *The Moon of Gomrath*). As well as these, this paper will discuss more recent works in which the landscape is integral to the characters and narrative, from N. K. Jemisin (*The Broken Earth* trilogy), Kazuo Ishiguro (*The Buried Giant*), and Zoe Gilbert (*Folk*).

In considering the landscapes of these texts, the discussion will draw on phenomenological approaches from archaeology, specifically ideas around the way landscapes are given meaning as a result of the ways people understand, experience, and relate to them, and what this can tell us about relationships and identity in the context of fantasy and science fiction landscapes.

*

> The landscapes we inhabit are rich in story. The lives of our ancestors have contributed to the shape and form of the land we know today ... Every bump, fold and crease, every hill and hollow is part of a narrative that is both human and prehuman. And as long as men and women have moved over the land these narratives have been spoken and sung.
> (Hugh Lupton, 2012 cited in Windling, 2017)

Landscape is important in fantasy and science fiction; one need only look at the myriad books that start with a beautifully drawn map to see that. Readers like to be able to visualise the lands that the characters are travelling through, especially in stories that involve journeying. However, for a constructed or fictionalised landscape to be truly engaging, it must go beyond being a simple backdrop or canvas against which characters move and act, and become an active participant in the story itself. This paper will discuss examples of books where the authors achieve this, and examine what role these landscapes play, in the narrative and in the characters' identity and relationships. It will draw on the idea of phenomenology from archaeological theory to explore how characters interact with and relate to their landscapes and how the land can sometimes almost seem to be a character in its own right.

Christopher Tilley, in *A Phenomenology of Landscape* (1994), sets out to interpret prehistoric landscapes using phenomenological approaches from philosophy, anthropology, human geography, and (newly, at the time) archaeology. It is an "attempt to understand the past through an experiential study of sites and landscapes" (O'Leary, 2013), a way of relating to places and spaces through perceiving and experiencing them. Tilley puts forward the idea of a mythological landscape, with meaning inscribed on it via human agency, and narratives constructed through what can be seen and remembered. In particular, the naming of features and places is important for establishing and maintaining identity.

He also centres movement; passage through the landscape linking people and places, and paths as a metaphor for stories and relationships. "Stories organize walks, making a journey as the feet perform it, organizing places by means of the displacements that are described" (Tilley, 1994, p.32), and there are right and wrong ways of making these journeys. Following the correct path connects people to those who have travelled it before, while if a path is neglected, physically or culturally, that movement and interconnectedness is lost.

Tilley's approach has been subject to criticism by some around the accuracy and practicality of its methods in reconstructing ideas about the past, as it is by necessity both subjective and open to interpretation. However, it is widely used and supported as a theoretical model, and many others have built on his work since the book was first published (O'Leary, 2013). For the purposes of this paper, though, it is interesting to consider how some of these principles might be applied to ideas of landscape and identity in fiction. In particular, we will consider the connection or relationship between people and the landscapes they know well, and conversely, the fact that such a relationship can be lacking if the landscape is not properly understood; the importance of movement and journeys in creating narrative; and the construction of identity in relation to knowing, naming, or experiencing a landscape.

Susan Cooper's *The Dark is Rising* Sequence (1984) is made up of five books, originally published between 1965 and 1977. It takes its young protagonists on journeys through various landscapes; the first and third books are set in Cornwall, the second in the Thames Valley, the fourth in Wales, and the fifth moves between the Thames, Wales and the Lost Land, a magical country fallen centuries earlier to time and the sea. In some cases these are friendly, familiar and welcoming, providing support and positive influences. In others they are dark and threatening, full of danger and horrors, hidden or otherwise.

In both *Over Sea, Under Stone* and *Greenwitch* (Cooper, 1984), the Cornish village of Trewissick is the backdrop against which Simon, Jane, and Barney Drew – first alone and then with Will Stanton – take up the fight of the Light against the Dark and join the search for artefacts that are desired by both sides. The first book is a treasure hunt; the children follow an ancient map that leads them up to the standing stones on the headland and down, racing the tide, to a cave under the cliffs. The Cornish coastline feels broadly neutral, rather than working against them, but there are certainly moments when it seems threatening. The stones on the headland are a "silent dominating circle", a "ghostly group of great stones" (Cooper, 1984 p.94-95). The cliffs trap them between their enemies and the incoming tide; "the sheer granite face towered implacably up, far, far above their heads" (Cooper, 1984, p.162). But there are also moments where the environment provides succour. When Barney, the youngest, is alone in the depths of the cave where he finds the grail, he feels "friendliness round him in the dark now as well as fear" (Cooper, 1984, p.155).

In the third book, *Greenwitch*, the children return to Trewissick, this time with Will, again seeking the grail (which has been stolen) and the key to understanding it. The main focus is Jane's connection to a construct called the Greenwitch, a figure built of leaves and branches by the village women and thrown into the sea as part of a local tradition. The Greenwitch is of the land – made of wood – and given to the water. Again it is threatening but not necessarily evil, although quick to anger; "The leafy head split horribly into a parody of a face, snarling, furious" (Cooper, 1984, p.395). A theme running through the whole sequence is that the land – the natural world – is wild, neither good nor bad, standing apart from the battle between the Light and the Dark. It has its own power, however. When the children return to their enemies' abandoned stronghold towards the end of the book, it is quickly being reclaimed by nature; as one of the characters comments, "The wild is taking Pentreath Farm, very fast" (Cooper, 1984, p.447).

Will Stanton, in the second book *The Dark is Rising* (from which the sequence takes its name), is who he is because of where he comes from, both his family and also where he grew up. He is intimately acquainted with the landscape of his childhood – the Thames Valley – which allows him to notice changes and dangers when something isn't right. When he awakens on his eleventh birthday to a world blanketed in snow, it is a landscape cast back in time, made unfamiliar by both the winter and the removal of modern landmarks.

> There were no roofs, there were no fields. There were only trees. Will was looking out over a great white forest: a forest of massive trees, sturdy as towers and ancient as rock. They were bare of leaves, clad only in the deep snow that lay untouched along every branch, each smallest twig … The only break in that white world of branches was away over to the south, where the Thames ran; he could see the bend in the river marked like a single stilled wave in this white ocean of forest, and the shape of it looked as though the river were wider than it should have been.
> (Cooper, 1984, p.196)

Will's walk through this strange-yet-familiar landscape is the beginning of his own personal journey to discovering his heritage as the last of the Old Ones. It is clear throughout the book that there are safe paths and places that are less safe. When Will encounters the Rider for the second time, the words "It was unwise to leave the road, Will Stanton" (Cooper, 1984, p.203) are an obvious threat, and later after his mentor Merriman saves him from an agent of the Dark, he tells Will, "It was lucky for you that you were standing on one of the Old Ways, trodden by the Old Ones for some three thousand years" (Cooper, 1984, p.231). As the book progresses, the landscape is transformed again, first by a great blizzard, and then by a flood as the snow thaws: "everything they saw became strange all over again, as the rain carved the snow into new lanes and hillocks" (Cooper, 1984, p.321). But Will, with the aid of the other Old Ones, is still able to find his way and complete his quest.

When we see Will in Wales on the other hand, in *The Grey King*, he is out of his comfort zone, alone in an "unfamiliar land of green valleys and dark-misted mountain peaks" (Cooper, 1984, p.482) where he can "feel tension mounting everywhere, advancing like a slow relentless flood from the high peaks brooding over the end of the valley" (Cooper, 1984, p.492). He needs the help of the mysterious white-haired boy Bran and the shepherd John Rowlands, and their local knowledge and connection to that landscape in order to succeed. To navigate these mountains and lakes, following the breadcrumbs of place names – in Welsh, a language he does not speak – and the meaning behind them, he must see them through the eyes of others.

Silver on the Tree, the fifth and final book in the sequence, begins with Will at home on the Thames with his family, and then sees him rejoin Bran in Wales, where they come together with Simon, Jane, and Barney. Once again they follow a trail of clues – hints hidden in descriptions and place names –

through the mountains, facing creatures of the Dark that try to turn them aside, and then for Bran and Will their journey takes them to the Lost Land of King Gwyddno Garanhir, drowned centuries earlier when its sea defences failed. The Lost Land is a beautiful, magical place; the two boys race the Dark across it from the cultivated fields outside the City through dense and oppressive woodland in the Country, where they are saved from a sinister attacker by the presence of a may tree (hawthorn). Finally they follow the river to the Castle surrounded by seven "guardian trees" (Cooper, 1984, p.724), each a different type.

Much like Cooper, Alan Garner uses a fictionalised version of a very specific real landscape – Alderley Edge – in *The Weirdstone of Brisingamen* (1984) and *The Moon of Gomrath* (1992), first published in 1960 and 1963 respectively. When the child protagonists, Colin and Susan, are first exploring it, it is largely described in positive terms:

> They left the shimmering road for the green wood ... they walked among fir and pine, oak, ash, and silver birch, along tracks through bracken, and across sleek hummocks of grass. There was no end to the peace and beauty. And then, abruptly, they came upon a stretch of rock and sand from which the heat vibrated as if from an oven. To the north, the Cheshire plain spread before them like a green and yellow patchwork quilt ... Here the Edge dropped steeply for several hundred feet, while away to their right the country rose in folds and wrinkles until it joined the bulk of the Pennines, which loomed eight miles away through the haze.
> (Garner, 1984, p.20)

They are told about the legends and folklore of the area by their hosts, and very quickly find themselves confronted by these in person, first threatened and pursued through a landscape that has turned dangerous by svarts, and then saved by the wizard Cadellin. In recovering the Weirdstone of the title, which has been stolen, they find themselves lost underground in a maze of tunnels and mine shafts, which they are guided through by the dwarfs Durathror and Fenodyree, who have a close connection to the place and can navigate it effectively. After escaping the mines, they must avoid their enemies and carry the stone back to Cadellin, across fields and moorland, through woods and tangled undergrowth, up hills and mountains. The countryside both hinders them, making movement difficult, and helps them, providing concealment.

At the start of the sequel, *The Moon of Gomrath* (Garner, 1992), Colin and Susan are searching the Edge and the area around it for Cadellin, whom they have not seen since the events of the first book. Without him, the landscape has lost much of its magic; "they found it unbearable that the woods for them should be empty of anything but loveliness, that the boulder that hid the iron gates should remain a boulder, that the cliff above the Holywell should be just a cliff" (Garner, 1992, p.14). Quickly, however, the children are catapulted into another adventure, and again they travel through country turned threatening, beset by foes on all sides. Huge tangled thickets of rhododendrons feature in both books, and in this one they are particularly oppressive, as Susan feels that "all those millions of leaves, each acrid, leathery, breathing, alive, were piled into one green-celled body, that together they had an awareness that was animal" (Garner, 1992, p.121).

Garner uses specific place names to give his description a sense of intimacy and plausibility, and also an urgency to the characters' movement through these locations, listing them one after another in quick succession:

They went by Adders' Moss, past Withenlee and Harehill, to

Tytherington, and then into the hills above Swanscoe, up and down across ridges that swelled like waves: by Kerridge and Lamaload, Nab End and Oldgate Nick, and down Hoo Moor above the Dale of Goyt: mile after mile of killing ground, bare of all trees and broken only by gritstone walls.
(Garner, 1992, p.108)

In N. K. Jemisin's *The Broken Earth* trilogy (2015; 2016; 2017), the Earth itself is in fact a living being, and, in contrast to the other landscapes discussed in this paper, is the ultimate antagonist of the whole series in many ways. The characters are not just striving against each other, but against their whole planet, which was turned against them in the distant past by the actions of a society reaching beyond its limits with no thought for the consequences.

"Like an old man lying restlessly abed it heaves and sighs, puckers and farts, yawns and swallows" is how Jemisin introduces readers to the Stillness, the single great continent, in *The Fifth Season* (2015, p.2), characterising it as alive from the very start. It moves and shakes, volcanic and unstable, and the lives of its residents are shaped by the need to prepare for, and live through, the dangerous and unpredictable Fifth Seasons which are triggered by eruptions, quakes, and other disasters. After the cataclysm that opens the narrative, it is a land of deserts, of stone forests formed of "tall sharp-edged black spires" (Jemisin, 2017, p.59), covered in ash and thoroughly inhospitable to most life; plant, animal or human.

In the early parts of the trilogy, Father Earth – the Evil Earth – is a somewhat distant concept, seeming to represent the struggles of living in such a volatile land, and the dangers of the Seasons. It is described as a "planet that wants nothing more than to destroy the life infesting its once-pristine surface" (Jemisin, 2015, p.146), but that is not something the majority seem to believe as anything other than metaphorical, although Alabaster and the stone eaters know the truth and other characters begin to realise this in The Obelisk Gate (Jemisin, 2016). In the final book, however, it becomes clear that this is neither a myth nor a metaphor, but a real and present threat, and one that has impacted all of their lives both directly and indirectly.

The orogenes in Jemisin's books are defined by their connection to the land, to the Earth itself. They cannot escape from it even if they want to. The sessapinae organs in their brain stems allow them to sense and control (to varying degrees) seismic activity and atmospheric conditions. They may not understand why, or even in many cases how, they can do this, but it is key to who and what they believe they are and how they are seen and discriminated against by others, and ultimately defines the relationships they are able to have. It is an orogene who is responsible for the act that starts the cycle of cataclysmic events chronicled in the trilogy, at the beginning of *The Fifth Season* (Jemisin, 2015), and it is an orogene who is responsible for the act that finally ends it, in the climactic moments of The Stone Sky (Jemisin, 2017).

Jemisin's protagonists, through all the interwoven story arcs, travel across the Stillness, again relating to the land via journeys. Sometimes they travel by their own choice, at other times they are forced to or taken against their will, but it is their movement through the world that progresses their inner journeys. This is particularly true for Essun and her daughter Nassun; although they take very different paths they both develop their understanding of themselves, their knowledge of the Stillness, and their eventual discovery of the greater story they are a part of, by travelling on the surface, beneath it, and finally through the centre of the planet in order to comprehend the truth about their world and its history.

The Earth even speaks to Nassun directly as she passes through its core, which to her feels like "drowning in energy and sensation and emotion" (Jemisin, 2017, p.245), and calls her its enemy. After everything she has experienced in her young life, all the horror and betrayal, she finds that she understands its hatred and its need for revenge. She feels a kinship with it, even though it wants to destroy her and she, in that moment, wants to destroy it. This mirrors in many ways her relationships with parental figures throughout her story; her mother Essun, her father Jija, and her Guardian Schaffa, all of whom in some capacity both love her and damage her, and who she both loves and hates by turns.

The Buried Giant by Kazuo Ishiguro opens with a description of the ancient British landscape in which it is set, that paints it as wild, treacherous, and potentially dangerous; it has "miles of desolate, uncultivated land; here and there rough-hewn paths over craggy hills or bleak moorland" (2015, p.3). The aging protagonists Axl and Beatrice set off on a journey across this land with an uncertain destination; however they continually struggle to remember and understand both their purpose and their direction. It is a land that sends forth creatures to attack them, from monstrous ogres to dog-like beasts and river pixies, wreathed in mists and scattered with places that conjure fear, such as the Great Plain they must partially cross, which causes Beatrice great anxiety even in the midday sun.

Woodlands in the book are also often imbued with a sense of mystery and unease. As events build towards their conclusion there is a scene in a grove of trees surrounding a frozen pool, where the young boy Edwin sees three drowned ogres trapped with their heads submerged, in a pose that makes him think of headless corpses. However in another passage the old knight Gawain appears to be in the same clearing, but describes instead "three great trees, yet each one cracked at the waist and fallen forward into the water" (Ishiguro, 2015, p.283). This disparity in what they perceive at the same location adds to the strange, dreamlike quality of the landscape, and gives the reader the sense that they are lost within it alongside the characters.

It becomes apparent through the narrative that there is a malady affecting the land of Britain, and this is also causing problems and memory loss in the people who live there. The land is a confused, hazy place, full of strange happenings and dangers, which mirrors and reflects the inner turmoil of the protagonists and others that they encounter. Fundamentally, the land is entirely tied up with the characters' identities – who they really are, and what they have done in the past – and all is revealed at the end when they lift the curse and break through the confusion. The dragon Querig, who is the cause of the strange mist and its effects, is under a spell cast many years before with the intention of bringing harmony between those who were previously enemies by causing them to forget past grievances: Britons and Saxons, now sharing the land. The book ends with both fear and hope. Before Axl and Beatrice take their final journey alone, they take their leave of Edwin and the warrior Wistan, and there is a hint that their rediscovered identities may not cause a descent into conflict in all cases:

> As he heard this, something else came back to Edwin: a promise made to the warrior; a duty to hate all Britons. But surely Wistan had not meant to include this gentle couple. And now here was Master Axl, raising a hand uncertainly into the air. Was it in farewell or an attempt to detain him?
> (Ishiguro, 2015, p.328)

Folk by Zoe Gilbert (2018) takes place on the fictional island of Neverness, and the island setting is integral to the stories being told. Different parts of the landscape have different myths and magic tied to them, and the characters both fear and are drawn to these as their tales progress. Some of them emerge from the land, some are taken by it, and some escape its clutches but are forever changed. Fundamentally, the islanders are who they are because of where they are, and what they believe about their homeland. The book starts and ends in the gorse maze, with the myth of the Gorse Mother, and the potential for tragedy: "Four seasons of growth and the gorse has doubled her spines. She has grown chambers and passageways, whole rooms of thorn. She has twisted her maze so cruelly that not one boy has been able to learn it" (Gilbert, 2018, p.1).

The river plays a key role in a number of Gilbert's interwoven tales, as does the sea. One girl is bewitched and taken by a strange man – a water bull – who comes from the river. In another story the river first hides and then reveals a sister's murder. A mother's true nature is revealed to her daughter, and the child must descend into the cove known as Swirling Cleft "on an endless hidden staircase" finding "footholds in rock and ivy" (Gilbert, 2018, p.93) to bring back the sea mist for her. Moving inland, a young boy has a strange encounter with an old beekeeper; the tale ends with the boy sitting in a hollow tree among the ivy, becoming one with the landscape as bees crawl on his skin. Much like Ishiguro (2015), Gilbert's book has dreamlike elements where the reader is unsure what is real and what is not, and the islanders' practices and beliefs call to mind the Cornish women's ritual construction and sacrifice of the Greenwitch in *The Dark is Rising* Sequence (Cooper, 1984).

Tolkien's characters in *The Hobbit* (1999a) – first published 1937 – and the three volumes of *The Lord of the Rings* (1999b, 1999c, 1999d) – first published between 1954 and 1955 – are all very closely tied to, and reflective of, the landscapes where they belong: the hobbits in the Shire, the elves in Rivendell and the woods, the dwarves deep underground or in the mountains, the riders on the grasslands of Rohan, the orcs in the ravaged land of Mordor, and perhaps most obviously, the Ents, who are truly a part of the forests. The Ents, in many ways, are the ultimate personification of the land; Treebeard even shares one of his names, Fangorn, with the ancient forest in which he lives, and speaks of how some Ents are "growing sleepy, going tree-ish" and some trees are "quite wide awake … getting *Entish*" (Tolkien, 1999c, p.77). They are initially a neutral, although benevolent, force, but choose (after a long debate) to side with good against evil, becoming instrumental in defeating Saruman at Orthanc.

There are times, however, when the landscape seems to be actively working against the characters, whether under an enemy's control or just because it is an evil, corrupted place. In *The Hobbit* (Tolkien, 1999a) Bilbo's ill-fated journey through Mirkwood with the dwarves is one of darkness, gloomy and confusing at best and outright dangerous at worst, and like Will Stanton in *The Dark is Rising* (Cooper, 1984) he discovers the perils of leaving the safety of the path. In *The Fellowship of the Ring*, the mountain pass the Company tries to take turns against them and becomes impassable, and Gimli in particular speaks of the mountain as a living thing with agency, saying "Caradhras was called the Cruel" (Tolkien, 1999b, p.379) and "Caradhras has not forgiven us" (Tolkien, 1999b, p.382).

The passage into and across Mordor that Frodo and Sam take in *The Two Towers* (Tolkien, 1999c) and *The Return of the King* (Tolkien, 1999d) is also fraught with danger. They traverse unforgiving rocky crevices, the stagnant and haunted Dead Marshes, the caves where the great spider Shelob lurks, and finally the plains of Mordor itself, where they come extremely close to death and defeat.

> Below them, at the bottom of a fall of some fifteen hundred feet, lay the inner plain stretching away into a formless gloom beyond their sight ... still only a grey light came to the dreary field of Gorgoroth. There smokes trailed on the ground and lurked in hollows, and fumes leaked from fissures in the earth ... Frodo and Sam gazed out in mingled loathing and wonder on this hateful land. Between them and the smoking mountain, and about it north and south, all seemed ruinous and dead, a desert burned and choked.
> (Tolkien, 1999d, p.235)

The characters are all shaped by their lands of origin, and when the land is damaged or sickened, the people are as well. This can be seen in what Saruman does to the Shire towards the end of *The Return of the King* (Tolkien, 1999d). It is not just how Saruman, in his guise as Sharkey, treats the hobbits that damages them, it is how he treats their homeland. That is what Frodo, Merry, Pippin, and especially Sam react to when they arrive back from their adventures; "they came to Bywater by its wide pool; and there they had their first really painful shock. This was Frodo and Sam's own country, and they found out now that they cared about it more than any other place in the world" (Tolkien, 1999d, p.341-342). Trees have been cut down, waters polluted, and the previously peaceful landscape has been industrialised, just as Orthanc was. After Saruman is defeated, part of Sam's role is to heal the Shire, using Galadriel's gift to him, planting trees including a *mallorn* from Lothlorien and ushering in a year of great abundance and fertility.

Three concepts from Tilley's *A Phenomenology of Landscape* (1994) were identified in the introduction to this paper as interesting in the context of landscape in fiction. The first is characters' connection to the landscape (or lack thereof). The second is journeys; movement through the landscape, and how that creates narrative. The third is the creation and reinforcement of identity via knowing, naming and experiencing the landscape.

On the face of it, Ishiguro's and Jemisin's stories are very different, but in both cases the protagonists do not fully understand their relationship or connection with the lands they inhabit, and through the journeys they take, the truth is revealed to them. Tolkien's hobbits rediscover the importance of their connection to the Shire through their difficult homecoming at the end of the journey. Gilbert's islanders, on the other hand, are solidly rooted in their landscape and its mythology, and there is no overarching journey undertaken, at least not in the same way that this can be identified in the other books discussed here. There is still movement in their stories though, writing and overwriting their connections to places and to each other.

The importance of taking the right path, and the danger of leaving it, can be seen explicitly when we look at Will Stanton in *The Dark is Rising* (Cooper, 1984) and Bilbo in *The Hobbit* (Tolkien, 1999a), both in the warnings they receive and the consequences or protections they reap with their actions. There is also a sense of following a trail – a quest that can only be achieved if you take the right road – more broadly in many of the texts: Cooper, Garner, Tolkien, and Ishiguro. The journey is not always the sole point of the story, but it is a key part of the narrative and is often linked to an inner journey undertaken at the same time, a process of discovery that the protagonists have to go through to reach their goals.

The naming of places in the landscape is important. In Garner's books it gives an immediacy and specificity to the locations described, bringing the reader closer to the characters' situation. For Cooper, names and the meaning behind them are vital in the tasks that the protagonists undertake, as they try to unpick clues from the past or from inscriptions and snippets of rhyme. Ishiguro's characters struggle to remember the names of places and locations, as their connection to the landscape has been disrupted by the spell cast on the land.

Knowledge and experience of the landscape is a key factor across all the narratives discussed. As well as more mundane connections – where a person is from, where they belong – there are characters and beings who are very much of the land in a deeper or even magical sense. Jemisin's orogenes and their ability to feel and affect their planet on a very fundamental level are an example of this. Tolkien's Ents are another, and there are also individual creatures who have this as a part of their identity; Cooper's Greenwitch, for instance, or Ishiguro's sleeping dragon Querig.

In considering all of these texts, we have discussed how the landscape can be set up by an author to help or hinder, acting almost as another character to either support or oppose the protagonists. Some landscapes, like Jemisin's, are clearly one or the other, while others, like Cooper's or Garner's, can be both, acting as mentor or antagonist by turns. On a deeper level though, the landscapes of story can tell us much about who the characters actually are, how they define themselves within their narratives, and how the reader views and understands their identities in relation to the places they come from and the paths they journey on.

References

Cooper, S., 1984. *The Dark is Rising* Sequence. London: Puffin.

Garner, A., 1984. *The Weirdstone of Brisingamen*. London: Collins.
—, 1992. *The Moon of Gomrath*. London: HarperCollins.

Gilbert, Z., 2018. *Folk*. London: Bloomsbury.

Ishiguro, K., 2015. *The Buried Giant*. London: Faber & Faber.

Jemisin, N. K., 2015. *The Fifth Season*. London: Orbit .
—, 2016. *The Obelisk Gate*. London: Orbit.
—, 2017. *The Stone Sky*. London: Orbit.

O'Leary, S., 2013. *How Can Phenomenological Methodologies help us understand past Landscapes?* [online] Available at: <https://www.theposthole.org/read/article/230> [Accessed on 30 October 2020].

Tilley, C., 1994. *A Phenomenology of Landscape: Places, Paths and Monuments*. Oxford: Berg.

Tolkien, J.R.R., 1999a. *The Hobbit*. London: HarperCollins
—, 1999b. *The Fellowship of the Ring*. London: HarperCollins.
—, 1999c. *The Two Towers*. London: HarperCollins.
—, 1999d. *The Return of the King*. London: HarperCollins.

Windling, T., 2017. *The landscape of story*. [online] Available at: <https://www.terriwindling.com/blog/2017/08/on-story.html> [Accessed on 30 October 2020].

Freedom Is Slavery:
The sociopolitical implications of worldbuilding in speculative fiction

Sébastien Doubinsky

Abstract

Worldbuilding is, if we consider myths a part of literature, as old as the written word. Imagining other worlds, or ages, strange creatures and supernspeatural heroes is the very fabric of what we call "fiction". From King Arthur's Avalon to the West visited by Sun Wukong and his allies, many worlds have been built and destroyed. Some of these world also reflect religious, philosophical or political concerns: Plato's "Atlantis", Thomas More's "Utopia", Rabelais's "Thélème" or Jonathan Swift's "Liliput" are classic examples. Since then, Aldous Huxley, George Orwell, Yevgeny Zamyatin, Le Guin, Abdouramahn Waberi, J. S. Breukelaar, Eugen Bacon, and myself have explored and built worlds that are not only a background for a fictional narrative, but also serve as a political commentary. With this specificity, "worldbuilding" appears through another angle, in which the political becomes a meaningful and essential element. The constructed world's "politics" thus becomes the blueprint of the fiction instead of the reverse. Using examples in classics of speculative fiction and contemporary writers, I will try to reflect upon the implications of such consciously orientated worldbuilding and its implications for what we call our everyday "reality" and for the reader, not as a passive agent of culture, but as a fully conscious citizen.

*

This is merely a copy, word by word, of what was published this morning in the State newspaper;
'In another hundred and twenty days the building of the Integral will be completed. The great historic hour is near, when the first Integral will rise into the limitless space of the universe. A thousand years ago your heroic ancestors subjected the whole earth to the power of the United State. A still more glorious task is before you, the integration of the indefinite equation of the Cosmos by the use of glass, electric fire-breathing Integral.'
Yevgeny Zamyatin, *We*, 1924.

A squat grey building of only thirty-four stories. Over the main entrance the words, CENTRAL LONDON HATCHERY AND CONDITIONING CENTRE, and, in a shield, the World State's motto, COMMUNITY, IDENTITY, STABILITY.
Aldous Huxley, *Brave New World*, 1932.

It was a bright cold day in April, and the clocks were striking thirteen. Winston Smith, his chin nuzzled into his breast in an effort to escape the vile wind, slipped quickly through the glass doors of Victory Mansions, though not quickly enough to prevent a swirl of gritty dust from entering along with him.
George Orwell, *1984*, 1949.

Thus begin three of speculative literature's most famous novels, Yevgeny Zamyatin's *We* (1924), Aldous Huxley's *Brave New World* (1932), and George Orwell's *1984* (1949). In just a few lines, the visual and psychological foundations of whole, grim new worlds are constructed for the reader to experience with either awe or anguish. But these new worlds are not unknown to us; they resonate clearly with our own history, both at the time when they were written, and today, from what we have learned through history.

This resonance is precisely the thin but clear line that separates science fiction and fantasy from speculative fiction. Where in sci-fi or fantasy, the reader is embarked in a true discovery of the "Unknown", she or he always has at least one foot remaining on the solid ground – our ground – when it comes to speculative fiction.

This "reality" referred to in speculative fiction is not however any kind of reality: it is a sociopolitical identity, that is to say a fictional reality coloured (or tainted, if you will) by ideologies and their correlated social structures. As Aldous Huxley famously said in his 1963 essay "The politics of Ecology": "In politics, the central and fundamental problem is the problem of power." The same could be said about most of (if not all) speculative fiction. Whether dealing with the future, an imaginary past or a parallel universe, speculative fiction worlds are always related to models one can find on this Earth, which will be used and transformed to welcome the narrative.

Worldbuilding in speculative fiction becomes thus a rearrangement of pre-existing elements more than finding out what our imagination can come up with in terms of weirdness and novelty. When Zamyatin, Huxley, and Orwell create their dystopias, they only have to stress details that already exist in capitalist, fascist, and Stalinian realities, just as Jonathan's Swift's "Lilliput" in *Gulliver's Travels* (1726) was a tiny version of 1700s England. More recently, Abdouramane Waberi's 2006 speculative novel *In The United States Of Africa* turns the all-too familiar trope of colonialism on its head and presents us with a rich Black continent having to deal with the immigration of destitute white Europeans and Americans.

As in horror, familiarity is key to bringing the uncanny in the speculative narrative, even if this "familiar" is transformed and sometimes only seemingly remotely connected to our own world. For instance, both Ursula Le Guin in *The Dispossessed* (1974) and Aldous Huxley in *Island* (1962) imagine what an anarchist-inspired society would look like in the future – in space for Le Guin and on Earth for Huxley.

What is striking is both the difference in the worlds described and the similarity of their construction. The major difference between the two texts lies in their social characteristics: Le Guin, obviously inspired by the Soviet experience, creates a dull, tough, and ideologically narrow colony, where absolute equality dominates over the notion of individual freedom and development. Although there is no political party to dominate and control the citizens, one can nonetheless feel the pressure of ideology. Combining both the varnish of a utopia and the harsh realities of a dystopia, the anarchist colony on the planet Anarres is an imperfect society reflecting the flaws of human ideologies. As Le Guin explained in a 2013 interview in *The Paris Review*, politics were at the core of the writing of the book:

> That is probably truest of *The Dispossessed*. Although it started as a short story. I had this physicist and he was in a prison camp somewhere. The story just went nowhere, but I knew that character was real. I had this lump of concrete and somewhere inside it was a diamond, but getting into the lump of concrete—it took years. For whatever reason, I started reading pacifist literature, and I was also involved in antiwar protests, Ban the Bomb and all that. I had been a pacifist activist of sorts for a long time, but I realized I didn't know much about my cause. I'd never read Gandhi, for starters.
>
> So I put myself through a sort of course, reading that literature, and that led me to utopianism. And that led me, through Kropotkin, into anarchism, pacifist anarchism. And at some point it occurred to me that nobody had written an anarchist utopia. We'd had socialist utopias and dystopias and all the

rest, but anarchism—hey, that would be fun. So then I read all the anarchist literature I could get, which was quite a lot, if you went to the right little stores in Portland.
(Wray, 2013)

Huxley's *Island* (1962), on the contrary, is presented as a near-perfect utopian experience, embodying equality, respect for the individual and spiritual and intellectual development. Set in an isolated island, it is a true paradise, embodying a positivist view of science, religion, and social interactions, which will finally be destroyed by human greed. Although opposite to Le Guin's Anarres, Huxley's utopia is also based first and foremost on a political reflection which began in 1946:

"If I were now to rewrite the book (*Brave New World*, author's note), I would offer the Savage a third alternative. Between the Utopian and primitive horns of his dilemma would lie the possibility of sanity... In this community economics would be decentralist and Henry-Georgian, politics Kropotkinesque and co-operative. Science and technology would be used as though, like the Sabbath, they had been made for man, not (as at present and still more so in the Brave New World) as though man were to be adapted and enslaved to them. Religion would be the conscious and intelligent pursuit of man's Final End, the unitive knowledge of immanent Tao or Logos, the transcendent Godhead or Brahman."
(Huxley, 2005, p.7)

Although these two novels seem miles apart at first sight, they do share striking elements in their worldbuilding features. First, both societies are isolated, which is the classic literary trope of the "Lost World" such as the city of El Dorado discovered by the naive Enlightenment antihero Candide in the eponymous 1759 novel by Voltaire, or the various islands Swift's Gulliver travels to in his journey. Secondly, these societies are not totally unfamiliar and can be linked to pre-existing models, whether historical, utopian or dystopian. Le Guin's Anarres anarchist colony can be retraced to the Soviet experience, while Huxley is obviously influenced by the "ideal societies" discovered in Polynesia in the 18th century by the French and English explorers, Louis Antoine De Bougainville and James Cook. The setting thus is more than a simple décor – it is an essential piece (if not the essential piece) of the entire narrative, as it sets it within a historical and non-fictional tradition, which is or should be familiar to the reader. In this way, worldbuilding does not appear as a purely creative endeavor, but as a clear and purposeful construction, with the intention of "guiding" the reader instead of losing her or him. This familiarity, both with historical and/or literary references, is the center of gravity of the narrative effect. We would not, as readers, feel angst in Orwell's *1984* (1949) and Huxley's *Brave New World* (1932), or use them today as political references, if these works weren't frighteningly close to our own reality. The closeness of reality and fiction in the speculative world creates a paradoxical cognitive dissonance that is not only necessary for the cohesion of the text, but is also a crucial element of its identity.

No novel can better illustrate this than Philip K. Dick's alter-historical *The Man In The High Castle* (1962), which functions precisely because it is a negative mirror image of 1950s America. It is a world built on the principle of transparencies, as beneath PKD's fictional Japanese-occupied California, the reader can clearly recognise the real State and its emblematic city, San Francisco. Dick doesn't need to actually *create* or *build* a fictional world – he embeds his imaginary nightmare within the existing and completely recognisable frame of what we call "reality". This transparency thus creates the aforementioned "cognitive dissonance" which places the reader right in the middle of the taoist sage Chuang Tzu's most famous riddle:

> "Once upon a time, I, Chuang Tzu, dreamt that I was a butterfly, flitting around and enjoying myself. I had no idea I was Chuang Tzu. Then suddenly I woke up and was Chuang Tzu again. But I could not tell, had I been Chuang Tzu dreaming I was a butterfly, or a butterfly I was now Chuang Tzu?"
> (Chuang Tzu, 2007, p.20)

The Man In The High Castle functions therefore like a "Pepper's Ghost", where an image in a mirror is projected on a windowpane, but here the reader doesn't know on which side of the window he is standing, and who is the ghost.

Another important aspect in speculative fiction worldbuilding is the type of characters or narrators involved. In science fiction or horror, characters are very often constructed with pre-existing models, or archetypes, from the unhappy wife to the bullied kid, the military astronaut or the dedicated scientist. The same is true in speculative fiction, with a slight twist. If the figures of the "explorer", the "outsider", the "distant witness", the "academic", the "obedient citizen", and so on are all familiar narrative figures that enable a quick empathy (or antipathy) with the main character, they also have a specific political and symbolic value which is often the key to the story's identity. The recurrent male "loser" figure in Philip K. Dick's novels and stories is not just any social and psychological type of character, it is a very *specific* type of character. As Dick explained himself in a 1979 interview:

> I am very conscious of the reader.(...) I identify with the weak person; this is one reason why my fictional protagonists are essentially antiheroes. They're almost losers, yet I try to equip

them with qualities by which they can survive. At the same
time I don't want to see them develop counter-aggressive
tactics where they, too, become exploitative and manipulative.
(Dick, 1979)

The "underdog", the "stranger" or the "outsider" are characters
that are vulnerable to the system, the world in which they are
living. Winston Smith, in 1984, is also the "middleman"victim
of the totalitarian system. And in Le Guin's *The Dispossed*
(1974), the main character, the scientist Shevek, who fled the
anarchistic colony on Anarraes for the capitalistic regime of
A-Lo on the neighbor planet Urras, is a misfit in both systems.
The feeling of strangeness, of permanent or sudden "otherness"
is essential in speculative fiction as it sets the reader into
an uncomfortable position, which is a "critical" one, as the
empathy felt with the main character also implies a political
judgement on the situation. By siding with Winston Smith, the
reader opposes Big Brother. There is no in-between possible:
one has to take a stand.

This "critical" position is the basis of all speculative fiction
worldbuilding, as opposed to science fiction and fantasy, which
can also have political traits, but used as a background accessory
for the narration. In *Brave New World* (1932) and *Island* (1962),
Huxley did want to show the two extremes of the political
spectre, dystopia and utopia. As he told an interviewer for *The
Paris Review* in 1960, the two novels are reversely linked:

At the moment I'm writing a rather peculiar kind of fiction.
It's a kind of fantasy, a kind of reverse Brave New World,
about a society in which real efforts are made to realize human
potentialities. I want to show how humanity can make the
best of both Eastern and Western worlds. So the setting is an
imaginary island between Ceylon and Sumatra, at a meeting

place of Indian and Chinese influence.
(Wickes and Fraser, 1960)

This confirms that the worlds built by Huxley in both novels were constructed in order to illustrate a political and critical point of view from the start, as we have also seen above with Ursula Le Guin and *The Dispossessed* (1974). Politics are not only the starting point of worldbuilding in speculative fiction, they also define the genre's entire fictional identity. Cory Doctorow formulated this very clearly in a 2020 interview:

For example, there's a lot of talk right now about the Green New Deal and its Canadian progenitor, the Leap Manifesto. But then there are all these questions about how will we pay for it and what it will look like on the ground. Those ideas actually aren't necessarily undertheorised, but the theoretical frameworks for them are abstruse. (...) So, I'm trying to write a post-successful Green New Deal novel in which modern monetary theory is the dominant organising principle for provisioning state activity and trying to take this very abstract idea and stick it into a narrative.
(Zacharia, 2020)

The "transparencies" mentioned in the beginning of this essay suddenly become obvious. Contrary to science fiction, which is based on the future, and fantasy, which is often based on different worlds, speculative fiction is based and focused on the present, or the possibilities of the present. As Doctorow explains in the interview, the world he is building is based on an economic theory he wants to illustrate, just as Orwell's *1984* (1949) was a criticism of Stalinist Russia.

This means that speculative fiction worlds are thus not only architectural and narrative constructions, but also commentaries on our political realities. In my own City-States series, I used the historical organisation of the city-states of the past (Babylon, Rome, Athens, etc.) in order to reflect on the new world order of today. As historical narratives are permanently threatened by new archaeological findings, speculative fiction is a constant reminder of the fragility of our current political certainties or beliefs. Speculative worlds are always built on solid ruins, or over solid buildings, even if they exist in the limbo of fiction. They are very similar to the French philosopher Jean Baudrillard's idea of a "*simulacra*", that is to say the projected image of reality that many mistake for reality, the difference being that the projected reality is a recognisable fiction. Yet, in many instances, just as Baudrillard's *simulacra* can replace their original, speculative fiction constructions can become an accepted substitute for actual reality. In an interesting reversal, the worlds built by Orwell, Huxley, and Atwood, for example, have now become the references that help us describe contemporary realities.

In this way, speculative fiction worlds become an interesting kind of mirror, because, as a simulation, a reflection or a *simulacra*, they reveal the true identity of our real systems. Orwell, Huxley, and Atwood, by using the vocabulary, references and modality of propaganda in their own fictions (whether capitalist, fascist, communist or religious) unmask the "realities" hidden behind both fictional and actual regimes' and political parties' narratives. Fiction becomes double, existing both within and outside the novel at the same time, and the world described in the books is like the reflection of a street in a door – it gives way to reality every time the door is pushed, but also becomes instantly visible when the door closes again.

Politics are thus not just one of the elements of worldbuilding in speculative fiction, but its very foundations, defining everything within its narratives. Architecture becomes both symbolic and referential and characters are carefully created so that their position will enable them to represent or denounce the system. The coherence of a utopia or a dystopia is not based therefore on the impressive imagination of its writer but, on the contrary, on the possible and credible identification with the real world. The strength of this credibility can be such that it becomes a "reality" in language and reference. For instance, today some are still building up expeditions in order to find Plato's Atlantis in the middle of the Mediterranean.

This is also why speculative fiction is sometimes considered as a "dangerous" form of fiction for the dominant political systems, and relevant for its opponents. Margaret Atwood's *The Handmaid's Tale* (1985) has thus become a manifesto for women's rights, and her fiction has helped visualise actual injustices taking place in the world around us, and the possibility of an even more sinister reality in a not so far future. The success of *The Handmaid's Tale* is interesting as it was first published in 1985, but gained much renewed attention in the past years because of the political situation in the United States. Philip K. Dicks's *Do Android Dream Of Electric Sheep?* (1968) (Now published as *Blade Runner*, because of the movies) has received the same renewed interest since artificial intelligence linked to centralised control seems to become more and more a reality.

Descriptions (and especially their esthetics) are therefore never innocent in speculative fiction. The depressing architectures of *1984* (Orwell, 1949) and *Brave New World* (Huxley, 1932) are reproductions of brutalist buildings, found both in Stalinist and capitalist countries. The archaic clothes of the Handmaids in *The Handmaid's Tale* (Atwood, 1985) are a clear reminiscence of the 1600s and the Witch Trials. One can immediately see that these esthetic choices are not random, just as the steel and glass skyscrapers in Zamyatin's *We* (1924) are a derivation of Suprematist and Futurist designs.

> This morning I was on the dock where the Integral is being built, and I saw the lathes; blindly, with abandon, the balls of the regulators were rotating; the cranks were swinging from side to side with a glimmer; the working-beam proudly swung its shoulder; and the mechanical chisels were dancing to the melody of an unheard Tarantella. I suddenly perceived all the music, all the beauty, of this colossal, of this mechanical ballet, illumined by light blue rays of sunshine. Then the thought came: why beautiful? Why is a dance beautiful? Answer: because it is an unfree movement.
> (Zamyatin, 2020, pp.10, 13)

This clearly transparent political resonance of the aesthetic described by the speculative fiction writers implies yet another specific trait of the genre, which is the impossibility of an "innocent" reading: by recognising the symbols or architecture displayed, the reader cannot ignore the political message contained in the novel. The notion of a solely "imaginative" fiction is immediately dissolved by the visual descriptions or references displayed. In an interesting way, one could almost say that the architectures shown in speculative fiction are the very structures of the narrative construction. Dick's 1962 *The Man In The High Castle*'s plot strength, for instance, lies for a very large part in the description of a still perfectly recognisable 1950s California, even under Japanese rule. The collision of the "American Dream" and a dictatorial foreign regime is an essential narrative element.

As worldbuilding in speculative fiction encompasses both an imaginary setting and the reality in which the reader exists, the relationship between the two becomes undeniable. More than an "echo" of reality, the speculative fiction world is a sort of *doppelganger*, that is to say an uncanny double. Fiction thus becomes an "in-between" zone, which questions the solidity and certainty of our reality. It is not for nothing that we use speculative fiction classics as references in articles we read, conversations we have or classes we teach: *Brave New World* (Huxley, 1932) and *The Handmaid's Tale* (Atwood, 1985) for instance, do not serve only as illustration, but also as explanation of what we feel we are living at the moment, in the same way fairy tales were used in the past. And it is to be noted that these references are "obvious" to those who use and share them. If a columnist criticises a political speech as being "Newspeak", everybody will understand the reference, whether they have read *1984* (Orwell, 1949) or not. It is a word that is now as embedded in our own reality that it is in the novel. The same goes for the terms "ultraviolence" from Anthony Burgess's *A Clockwork Orange* (1962), and "robot", which comes from Karel Čapek's dystopian play *R.U.R.* (1920). The speculative fiction world is therefore a non-waterproof object, perhaps a sort of a sponge, which not only absorbs water, but seeps it out when pressed. Its borders are fluid and difficult to trace clearly, although it has a clear and defined purpose. In a way, we could suggest that a speculative fiction novel is a political quantum object: immaterial, impossible to pin down, yet defining of our own reality by challenging it with its very existence.

If building a fictional world is often compared to an act of a Demiurge or a God, then those building speculative fiction worlds are very specific: by deliberately creating them within an already existing human history and political experience, they paradoxically give the readers an added freedom, which is to actually experience this fiction as a simultaneous reality that forces them to reflect on their own. The worlds built by those "gods" are thus neither marvels nor horrors of the imagination, but carefully thought-out political architectures. Whether utopian or dystopian, these deeply political structures always serve a purpose that not only serve to embellish a fiction, but to give it its innermost radical identity – and by doing so, shaking the foundations of the political narratives that are shaping us in real life.

References

Atwood, M., 1998 (1985). *The Handmaid's Tale*. New York: Anchor Books.

Baudrillard, J., 1994 (1981). *Simulacra and simulation*. Ann Arbor: University Of Michigan Press.

Chuang Tzu, 2007. *The Book Of Chuang Tzu*. London: Penguin Books.

Dick, P. K., 2010 (1968). *Do Android Dreams Of Electric Sheep?*. London: Gollancz.
—, 2012 (1962). *The Man In The High Castle*. Boston: Mariner Books.

Dick, P. K., Pratt, C., 1979. Killing The Rat. In: D. Streitfeld, ed. 2015. *Philip K. Dick: The Last Interview*. Brooklyn: Melvin House Publishing, p.69.

Huxley, A., 1988. *The politics of Ecology*. [online] Available at: <https://www.microdutch.org/guru/Huxley-Online/politics_of_ecology.html> [Accessed 4 March 2020].
—, 2005 (1932, 1958). *Brave New World and Brave New World Revisited*. New York: Harper Perennial Modern Classics.
—, 2009 (1962). Island. New York: Harper Perennial Modern Classics.

Le Guin, U., 2014 (1974). *The Dispossessed*. New York: Harper Perennial Modern Classics.

Waberi, A., 2009 (2006). *In The United States Of Africa*. Winnipeg: Bison Books.

Wickes, G., Fraser, R., 1960. *Aldous Huxley, the art of fiction number 24*. [online] Available at: <https://www.theparisreview.org/interviews/4698/the-art-of-fiction-no-24-aldous-huxley> [Accessed 3 March 2021].

Wray, J., 2013. *Ursula K. Le Guin, The art of fiction number 221*. [online] Available at: <https://www.theparisreview.org/interviews/6253/the-art-of-fiction-no-221-ursula-k-le-guin> [Accessed 3 March 2021].

Zachariah, J., 2020. *The machine without the engine: an interview with Cory Doctorow*. [online] Available at: <https://brookfieldinstitute.ca/the-machine-without-the-factory-an-interview-with-cory-doctorow/> [Accessed 4 March 2020].

Zamyatin, Y., 2020 (1924). *We* in *1984 & Brave New World & We*. Mumbai: Sanage Publishing House.

Worldbuilding with Sex and Gender

Cheryl Morgan

Abstract

Science fiction is fond of creating new worlds populated by new types of creatures, but often the imagination of authors is somewhat limited. TV and movies can perhaps be forgiven for sticking to the basic humanoid shape because they have to turn human actors into aliens, but written fiction has no such excuse. Nevertheless, we see far too many examples of alien species that are bipedal, have two sexes and, apparently most importantly, whose females have two (and only two) large breasts.

Fortunately, help is at hand. The natural world on our own planet is full of creatures that do sex and gender very differently from humans. Many animal species have same-sex liaisons. Most animals determine their sex in a very different way to the XX/XY chromosome system used by mammals. Some animals change sex naturally as part of their lifecycle. Some exhibit what we might recognise as transgender identities. And some have a lot more than two sexes.

Taking the natural world as its inspiration, and the work of pioneering biologists such as Professor Joan Roughgarden, this essay will provide examples of how aliens can be very different from humans. Along the way it will look at a few examples, such as Le Guin's *The Left Hand of Darkness*, and Martha Wells' Raksura novels, that have successfully created interestingly alien aliens.

Introduction

A common joke about *Star Trek* is that their aliens are just humans with funny lumps on their heads, but *Trek* is by no means the only piece of science fiction to be unimaginative about creating aliens. In art, aliens are all too often bipedal, with two arms, two legs, and other human-like characteristics. Even when we base our aliens on well-known Earth animals, we generally make them very human-like.

A common figure in SF art is the sexy cat girl. She'll have a cat's head, but a lithe body based on a human female, including two (and only two) prominent breasts. Anyone who has owned cats will know that the females do not have breasts, and that they have more than two nipples. Something strange is happening here. Then there's Madame Vastra from *Doctor Who*. She is a lizard woman, but she too has human-like breasts. This is odd, because lizards lay eggs and have no need to suckle their young.

Part of the problem is a common assumption that the natural world is a mirror of humanity. A clear example of this is the story of Noah's Ark, in which every animal species on Earth is assumed to be heterosexual and form nuclear families. People who campaign against LGBT rights often double down on this, claiming that being gay, or trans, is "not natural". And yet sex and gender in the animal world is often very different from this assumed norm. That means that the natural world is full of interesting ideas for creating different aliens.

In school biology we learn about amoebae, that reproduce by cloning, and about sexual reproduction that involves the fusion of gametes. Gametes come in two types, eggs and sperm, and the creature that produces the eggs is defined as female. This is a biological definition. It says nothing about how males and females should look, or behave, or even that there should be only one variety of each. Gametes aside, everything else is up for grabs, including the chromosome system, gendered behaviour, family structure, and so on.

In this essay I will be using this biological definition of sex, mainly because I'll be referencing a lot of biological studies.

This is not the same thing as the human concept of sex, which we generally assign based on appearance and which can be legally determined.

I will also be talking about sexuality, because most animal species are known to engage in sexual activity between individuals of the same sex. We can't know whether these animals are "in love" in the way that humans would understand it, but at the same time we can't attribute it all to "dominance behaviour" because that is also imposing human ideas on animals.

Finally, I will be talking about gender, which in humans is often a matter of behavioural expectations. We see gender in terms of what clothes people wear, what mannerisms they use, what jobs they do and so on. People who claim to oppose gender, or be "gender critical", generally oppose any gendered behaviour that does not conform to narrow social stereotypes of "correct" performance for males and females.

Biologically, animals can be said to exhibit more than two genders when there are clear varieties within a species that are of the same sex but have very different behaviours when it comes to mating. For example, a species may have three genders, one of which is female, and the other two are different types of males that have different sizes, different colourations, and different mating strategies. There is an assumption that these varieties can be biologically distinguished in some way, though we do not always know what markers to look for.

These biological genders are not the same as gender identity, a term we use in connection with human trans people. There is no known biological cause for human beings to be trans, and trans identities are often assumed to have purely psychological causes. However, as we will see, trans-like behaviour also exists in some animal species.

Some creatures, such as leopard slugs, are true hermaphrodites. They produce both eggs and sperm and can fertilise themselves. However, they prefer the sex act as they have one of the most beautiful and romantic mating processes in the world. They hang from a tree branch, side-by-side, and both extrude a bright blue sex organ. They curl these around each other and enjoy each other's company. (Attenborough, 2010).

Other animals are much less romantic. Spiders, for example. Adrian Tchaikovsky did a wonderful job of creating a spider race in *Children of Time*, but even the leaders of this great civilisation see nothing wrong in eating your male partner after sex:

> The killing of males under the protection of another peer house is a crime that demands restitution; the needless killing of males garners sufficient social disapprobation that it is seldom practiced, and the culprits usually shunned as wasteful and lacking the golden virtue of self-control. However, to kill a male for a good reason, or after coitus, remains acceptable, despite occasional debates on the subject.
> (Tchaikovsky, 2015, p.329)

You might think that male spiders have a rough time of it, but for many male animals mating is just as dangerous, if not more so, because the females are so much bigger. Take the angler fish, for example. The female is huge and armed with masses of teeth. The male is about the size of one of her fins, and could easily end up as a tasty morsel if he isn't careful.

The paper nautilus has it even worse. The males are about 600 times smaller than the females. When a male spots a likely female, he sneaks up to her, detaches his penis, and swims away fast before she can eat him. The penis, which looks and acts like a small worm, is left to get on with mating by itself. The detached penis has just enough self-awareness to burrow into the female's shell. She may collect several of these before deciding to fertilize her eggs with one or a combination of them. Scientists have not observed any live males without their penises in the wild, and it is thought that they might die without them, though perhaps they regrow (Edmonds & Van Der Berg, 2019).

The world record for size mismatching is held by the green spoon worm, where the females are 200,000 times larger than the males. The males live inside the females as a sort of parasite. Of course, when born the baby worms are all the same size. Whether one grows into a giant female, or stays a tiny male, is dependent on which sex of adult the baby first meets. If they meet a female, the baby worm climbs inside her and becomes male, but if they meet only males, or no other worms, they become female.

Some science fiction writers have played with this idea of sex and gender being indeterminate at birth. In *Questors* (2007), a middle-grade novel by Joan Lennon, there is an alien species that does not develop any sex characteristics until puberty. Ann Leckie, in *Provenance* (2017), has a society in which social gender is chosen at adulthood.

While we might think of amoebae as simple organisms, they are by no means the only creatures to reproduce by cloning, or parthenogenesis as it is termed. In Japan there are nests of termites that are all female. Whip-tailed lizards in Arizona also have the ability to produce offspring without the help of a male. Charmingly they seem to only be able to do so after rubbing against each other in what appears to us to be a lesbian sexual encounter.

In *Motherlines* (1978), Suzy McKee Charnas introduces a society of women who have developed the ability to reproduce through parthenogenesis, though apparently they need some help from their horses. Kameron Hurley's *The Stars are Legion* (2017) features a society with exceptionally advanced biological science. In the world of the book, nothing male exists, and wombs are used to grow things other than babies.

The effectiveness of cloning as an evolutionary strategy is a matter for great debate among biologists. Without the mixing of DNA, opportunities for evolution are limited. Mutations can take place, but that can be bad for the species as well as good. Nevertheless, cloning species appear successful. The Japanese termite colonies have been at it for around 14 million years and show no sign of going extinct. But their record is dwarfed by the bdelloid rotifer, a microscopic marine creature that has been all-female for 84 million years.

Recently Chinese scientists succeeded in breeding mice with two mothers, though they did need to grow sperm, taken from a stem cell of one of the mothers to do so (Rehm, 2018).

Penises are a matter of great pride for human males, but in other species the female has a penis too. Hyenas are the best-known example. It doesn't appear to be a smart strategy as the penis is an extension of the vaginal canal and the female hyenas give birth through it. The morality rate of both mothers and cubs is horrific.

Human males, however, have nothing to crow about. Elephants, obviously, have much bigger penises. What's more they are prehensile, like a tail. Elephants are very bulky animals and they need a bit of length and flexibility to ensure that copulation is possible.

The record for size is held by blue whales, which have penises that are between 2.5 and 3 metres long, but they still only have one. Some lizard species have two penises. The latter is all to do with how the organ evolved. In mammals, penis cells are modified tail cells, but in lizards they are modified leg cells, hence you can get two. They can only use one at once, unlike the man in Iain M Banks's *Hydrogen Sonata* (2013) who has over 50 penises grafted all over his body.

Not to be outdone, female kangaroos have 3 vaginas. The same is true for other marsupials such as koalas and wombats. However, this isn't as unusual as it seems. They still only have one vulva, but the tube splits into three inside the body. The central tube is used by the baby emerging from the womb, while the other two are used by sperm. This arrangement allows sperm to fertilise a new egg while an embryo is still growing in the womb. Female kangaroos are pregnant pretty much all the time. While a joey is growing in the pouch, another is waiting in the womb to take its place.

Although producing an egg is the biological definition of being female, incubation can be done in a variety of ways. Male seahorses incubate eggs and give birth to the babies through a hole in their chests. The Darwin's frog incubates eggs in its vocal sac, and appears to give birth though its mouth. While the male frogs do have very big vocal sacs, all the better to croak with, they are not big enough for a whole brood, so there can be violent competition between females to gather a harem of males to raise their babies.

Family structures in the animal world vary wildly. Most mammals practice polygamy, because having an extended family makes it easier to raise children over months, if not years. Most birds are monogamous, as it takes far less time to raise their young.

This does not mean that birds are always faithful to their partners. Razorbills live in big clifftop colonies. They mate in the middle of the colony in full view of everyone. Females can often be seen coupling with males other than their nest partner. The theory is that they are building friendly relationships with other males, just in case their nest partner dies and they need a replacement.

Naked mole rats are remarkable for all sorts of reasons, but one is that their family structure involves a queen and workers, just like bees.

Are vampires gay? I'm sure that's a question that many writers have asked. When it comes to bats, the answer is yes. Being a bat is a risky business. All that high-speed flitting around requires a lot of energy. A poor night's feeding can mean trouble, especially if you are pregnant. So vampire bat colonies practice a lot of mutual aid, with well-fed bats helping out their hungry neighbours. Among the males this also involves a lot of sexual activity.

Bats are by no means the only species to indulge in same-sex activities. A study of giraffes, which has yet to be repeated, found that 94% of sexual activity by males was with other males, much of it clearly affectionate.

Japanese macaques, the ones that spend a lot of time in hot springs, are famous for same-sex activity among females. Some of the ladies can be very aggressive about it. I am a bit sad that Gareth L Powell's *Ack-Ack Macaque* (2013) was not a butch lesbian, as that would have been entirely plausible.

It is well known that some animal species can change sex naturally. Clown fish, for example, will change from male to female if a colony has a shortage of females. The film, *Finding Nemo* (2003), might have been much shorter if it had featured traditional clown fish behaviour, but Hollywood has never cared much for realism.

In the first episode of *Blue Planet II* (2017) David Attenborough had some amazing footage of a sheep's head wrasse changing sex. When the male of a group dies, the females fight among themselves to see who will inherit the job, and the winner becomes male.

The best-known animal to change sex is the chicken. Hens have only one functional ovary. The other remains dormant. If the functional ovary stops working for any reason, the dormant one activates, and under some circumstances it can produce androgens (male sex hormones). This causes the hen to go through a second puberty and develop male secondary sex characteristics.

Ursula K Le Guin's *The Left Hand of Darkness* (1982) is a famous example of an alien species that changes sex. The Gethenians are sexless for much of their lives, only acquiring a sex during occasional short periods when they become fertile. Le Guin uses this to demonstrate how important stereotypical ideas about gender are to the ways in which humans relate to each other (and to other human-like species).

The Earthly animal most like the Gethenians in nature is right below our feet; well, right below Spanish feet. The Iberian mole is believed unique among mammals in having gonads that can behave like ovaries or testes. All that digging requires prodigious amounts of muscle power, and the female moles have evolved to be able to pump up their bodies on testosterone. Thanks to this, for most of the year they are outwardly indistinguishable from males. Come mating time, testosterone levels drop, and the moles develop vulvas allowing them to mate. (Graves, 2020)

Some animals are both male and female, not just in their sexual function like the leopard slugs, but in their whole bodies. Animals exhibiting this condition are known as gynandromorphs. The condition is most striking in species such as birds, butterflies and spiders, where the male and female look very different. The most famous example is the Cardinal, a common bird species in North America (Seaberg, 2019). The males have bright red plumage, and the females vary from grey to olive. Gynandromorphs have red plumage on one side of their body, and a female colour on the other side.

There's no reason to have just two sexes. Slime moulds have eight different types of gametes rather than two. With variation within those types they have over 500 different sexes. Finding a mate is so much easier when there are 500 options to choose from, not just the "opposite sex."

While most animals do only have two types of gametes, that doesn't mean that they have only two genders. As noted above, there are many animal species where individuals of the same sex express their maleness or femaleness in very different ways. Many fish, including the arrow squid and the bluegill sunfish, have two types of males with different mating strategies. The larger males tend to be very macho and territorial, while the smaller type will sneak in, mate with a female, and then run away.

We see similar behaviour in birds. The ruff, a type of sandpiper, has two types of male, distinguished by the colour of their display features. Those with brown ruffs are more macho, and arrive first at the nesting grounds to stake out a territory. Next to arrive are the white-ruffed males, who are courted by the brown-ruffs. When the females finally arrive, they prefer to hook up with an existing gay couple than with a lone brown-ruff.

Side-blotched lizards have five genders altogether: three males and two females. Orange males are highly dominant with big territories and multiple wives. Blue males are territorial but monogamous. Yellow males have no territory and are sneaky, specialising in affairs with the territorial lizards' wives. Orange females are territorial, but yellow females are not. It is believed that this variety of mating strategies helps the lizard population thrive in the difficult desert conditions where they live.

Some science fiction writers have postulated alien societies with multiple biological genders. The Raksura, created by Martha Wells in books such as *The Cloud Roads* (2011), have seven genders, three of which have wings and four of which do not. There is a certain amount of biological determination of social roles. They are a fascinating alien species.

Anne McCaffrey's dragons from the Pern novels have multiple biological genders, and they also have relations with humans. The Impression process creates such a strong link between human and dragon that when the dragons mate, sexual arousal is passed on to the riders. Women only ride gold dragons, but green dragons are female and are traditionally paired with gay men.

A similar situation exists in the Iskryne World books of Sarah Monette and Elizabeth Bear, starting with *A Companion to Wolves* (2008). Here the humans ride wolves, and while the riders are all male their mounts are not.

Humans have multi-gender societies too, though as yet there is no evidence of a biological basis for these. Long before we discovered gametes, chromosomes and hormones, we noticed that queer people existed, and we made space for them in society. Human societies have had three, four, five or even more social genders.

In 1993 the biologist, Anne Fausto-Sterling, wrote a famous paper that argued that humans had five sexes. Most people, including the author, now agree that it was a bit simplistic, and she should probably have said five genders rather than five sexes, but the paper inspired Melissa Scott to write *Shadow Man* (1995). In this book a side effect of faster-than-light travel has been to make humanity a genuinely five-gender species. The action is set on the one planet in the galaxy that steadfastly refuses to accept this and tries to enforce the gender binary on its population.

We have seen many examples of animals that have multiple genders, multiple sexes, and can even change sex, but human trans people are not exactly like that. The usual definition of a trans person is someone whose gender identity is at odds with their apparent biology. Do we see this in the animal kingdom too? Of course we do.

One famous example is a pair of jackass penguins who live in the Ramat Gan Zoological Centre in Tel Aviv, Israel. From their behaviour, Suki is clearly female and Chupchikoni is clearly male. Indeed, Chupchikoni is so macho that the keepers gave him a name that is a Hebrew slang word for penis. However, when a scientific study required the penguins to be taken into a lab and examined, Chupchikoni was found to have female genitals. Despite his macho presentation, poor Chupchikoni was misgendered in all of the news reports of the story.

That's a single example. A far better illustration is the case of bighorn sheep. Like many such animals, bighorns have a family structure where a single, dominant male has ownership of the female herd, and the rest of the males go off elsewhere sulking and plotting a coup. However, biologists have noticed that a small number of males stay with the female herd. Not only that, but they adopt female behaviours such as flirting with the ram and squatting to pee. They appear convinced that they are female.

Hopefully this essay has shown you that Earth's animals are far more fabulous and queerer than most people think. So next time you design an alien species, why not get creative with sex and gender. If you'd like to follow up on these, and any other examples of fascinating animal biology, I warmly recommend two books that I used to research much of this essay. *Evolution's Rainbow: Diversity, Gender, and Sexuality in Nature and People* is by Emeritus Professor of Biology at Stanford University, Joan Roughgarden (2003). A trans woman herself, Roughgarden has a refreshingly uninhibited view of the natural world, while remaining strictly scientific. A more entertaining but somewhat less scholarly view is available in *Dr Tatiana's Sex Advice to All Creation: Definitive Guide to the Evolutionary Biology of Sex* by Olivia Judson (2003).

The more that we study the animal world, the more varied, wonderful and queer we find it to be. Given such diversity of sexuality and gender on Earth, there is really no excuse for creating aliens that have only two genders and are heterosexual and monogamous. The next time you are creating a new world, go wild!

References

Attenborough D., 2017. *Blue Planet II*. Bristol: BBC.
—, 2010. *Who Knew Slugs Could Be So Romantic* [online] Available at: <https://www.youtube.com/watch?v=wG9qpZ89qzc> [Accessed 17 October 2020]. Bristol: BBC.

Banks, I.M., 2013. *Hydrogen Sonata*. London: Orbit.

Bear, E. & Monette, S., 2008. *A Companion to Wolves*. New York: Tor.

Charnas, S.M., 1979. *Motherlines*. New York: Berkeley Publishing Group.

Edmonds, P. & Van Der Berg, E., 2019. *To mate, this octopus gives life and limb*. [online] Available at: <https://www.nationalgeographic.com/magazine/2019/07/argonaut-octopus-detaches-his-tentacle-to-impregnate-his-mate/> [Accessed 21 November 2020].

Fausto-Sterling, A., 1993. The Five Sexes: Why Male and Female are Not Enough. *Science,* 33.

Graves, J., 2020. *Fierce female moles have male-like hormones and genitals. We now know how this happens*. [online] Available at: <https://theconversation.com/fierce-female-moles-have-male-like-hormones-and-genitals-we-now-know-how-this-happens-149174> [Accessed 21 November 2020].

Hurley, K., 2017. *The Stars Are Legion*. Nottingham: Angry Robot.

Judson, O., 2003. *Dr Tatiana's Sex Advice to All Creation: Definitive Guide to the Evolutionary Biology of Sex*. New York: Vintage.

Leckie, A., 2018. *Provenance*. New York: Orbit.

Le Guin, U.K., 1982. *The Left Hand of Darkness*. New York: Orbit.

Lennon, J., 2007. *Questors*. London: Puffin.

McCaffrey, A., 1978. *Dragonflight*. New York: Ballantine.

Powell, G., 2013. *Ack-Ack Macaque*. Oxford: Solaris.

Rehm, J., 2018. *Healthy mice from same-sex parents have their own pups*. [online] Available at: <https://www.nature.com/articles/d41586-018-06999-6> [Accessed 21 November 2020].

Roughgarden, J., 2003. *Evolution's Rainbow: Diversity, Gender, and Sexuality in Nature and People*. Berkeley: University of California Press.

Schuster, R., 2013. *Surprise! Lesbian Penguin Couple Shacking Up at Israeli Zoo*. [online]. Available at: < https://www.haaretz.com/lesbian-penguins-shack-up-in-israel-1.5301243> [Accessed 17 October 2020].

Scott, M., 1995. *Shadow Man*. New York: Tor.

Seaberg, M., 2019. *Rare half-male, half-female cardinal spotted in Pennsylvania*. [online]. Available at: <https://www.nationalgeographic.com/animals/2019/01/half-male-half-female-cardinal-pennsylvania/> [Accessed 21 November 2020].

Stanton, A., 2003. *Finding Nemo*. Los Angeles: Disney Pixar.

Tchaikovsky, A., 2015. *Children of Time*. New York: Tor.

Wells, M., 2011. *The Cloud Roads*. San Francisco: Night Shade.

Town Planning in Viriconium:
M John Harrison and Worldbuilding

Peter Garrett

Abstract

In 2007, M John Harrison's characterisation of worldbuilding as "the great clomping foot of nerdism" provoked an internet storm. This essay explores aspects of the online debate and reviews associated academic papers and formal publications, before examining the influences and techniques used by Harrison in the Viriconium series in order to subvert encyclopaedic worldbuilding. Methods identified include imagism, absurdist and surrealist techniques, intertextuality, allusional montage, and a complex system of internal reference. Finally, the essay considers the merits of application of Wolfgang Iser's reader-response theory to the Viriconium opus.
Iser's methodology is a powerful tool that can be used to illuminate the nature and purpose of Harrison's subversion of concord fiction, exemplified by comprehensive worldbuilding.

Introduction

Worldbuilding – the creation of a consistent imaginary framework to provide credible support for a story – is generally regarded as a necessary aspect of any work of fiction. The term is applied particularly to science fiction and fantasy, where the setting may be completely separate from, rather than a subset of, the world of our direct experience.

The accepted paradigm for worldbuilding within this genre is Tolkien's Middle-earth, an environment where detailed topography, history, mythology, ethnography, and, especially, philology all contribute to the intricate milieu in which his characters exist and the narrative develops. According to fantasy writer Chuck Wendig (2013), "...worldbuilding covers *everything and anything inside that world*. Money, clothing, territorial boundaries, tribal customs, building materials, imports and exports, transportation, sex, food, the various types of monkeys people possess..." (emphasis in original). This encyclopaedic notion of worldbuilding as the creation of a necessarily complete and consistent environment has perhaps reached its zenith in collaborative role-playing games projects (see Hergenrader, 2018), in which several individuals are commissioned to develop different specialist aspects (history, biology, politics, economics, geology, linguistics, etc) of an imagined setting.

Is, though, a detailed and consistent framework really necessary, or even desirable, for a work of speculative fiction? In a notoriously controversial blog, the genre-fluid writer M John Harrison (2007) maintained that it wasn't. "Worldbuilding is dull," he wrote.

> Worldbuilding literalises the urge to invent. Worldbuilding gives an unnecessary permission for acts of writing (indeed, for acts of reading). Worldbuilding numbs the reader's ability to fulfil their part of the bargain, because it believes that it has to do everything around here if anything is going to get done. Above all, worldbuilding is not technically necessary. It is the great clomping foot of nerdism. It is the attempt to exhaustively survey a place that isn't there...

Unsurprisingly, the blog sparked furious online debate.

In this essay I propose to examine aspects of the internet discussion; to review related academic and formally published literature addressing the value of comprehensive worldbuilding in speculative fiction in the light of Harrison's opinion; to analyse some influences and techniques used by Harrison, especially in the Viriconium series, that distinguish his work from epic worldbuilding fantasy; and to consider the reader-response theory of Wolfgang Iser as a suitable lens for the examination of Viriconium.

*

Harrison (2001) had already questioned the over-literalisation of the great modern fantasies, arguing that the apparent depth created by Tolkien and other writers was a threat to commercial concerns, who wanted to assert control over such secondary worlds. Corporate control could then be used as an invitation to consumers and a source of more profit. Asking what it might be like to live in an invented world, wrote Harrison, is a category error, a question that should not be posed and certainly should not be answered. In order to prevent this, he made clear, Viriconium is not only shifting and complex, but without rules; it cannot be mapped or understood. It's a "theory about the power structures culture is designed to hide; an allegory of language, how it can only fail; the statement of a philosophical... despair." It's also, though, an "unashamed postmodern fiction of the heart", an implied demonstration of depth, adventure, and vertiginous experience. Its lack of identifiable values is designed to oblige readers to reassemble and reexamine their value systems. It is thus intended to act as a metaphor for life, and in particular to demonstrate that any notion of control is an illusion.

The later, more direct blog (Harrison, 2007), however, attracted much more comment (see, for instance, Asoiaf, 2007; Reddit, 2015). Other prominent writers of speculative fiction praised the post. According to Warren Ellis (2007), "This is just glorious". Jeff VanderMeer (2008) described it as "a fascinating post" and characterised parts as "particularly resonant". China Miéville (2011) said: "...I think one of the most productive things anyone interested in World-Building can do is to go straight to (Harrison's) now notorious, and magnificent, diss of the whole project..."

On the other hand, fantasy novelist R Scott Bakker (2008), representing the robust objections of very many posts, took issue with the blog as over-intellectual. "For better or worse," he wrote,

> ...readers without literature degrees *tend to hate this stuff*. They like coherent characters and stories and settings. So when you start screwing with "representational expectations" (in other words, *unilaterally rewriting* the "bargain") by and large all you end up doing is preaching to the choir, writing for people with literature degrees, which is to say, for people who *already share your values*. In other words, you simply end up *catering to their expectations*. You become an "upscale" version of the very commercial entertainers you continually denigrate.
> (Bakker, 2008; emphasis in original).

Bakker speculated that what he regarded as Harrison's post-modernist elitism could be ultimately be self-defeating. "But what if it works the other way?" he concluded;

> What if the canned experimentalism of post-modernism, by leaving so many readers behind, reinforces the general anti-intellectualism that seems to characterize our culture, and so makes anti-intellectual politicians like (George W) Bush more appealing? This only needs to be an open question to throw

a rather severe light on the political undertones of Harrison's position. He could be the very scourge he's disparaging. (Bakker, 2008).

Building on Harrison's post, writer and editor Lincoln Michel (2017a; 2017b) provided a detailed critique of comprehensive worldbuilding. His points included Kelly Link's comment that it's necessary to make the reader do most of the work (Link, 2015); an observation that the lack of a detailed guide to the Dothraki language in George RR Martin's *A Song of Ice and Fire* (unlike Tolkien's Elvish) is no impediment to the developing narrative of individual characters involved in power struggles; that Ray Bradbury's Martian houses don't have to be structurally plausible to support the story; that internally consistent worldbuilding isn't regarded as necessary in surrealist, magic realist, and post-modernist literature – an established theory of magic is not required to invest magical events in, say, *One Hundred Years of Solitude* (Márquez, 1967) with their power; and that the world of the ground-breaking cyberpunk novel *Neuromancer* was considered insufficiently comprehensive to form the basis for a computer game (Gibson, 2014). Poor storytelling, said Michel, is unlikely to be because of defective worldbuilding, and the writer must not clutter the narrative path with unnecessary detail. He concluded that there is a need to distinguish between, on the one hand, use of "thematically resonant material", allowing the reader to fill in the gaps, and, on the other, inappropriate striving for an apparently "real" version of a fake world.

In response, game designer Martin Rezny (2017) argued at length (if unconvincingly) that logical consistency trumps artistic frippery, finally admitting that what is left undefined may be more interesting than what is explained. Novelist

Emily Temple (2017) contended that worldbuilding is whatever internal consistency is required to make a fiction credible. Temple, however, seemed to miss Michel's adoption of the Wendig (2017) definition of worldbuilding as a comprehensive framework. Similarly, fantasy novelist Daniel Stride (2018) considered that Michel had created a "straw man" in his definition of worldbuilding, and argued that the term includes imaginative suggestion of depth by allusion: "...worldbuilding is creating an immersive setting through the judicious application of particular details." As Harrison (2007) though made clear in the index post, comprehensive, all-encompassing, and commercially-driven worldbuilding has become the standard in fantasy and is very much a valid target of criticism.

In summary of this section, some of the controversy generated by Harrison's 2007 blog is based on variable definitions of the term "worldbuilding". Another major objection is that Harrison's post-modernism represents intellectual elitism. Academic opinion on the relative virtues of literary analysis versus populist commercialism will be reviewed in the next section.

*

In contrast to the high volume of online debate, the body of academic and formally published literature provoked by the topic is relatively slim, and, other than the discussion by Blackmore (2009) of techniques used by Harrison to counter the consolations of worldbuilding fiction, has developed only recently.

Makai (2019) expands on the theme of encyclopaedic worldbuilding as a capitalist reaction to the commercially threatening perceived depth of allusive and evocative fantasy and science fiction. "In the contemporary media landscape," he writes, "the proliferation of world-building fiction is largely due to the desperate need for the limitless expansion of successful intellectual property franchises." (Makai, 2019, p.57). Science fiction and fantastic literature create storyworlds in order to dislocate readers from the environment of their direct experience, in turn providing a way to make social, economic, and cultural (and political) comment on the primary world. This process can, however, become perverted; commercially acquired intellectual properties depend on the plausibility of the world, rather than its characters or narrative, for their success. The reader's "knowability" of the story-world then becomes the subject of "authoritarian high modernism" (Makai, 2019, p.68), supporting capital and with regressive political potential. The Viriconium series and Area X in Jeff VanderMeer's *Southern Reach Trilogy* both subvert this trend by frustrating the logic of internal world consistency.

Elliott (2019) further develops this theme, examining the overt fictional demonstration of a failure of worldbuilding in *The Course of the Heart* (Harrison, 2006). Worldbuilding, Elliott contends, seeks to replace "setting" with "world", denying any ambiguity of language and aiming to prevent any variations in interpretation of text. This aim, in turn, feeds into the reification of popular culture by massive franchises. Invented secondary worlds allow access to supposedly desirable qualities: consistency, comprehensibility, and closure. These are exactly the qualities that Harrison's doomed characters desperately seek, but which are denied to them.

According to Elliott, the techniques used by Harrison to subvert orthodox worldbuilding include "versioning": the presentation of the same characters, events, or places in different and mutually contradictory contexts. This allows Harrison to contradict "the frictionless and amiable fashion that is the dream-portrait that corporations paint of capitalism and themselves" (Elliott, 2019, p.120).

Fraser (2019), transposing the concept of hauntology – the politically populist characterisation of opposed ideologies as horrifying spectres from the past – from Jacques Derrida, characterises Viriconium as a ghostscape, haunted by the spectres of its own past. Like these spectres, the reader cannot "live in" the city, but must "haunt" it. Thus one can come to "know" the "excluded, lost, unacknowledged (and) shifting" things that one would not seek to know, or to know in the same way, in the worldbuilding model. (Fraser, 2019, p.63).

Izzo (2019) claims that, whereas Tolkien achieved an appropriate balance between encyclopaedic worldbuilding and mythopoiesis, modern authors tend to focus too much on one or the other: either choking the narrative with mundane details of the imaginary world, or overemphasising mythmaking. In the former category, Izzo includes works by Brandon Sanderson, Robert Jordan and, in contrast to the assessment of Michel (2017a), George RR Martin; he places M John Harrison, along with Peter S Beagle, Neil Gaiman, and Catherynne M Valente, in the latter.

A dissenting voice is that of writer, academic, and champion of worldbuilding-by-committee for fiction and games, Trent Hergenrader. Citing the views of Harrison and Michel, Hergenrader (2018) considers that they may have missed a broader point, which is that every form of creative writing may not always need to be in service of a story. And yet, Harrison is, precisely, subverting narrative as well as detailed setting in order to oblige the reader to review the world of their experience.

Thus, the body of published opinion in this area recognises that a concept of comprehensive worldbuilding exists and that its application has potential not only to compromise the quality of a narrative, but to reify a reader's imaginative conception of the real world in the service of commercial gain; and that this simultaneously encyclopaedic and reductionist concept of worldbuilding can be subverted by techniques used by Harrison and others to challenge the internal consistency of invented worlds.

*

Makai (2019) has commented that commercially acquired intellectual properties depend on the plausibility of the world, rather than its characters or narrative, for their success. In the absence of such a plausible framework, how does Harrison engage the reader's interest?

It isn't by empathic character development. Harrison's narrative voice is strongly authorial, and sometimes presents the perspectives of several characters in a single page. The reader is told rather than shown their feelings. As in absurdist literature, the characters' motivations and actions are neither explained nor judged. There are few sympathetic figures in the Viriconium series; St Elmo Buffin in *A Storm of Wings*, whom we are actually told is "decent" (Harrison, 1987a, p.126), and his reimagining as the astronomer Emmett Buffo in *In Viriconium* (Harrison, 1984) are exceptions. Male characters especially tend to share traits, are not always easily distinguishable, and frequently fall back on violence in a hopeless attempt to resolve their confusion. This is deliberate; the characters are surrogates for the reader. Their behaviour reflects their perplexity in the face of the irresolvable unknowability of their (and our) world, the inconsequentiality of their actions, and their frustrated attempts to retain control. Character development isn't, however, by itself a sufficient vehicle to carry the reader's interest alone.

The Viriconium stories all retain narrative plot, but this is generally a broad vehicle for the story and lacks intricacy. While plot twists do occur, they are rarely subtle and often telegraphed, subverting literary devices by drawing the reader's attention to their own artifice: in *The Pastel City* (Harrison, 1987b), the missing hero Norvin Trinor turns out, unsurprisingly, to be fighting for the enemy. Narrative flow is at times obstructed by detail, as in the closing sections of *A Storm of Wings*. Literary devices are sometimes used to introduce an ironic element of melodrama: in "A Young Man's Journey to Viriconium", the final story in *Viriconium Nights* (Harrison, 1986), two consecutive sections begin with a quote from a preceding section: "That man's name is Dr Petromax." The weighty implications of the quote, however, are inconsistent with its rather ordinary subject. Harrison does not set out to enthral the reader by the planned unfolding of an intricate plot; in line with the absurdist approach to character action and motivation, dramatic resolution is more likely to be precipitated by a random accident than by purposeful intervention.

Despite its deliberate inconsistency, the hook in the Viriconium series is indeed the setting. Harrison, though, uses very different methods from both encyclopaedic worldbuilding and Tolkien's mythopoiesis to create a very different atmosphere: the ephemeral environment of Viriconium. The application of multiple techniques leads to evocation of a world whose very inconsistency contributes to its dynamic status. The dialectic contained within the setting itself abolishes the reader's requirement for consistent development of character or plot. Immersed in this dreamlike, hallucinatory milieu, the reader is able to experience the narrative without judgement.

Harrison acknowledges his early exposure to TS Eliot

(Darlington, 1984) and uses similar imagist techniques, employing strongly visual language in his evocation of Viriconium:

> Viriconium.
> Its achingly formal gardens and curious geometries, its streets that reek of squashed fruit and fish; its flowers like purple wounds on the lawns of the Hermitage at Trois-Vertes; its palace like a shell; how can one deal with it in words? (Harrison, 1987a, p.187).

(The apparently rhetorical question is ironic; Viriconium, as Harrison (2001) says, is indeed "just words").

Images combining olfactory and visual aspects are very common: "At once a smell filled the room, thick and stale like wet ashes in a dustbin. Pallid oval motes of light, some the size of a birch leaf, others hardly visible, drifted up towards the ceiling." (Harrison, 1986: 27); "It was the smell of a continent of wet cinders, buzzing with huge papery-winged flies under a poisonous brown sky..." (Harrison, 1986: 28); "Sour earth... strewn with dark red petals that give forth a sad odour in the rain." (Harrison, 1986: 32).

Harrison's descriptive language consistently succeeds in establishing an imagist landscape more evocative of dreams than reality, termed by Blackmore (2009) as "hyper-real style". Light has a different quality:

> In Viriconium the light was like the light you see only on record covers and in the colour supplements. Photographic precision of outline under an empty blue sky is one of the most haunting features of the Viriconium landscape. Ordinary subjects – a book, a bowl of anenomes, someone's hand – seem to be lit in a way that makes them very distinct from their background. (Harrison, 1986, p.142).

(The didactic tone of the quote is a metatextual comment, deliberately drawing attention to Harrison's own descriptive technique).

Perspective is portrayed as subtly altered:

> From here he had a view of the Low City, some odd quality of the moonlight giving its back and foreground planes equal value, so that it had no perspective but was just a clutter of blue and gamboge roofs filling the space between his eyes and the hills outside the city.
> (Harrison, 1984, p.10).

And again:

> The mosaic of its roofs, whited by moonlight and last week's frozen snow, lay like the demonstration of some equivocal geometry.
> (Harrison, 1987a, p.143).

Vector and perspective are dissociated. An airboat flying towards the protagonist "...appeared to be stationary, merely growing larger as it neared the tower." (Harrison, 1987b, p.13). The time sequence of movement is disordered:

> Overlaid [...] was a woman in a brown cloak. At first she was tiny and distant, trudging up Henrietta Street towards him; then, without any transitional state at all, she had appeared in the middle ground, posed like a piece of statuary between the puddles, white and naked with one arm held up [...]; finally, with appalling suddenness, she filled his whole field of vision, as if on the Unter-Main-Kai a passerby had leapt in front of him without warning and screamed in his face.
> (Harrison, 1986, p.22).

Other techniques employed by Harrison to emphasise an atmosphere of strangeness are similar to those used by surrealist and absurdist writers. The characters of *In Viriconium* frequently become lost in familiar surroundings. In *The Street of Crocodiles* (2011), the surrealist author Bruno Schulz describes the adventures of a boy sent on a minor errand in a familiar but disorientating city:

> ...the streets multiply, becoming confused and interchanged. There open up, deep inside a city, reflected streets, streets which are doubles, makebelieve streets. One's imagination, bewitched and misled, creates illusory maps of the apparently familiar districts...
> (Schulz, 2011, p.61)

Other than the absence of Harrison's fantasy repertoire, the reader might find it difficult to distinguish this setting from Viriconium. Indeed, in the closing stages of *In Viriconium*, the portrait painter Ashlyme writes in his journal:

> ...a new disorder of the streets. It was a city I knew and yet I could not find my way about it. Avenue turned into endless avenue. Alleys turned back on themselves. The familiar roads repeated themselves infinitely in rows of dusty chestnut trees and iron railings.
> (Harrison, 1984, p.113).

In "Viriconium Knights", a story in *Viriconium Nights* (Harrison, 1986), a wall hanging displays changing topographic scenes that may or may not reflect reality. This echoes Schulz's work, in which maps may take on aspects of the real topography they represent:

> Hung on the wall, the map covered it almost entirely and opened a wide view on the valley of the River Tysmienica, which wound itself like a wavy ribbon of pale gold, on the maze of widely spreading ponds and marshes, on the high ground rising towards the south, gently at first, then in ever tighter ranges [...] . From that faded distance of the periphery, the city rose and grew towards the centre of the map, an undifferentiated mass at first [...] . In that section of the map, the engraver concentrated on the complicated and manifold profusion of streets and alleyways, the sharp lines of cornices, architraves, archivolts, and pilasters [...]. They dramatized and orchestrated in a bleak romantic chiaroscuro the complex architectural polyphony.
> (Schulz, 2011, p.69).

The frequent allusions to strange headgear in Viriconium (horses' skulls, heads of locusts, horned masks) as expressions of menacing, poorly-understood folk culture also recapitulate surrealist writers:

> Ancient, mythical tribes used to embalm their dead... I knew a certain sea captain who had in his cabin a lamp, made by Malayan embalmers from the body of his murdered mistress. On her head, she wore enormous antlers. [...]
> (Schulz, 2011, p.47).

Harrison uses many other absurdist and surrealist techniques, including juxtaposition. Epic events are contrasted with banal circumstances. St Elmo Buffin, in the immediate aftermath of the chaotic and total destruction of his fleet of exquisite warships, asks of visitors he believes, mistakenly, to be bringing help from the city: "Would you like some of this dried herring?" (Harrison, 1987a, p.115). Then, later: "I'm sorry, the fish is awful." (Harrison, 1987, p.116). An almost identical episode is recycled in *In Viriconium* (Harrison, 1984, p.43).

In the final story of *Viriconium Nights* (Harrison, 1986), Polaroid snaps of three pairs of women's shoes thrown into a ditch assume undefined importance, perhaps as a key to access to Viriconium.

In addition to imagism, TS Eliot's intertextuality is transferred to the world of Viriconium, frequently including direct and indirect references to the work of Eliot himself. The tarot card episode in *The Waste Land* is retold in *A Storm of Wings*. "Fear death by water," says Madame Sosostris (Eliot, 1922), while Fat Mam Etteilla prophesies: "Fear death from the air." (Harrison, 1987a, p.26). The range of intertextual allusions, including Rilke and Dante, goes well beyond the standard repertoire of fantasy, helping to enhance the perceived richness and mystery of the setting.

Like Tolkien, Harrison uses different languages to contribute to the depth of the milieu. However, whereas Tolkien employs mostly English for proper names associated with the Shire, and Anglo-Saxon for Rohan, much of the mythopoiesis of *The Lord of the Rings* is associated with the invented language of Elvish.

Harrison, on the other hand, proposes no invented tongue. The Viriconium series contains very few genuine neologisms as proper names; "Erecthalia" and "Alstath Fulthor" in *A Storm of Wings* are rare examples. Many toponyms, usually outside the city, are similar to places in Yorkshire or the rural English midlands; English transliterations of Scots Gaelic are used for many more names of places and characters. In contrast, street names in Viriconium itself are often slightly adapted from real street names in German or French, providing an air of decadent Paris or Weimar Berlin. Others, such as the variously-titled Plaza of Unrealised (or Realised) Time and the Piazza of Inherited Tendencies, nod to surrealism.

Harrison's atavistic languages are not intended to be understood. They are there to provide atmosphere, not meaning. "East and south of Monar runs a strip of heathland whose name, when it still had one, was a handful of primitive syllables scattered like a question into the damp wind." (Harrison, 1987a, p.20).

These touches help to provide a rich, if not readily tangible, contribution to the atmosphere which might not be achieved by a structured invented language.

Fraser (2019) characterises Harrison's recursive montage of allusions, especially those with an atavistic or self-contradictory historical component, as "hauntology". He compares this technique to Walter Benjamin's *The Arcades Project*. "...the 'Viriconium effect'," he writes, "– a disconnected, eternally returning, equivocal present – is the sign of the ghost in the fictions." (Fraser, 2019, p.70).

Fraser also describes the reader's sensation of the city assembling itself for their perception, dissolving again as they move on to a fresh and engrossing montage, and how the characters themselves draw attention to this: "As you walk," says Tomb the dwarf, "...the streets create themselves around you. When you have passed, everything slips immediately back into chaos again." (Harrison, 1987a, p.149)

Harrison's recycling of "images, descriptions, scenes, characters and narrative structures" within and between his texts is styled by Ryan Elliott (2019, p.105) as "versioning". In different accounts and contexts, characters diverge: Ansel Verdigris, a drunken, talentless, and treacherous wannabe poet in *A Storm of Wings* (Harrison, 1987a) and in the stories "The Luck in the Head" and "The Dancer from the Dance" from *Viriconium Nights* (Harrison, 1986), is simultaneously a revered historian and "poet of the city" in *A Storm of Wings* (and ironically styled thus in "The Dancer from the Dance"), and provides the epigram for another *Viriconium Nights* story, "The Lamia and Lord Cromis". Murdered by the agents of the Sign of the Locust amidst the gravestones of Allmen's Heath in *A Storm of Wings*, Verdigris also dies as collateral damage in Ardwick Crome's assassination attempt on Mammy Vooley in "The Luck in the Head". Characters from different scenes and different stories may also converge: St Elmo Buffin in *A Storm of Wings* is essentially the same as Emmet Buffo in *In Viriconium*.

Like Harrison's obvious plot manipulations, versioning renders the authorial process visible, challenging the reader to analyse the versions and their contexts and to question the basis of immersive popular fiction. Whereas the seamless arrangement of internal references in comprehensive worldbuilding fiction dampens resonance and "fuses the separate components together by methodically eliminating the distinctness of the contexts in which components occur, rendering the connectivity between texts inert", versioning, by drawing attention to the different contexts of a recycled element, "employs language's allusive capacities to encourage interpretive resonance within and between texts." (Elliott, 2019, p.119).

In short, Harrison uses methods including imagism, surrealist and absurdist techniques, intertextuality, allusional montage, and complex internal reference to create a shimmering, perplexing, and dreamlike perception of the present moment, in which the direct provenance and consequences of the narrative lose their importance. The reader is simultaneously enthralled and unsettled, challenged to question the inert conventions of worldbuilding fiction, achieving a richer experience as a result.

*

Comments such as "the reader doing the work", "filling the gaps", and "joining up the dots" are frequent in discussions about Harrison's writing. Fraser (2019) devoted a section of an essay on Harrison to examining the role of the reader as author. Nevertheless, there are no identified records of application of Iser's reader-response theory to Harrison's work.

In *The Implied Reader* (1978) and *The Act of Reading* (1980), Wolfgang Iser stressed the phenomenological aspects of reader reception theory: that is, the experience of the reader as foremost in determining the realisation of the text in order to form the "work". Every text has two poles: an artistic pole, determined by the author, and an aesthetic pole, achieved by the reader's concretisation of the text. The final literary work is created by the convergence of text and reader.

If a text fails to sustain the reader's illusory model, they will be unable to engage. On the other hand, an all-embracing illusion (including, perhaps, encyclopaedic worldbuilding) will reduce the polysemantic potential of the text to a single level of meaning and also fail to maintain interest. In order to engage the reader, therefore, the author must put into place "a network of response-inviting structures". This textual structure Iser identifies as "the implied reader".

The implied reader, however, although distinct from the real reader, is also a "structured act", brought into play by the reading process and facilitating the actualisation of the text.

The scene for the dynamic and creative interaction between text and reader is set by what Iser labels "repertoire": a framework of literary patterns, themes, and social contexts familiar to the reader. "The repertoire consists of all the familiar territory within the text. This may be in the form of references to earlier works, or to social and historical norms, or to the whole culture from which the text has emerged." (Iser, 1978, p.69).

The release of the aesthetic experience by the reader in their interaction with the text is in effect a performance. In order to achieve this the reader must both look back at the information gained from the text and anticipate what will happen next. This involves a dynamic process of anticipation, frustration, retrospection, reconstruction, and satisfaction.

As well as filling in blanks in the text, the reader must resolve "negations": contradictions in the repertoire, allowing words to transcend their literal meaning. The organised structures of familiar knowledge may be deformed, and the reader is obliged to examine accepted norms dislocated from their external context. Their continuing search for consistency is thus a non-linear process; rather than being an intrinsic property of the text, coherence of meaning is projected onto the text by the reader. This process facilitates assimilation of the text into a synthesis that allows the reader to learn something of themselves and mimics the experience of real life. Thus "... the reading experience can illuminate basic patterns of real experience." (Iser, 1978, p.281).

Alter (2011) examines the application of reader-response theory to the creation of a sense of place in fantasy literature, determining what lessons can be learnt by a prospective author. Concentrating on the repertoire of the text and the reader's horizon (a term in fact due to Hans Robert Jauss rather than Iser, and used by Alter to indicate the reader's process of anticipation and retrospection), she argues that communication of a fantasy setting can be developed, contested, and adapted in the same way as can plot or character in order to maintain reader interest.

The repertoire of the Viriconium series is immensely rich, borrowing themes not only from high fantasy (incorporating folklore and mythology) and Golden Age science fiction, but from mediaeval romance, 19th century urban fiction, romanticism, decadent literature, occultism, classical horror, weird fiction, surrealism, and high adventure stories. In addition, there are intertextual allusions to canonical authors including Dante, Rilke, and Heine. While even the most erudite reader of fantasy may not be familiar with the complete repertoire, they may still be engaged by the suggested mystery of the arcane allusions.

How, though, will the lack of fixed points in the text of Viriconium influence the reader's search for consistency?

In his analysis of a writer even less affirmative than Harrison, Samuel Beckett, Iser (2014) shows that Beckett, by exploring the anatomy of fiction through fiction itself, challenges the central conceit of concord fiction: that the falseness of its comforting answers must not be acknowledged. Beckett's frequent theme of an endpoint demonstrates that our overwhelming human need to imagine a conclusion is itself false; as the reader progresses through a Beckett text the end that obsesses the characters becomes even more ill-defined than at the beginning while, paradoxically, the characters' concern about the ending seems to diminish.

If memory is used to link different aspects of the ego then this becomes habit, which in turn vetoes the perception of an object as novel and a source of enchantment. Literature is necessary to confront us with strangeness and perhaps to understand how we acquire experience. "We can only talk of experiences if our preconceptions have been modified or transformed by them." (Iser, 2014, p.40).

We cannot know what it means to be alive, and attempts to do so must result in images which can only be fictions. Although we cannot help the continual invention of images we must reject their claims to truth. We cannot abandon our fictions, but must appreciate that they are indeed fictions. Accepting the incomprehensibility of reality allows us to see through the artifice of fiction that pretends to know the unknowable, but it's our incomprehension itself that gives rise to the need for fiction. Precisely because we can settle on no finality, we continue to be active. The destruction of meaning by a Beckett text allows the text to be experienced.

Beckett's subversion of meaning (labelled by Iser "negativeness") is the technique used to synthesise fictions while demonstrating the nature of fiction itself. The reader, continually obliged to reject meanings stimulated by the text but invented by themselves, may gain insights into the factors that guide their own interpretation and perhaps free themselves from the constrictions of their preconceived outlook.

Harrison (2001) makes it clear that his aim, since Viriconium has been swept clear of values, is to oblige the reader to reinsert them and, in the process, reexamine their value system. "Recognise this procedure?" he asks. "It's called life. This is one of Viriconium's many jigsawed messages to the reader. You can't hope to control things. Learn to love the vertigo of experience instead."

The Viriconium stories do reach conclusions, but these themselves deliberately subvert the form of the novels and stories. The main character of The Pastel City misses the litany of triumphant endings recounted by the author, but in an epilogue agrees to return to service on the condition that another character refrain from explaining to him the meaning of the Name Stars; that is, as long as his incomprehension of the past can be maintained. In *A Storm of Wings*, the shock wave caused by the destruction of the bloated and epically perplexed Benedict Paucemanly enters Viriconium "to empty those ancient streets of all illusions but their proper human ones" (Harrison, 1987, p.185). Memory and history are inconsistent and unreliable; any attempt to use them to guide action is bound to fail.

In Viriconium, the reader will appreciate that the reference points of the text are not fixed and that no template to establish control is available. They will become enmeshed in a web of allusion, imagery and action, simultaneously dense and ephemeral; an advancing wavefront of the moment. As the city dissolves and reassembles itself, they will be subject to the illusion of an intricately unfolding plot that doesn't exist, and will appreciate this as well. Perhaps the experience will allow them to examine their values afresh and contribute to their realisation of the essential unknowability of life and the true role of fiction.

References

Alter, N., 2011. *Creating a sense of place in fantasy fiction*. [online] Available at: <http://www.textjournal.com.au/april11/alter.htm> [Accessed 27 August 2020].

Asoiaf, 2007. *Viriconium (M. John Harrison)*. [online] Available at: <https://asoiaf.westeros.org/index.php?/topic/24301-viriconium-m-john-harrison/#comments> [Accessed 27 August 2020].

Bakker, R. S., 2008. *New R. Scott Bakker Q&A*. [online] Available at: <http://fantasyhotlist.blogspot.com/2008/01/new-r-scott-bakker-q.html> [Accessed 27 August 2020]

Blackmore, L., 2009. Undoing the mechanisms: Genre Expectation, Subversion, and Anti-Consolation in the Kefahuchi Tract Novels of M. John Harrison. *Studies in the Fantastic* (2), pp.21-47.

Darlington, A., 1984. The Condition of Falling: interview of M. John Harrison. *Vector* 122(3), pp.3-6.

Eliot, T. S., 1922. *The Waste Land*. [online] Available at: <https://www.poetryfoundation.org/poems/47311/the-waste-land> [Accessed 27 August 2020].

Elliott, R., 2019. On Versioning. In: R. Williams and M. Bould, eds. *M. John Harrison: Critical Essays*. Canterbury, Gylphi Limited. Ch.7.

Ellis, W., 2007. *M. John Harrison on worldbuilding*. [online]. Available at: <https://warrenellis.com/m-john-harrison-on-worldbuilding/> [Accessed 27 August 2020].

Fraser, G., 2019. Viriconium Ghostwalk. In: R. Williams and M. Bould, eds. *M. John Harrison: Critical Essays*. Canterbury, Gylphi Limited. Ch.5.

Gibson, W., 2014. *William Gibson on the Apocalypse, America, and The Peripheral's Ending.* [online] Available at: <https://io9.gizmodo.com/william-gibson-on-the-apocalypse-america-and-the-peri-1656659382> [Accessed 27 August 2020].

Harrison, M. J., 1984. *In Viriconium*. 2nd ed. London: Unwin Paperbacks.
—, 1986. *Viriconium Nights*. 2nd ed. London: Unwin Paperbacks.

—, 1987a. *A Storm of Wings*. 2nd ed. London: Unwin Paperbacks.
—, 1987b. *The Pastel City*. 2nd ed. London: Unwin Paperbacks.
—, 2001. *What It Might Be Like to Live in Viriconium*. [online] Available at: <https://fantasticmetropolis.com/i/viriconium> [Accessed 27 August 2020].
—, 2006. The Course of the Heart. San Francisco: Night Shade Books.
—, 2007. *very afraid*. [online] Available at: <http://web.archive.org/web/20080410181840/http://uzwi.wordpress.com/2007/01/27/very-afraid/> [Accessed 27 August 2020].

Hergenrader, T., 2018. *Collaborative Worldbuilding for Writers and Gamers*. London: Bloomsbury Academic.

Iser, W., 1978. *The Implied Reader: Patterns of Communication in Prose Fiction from Bunyan to Beckett*. Baltimore: The Johns Hopkins University Press.
—, 1980. *The Act of Reading: A Theory of Aesthetic Response*. Baltimore: The Johns Hopkins University Press.
—, 2014. When is the end not the end? The idea of fiction in Beckett. In S. E. Gontarski, ed. *On Beckett: Essays and Criticisms*. London: Anthem Press.

Izzo, M., 2019. Worldbuilding and Mythopoeia in Tolkien and post-Tolkienan Fantasy Literature. In: D. Fimi and T. Honegger, eds. *Sub-creating Arda: World-Building in J. R. R. Tolkien's Works, its Precursors and Legacies*. Zollikofen: Walking Tree Publishers. Ch.4.

Kelly, L, 2015. *Kelly Link and Lev Grossman discuss world building at WORD Jersey City*. [online] Available at: <https://youtu.be/CJTS7FNQKQE> [Accessed 27 August 2020].

Makai, P. K., 2019. Beyond Fantastic Self-indulgence: Aesthetic Limits to World-building. In: D. Fimi and T. Honegger, eds. *Sub-creating Arda: World-building in J. R. R. Tolkien's Works, its Precursor,s and Legacies*. Zollikofen: Walking Tree Publishers. Ch.5.

Márquez, G.G., 1967. *One Hundred Years of Solitude*. Buenos Aires: Editorial Sudamericana.

Michel, L., 2017a. *Against Worldbuilding*. [online] Available at: <https://electricliterature.com/against-worldbuilding/> [Accessed 27 August 2020].

Michel, l., 2017b. *More Thoughts about Worldbuilding and Food*. [online] Avaiable at: <https://electricliterature.com/more-thoughts-about-

worldbuilding-and-food/> [Accessed 27 August 2020].

Miéville, C., 2011. *Mind Meld Make-Up with China Miéville on Worldbuilding.* [online] Available at: <http://www.sfsignal.com/archives/2011/05/mind_meld_make-up_with_china_miville_on_world-building/> [Accessed 27 August 2020].

Reddit, 2015. *M. John Harrison's critique of "worldbuilding" in fiction.* [online] Available at: <https://www.reddit.com/r/literature/comments/2p7l25/m_john_harrisons_fascinating_critique_of/> [Accessed 27 August 2020].

Rezny, M., 2017. *How (and Why) to Write Realistic Aliens and Magic.* [online] Available at: <https://medium.com/electric-literature/how-and-why-to-write-realistic-aliens-and-magic-a6e4427c94a5> [Accessed 27 August 2020].

Schulz, B., 2011. *The Fictions of Bruno Schulz: The Street of Crocodiles & Sanatorium under the Sign of the Hourglass*. Translated from Polish by Celina Wienwieska. Basingstoke: Picador.

Stride, D., 2018. *A World of Straw: Lincoln Michel on Worldbuilding.* [online] Available at: <https://phuulishfellow.wordpress.com/2018/09/25/a-world-of-straw-lincoln-michel-on-worldbuilding/> [Accessed 27 August 2020].

Temple, S., 2017. *In Defense of Worldbuilding.* [online] Available at: <https://lithub.com/in-defense-of-worldbuilding/> [Accessed 27 August 2020].

Vandermeer, J., 2008. *M. John Harrison on "World-Building".* [online] Available at: <https://www.jeffvandermeer.com/2008/01/21/m-john-harrison-on-world-building/> [Accessed 27 August 2020].

Wendig, C., 2013. *25 Things You Should Know About Worldbuilding.* [online] Available at: <http://terribleminds.com/ramble/2013/09/17/25-things-you-should-know-about-worldbuilding/> [Accessed 27 August 2020].

Worldbuilding in Ngũgĩ wa Thiong'o's
The Perfect Nine:
The Epic of Gĩkũyũ and Mũmbi

Eugen Bacon

Abstract

"Life has and has not a beginning.
Life has and has not an end.
The beginning is the end and the end is the beginning."
(wa Thiong'o, 2020, p.189)

Creating imaginary worlds is essential in all forms of speculative fiction, whether the work is a novel or a short story. It is an investment that compounds the credibility of the work to the reader. Richly invented worlds, made-up languages, visionary topography and ingenious perspective teleport the reader to infinite possibilities inside the fictional realms of the author's inventiveness. Ngũgĩ wa Thiong'o's *The Perfect Nine: The Epic of Gĩkũyũ and Mũmbi* is an epic story on the founding of the nine clans of the Gĩkũyũ people of Kenya, told from a feminist perspective. This essay explores the worldbuilding, as it applies through creation mythology, culture, nature and the otherwordly, in a verse narrative that blends folklore, mythology, adventure and allegory. The author frames a large-scale metaphoric world that's also accessible to the reader, in this lush chronicle on the genesis of Gĩkũyũ clans through valour, family, nature and nurture. The success of his creation validates Ngũgĩ wa Thiong'o as a leading literary African author and scholar, a recipient of twelve honorary doctorates, and a nominee for the Man Booker International Prize.

Introducing the novel

Ngũgĩ wa Thiong'o's black speculative fiction is a translation of its original Gĩkũyũ version titled *Kenda Mũiyũru* (2018). *The Perfect Nine: The Epic of Gĩkũyũ and Mũmbi* (2020) is a quest narrative that reimagines the mythology of Gĩkũyũ and Mũmbi (Kariuki, 2019)—who are the respective traditional 'Adam and Eve' of the Gĩkũyũ people, one of the forty-two tribes in Kenya, East Africa (Gĩkũyũ Centre for Cultural Studies, 2020).

The novel follows Christopher Vogler's mythic structure as explored in his book *The Writer's Journey* (1998), interrogating the relationship between mythology and storytelling. Vogler's template is itself borrowed from mythologist Joseph Campbell, who wrote *The Hero with a Thousand Faces* (1949), and who in turn took his template from Carl Jung's theories of archetypes, the personal and collective unconscious, and the human psyche. Campbell's ideas, including those on myth, the modern world, and the hero's adventure, appear in *The Power of Myth* (Campbell & Moyers 1988). In *The Hero's Journey* (1990) Campbell studied the hero's call to adventure, the road of trials, the vision quest … all the way to the return to the threshold, where the hero/ine reappears triumphant, to deserved recognition. To Campbell, myths are the masks of God through which persons seek to relate themselves to the wonders of existence. But in *The Perfect Nine*, there's not one hero/ine, but manifold potential heroes and heroines, as ninety-nine suitors embark on a quest rife with trials and tribulations, to win the hands of nine (plus one) daughters of Gĩkũyũ and Mũmbi.

The story starts with the ordinary world, in which the parents, Gĩkũyũ (man) and Mũmbi (woman), survive their own creation and hurdles to reach their home in a place called Mũkũrũweinĩ.

Their nine beautiful daughters, who are actually ten, are now mature for marriage. The daughters (Wanjirũ, Wambũi, Wanjikũ, Wangũi, Waithĩra, Njeri, Mwĩthaga, Wairimũ, Wangarĩ, and Warigia), despite their own self-sufficiency—they have grown without brothers and don't need men to complete them— understand the trinity of life: birth, life, death.

Each daughter has a role to build a clan, and suitors aren't lacking. Handsome young men arrive from far afield, lured by the silhouettes of the daughters' beauty in their dreams, girls in fantasies who lead them down valleys to rivers with song. In a feast of song and dance, the suitors perform their own songs and dances of their regions, some picked up on the way. Gĩkũyũ and Mũmbi place upon the suitors many challenges—initially meek ones: building a hut in one day, finding the daughters hidden in a black forest, making clothes from slaughtered animal skin, shooting an arrow in the eye of a tree at climbing distance. The remainder must go on a final challenge that is two-fold: to travel to the mountain of the moon and catch a piece of the moon in a gourd and mix it with water from the lake; and to find the cure-all hair of the unseen king of the human-eating ogres—healing hair that grows in the middle of the ogre's tongue. It's a special hair that will restore Warigia, the unspoken tenth, born with a disability.

Typical of the quest narrative, some suitors refuse the call to adventure. Those that accept it find that they must rely on the daughters in their wisdoms to serve as mentors as they cross thresholds—obstacle after obstacle—to reach the fruition of their quest. But once the treasures are achieved, there's an ordeal to make it back, the journey home as perilous as the adventure from it, and it's life or death for many. Finally, only ten suitors are the last ones standing, a man for each daughter.

For those who have read Ngũgĩ wa Thiong'o's fiction—

comprising *Wizard of the Crow* (2006), *Petals of Blood* (1977), *The River Between* (1965)—some curriculum in African literature, for those who have seen his plays, like *The Black Hermit* (1963), or read his essays and memoirs, there's always the unexpected. Having overcome the novel's arrival in verse form, there's a whole new world for the reader to understand and find immersion, and herein comes the author's critical role of worldbuilding.

The importance of worldbuilding

Creating imaginary worlds is essential in all forms of speculative fiction, whether one is writing a novel or a short story. Orson Scott Card in his book *How to Write Science Fiction and Fantasy* (1990) speaks to the importance of worldbuilding in hooking the reader:

> Many readers, having once discovered a strange world that they enjoy, want to return to that same world again and again, until they're more familiar with that imaginary place than they are with the real-world town they live in.
> (Card, 1990, p.24)

Assigning a whole chapter on world creation, Card emphasises the importance of making rules for the invented world, rules that do not obstruct the reader but rather open possibilities and make the new world—however removed from the real world— credible to the reader. Worldbuilding gives evolution, history, culture, language, biography to the new world, and the reader can relate to it.

Istvan Csicsery-Ronay Jr in his essay 'Who Framed Science Fiction' (2004) that's an analysis of Peter Stockwell's *The Poetics of Science Fiction* (2000), asserts that science fiction (and this applies to speculative fiction) specialises in producing large-scale metaphoric structures that engage the reader through the author's architecture of a rich, textual universe that can map into the reader's reality (Csicsery-Ronay, 2004, p.125). While in short fiction worldbuilding need not be elaborate, if one goes with Raymond Carver's approach to writing the short form as 'Get in, get out. Don't linger. Go on' (1981), a good writer must take time on setting in their speculative world, big or small. Worldbuilding is the essence, and Ngũgĩ wa Thiong'o in his novel applies various forms of literary devices to achieve effective worldbuilding.

Worldbuilding through creation mythology

> "Making things is a matter of hands and eyes.
> *All my daughters are makers of things."*
> (wa Thiong'o, 2020, p.70)

The novel borrows from the folklore on the founding of Gĩkũyũ clans that begot a nation. The god of the mount, who is also the giver supreme, the god of many names, known as Mulungu, Unkulunku, Nyasai, Jok, Ngai, Yahweh and Allah, is a he/she that is a unifying god. The giver puts Gĩkũyũ and Mũmbi at the top of the snow-capped Mount Kenya (like the Garden of Eve) and they survey the lands around.

They stand in awe at the summit, 'white and massive as the moon' (wa Thiong'o, 2020, p.5), and gaze out at undulating plains, hills, valleys, rivers that flow through lilies. As they take in grass plains populated by giraffe, gazelles, zebra, antelope, buffalo, lions, ostriches, partridges, and listen to chirping birds all around the mountain, Gĩkũyũ and Mũmbi determine that the lands out yonder and swollen with fig trees and olive trees, those forests and mounts full of melodies, will become home. But to reach Mũkũrũweinĩ—where swallows sing in the air, time flows like an endless river, pregnant clouds let down rain, and earth drinks the water to grow roots and bear fruits and flowers—Gĩkũyũ and Mũmbi must first beat obstacles in malevolent nature.

Later, they will return to the same snow-capped mountains, the mountain top where the giver supreme put them, this time to ask for suitors for their daughters.

Leveraging from the creation mythology of the Gĩkũyũ people, Ngũgĩ wa Thiong'o gives the story a credible beginning and makes the characters—teeming with life purpose—matter. This supports the quest narrative's construction and encourages the reader's immersion.

Worldbuilding through culture

Csicsery-Ronay Jr speaks of language as part of worldbuilding in the physics and biologies of imaginary worlds. Language as culture is part of worldbuilding. Ngũgĩ wa Thiong'o uses the strong Gĩkũyũ slant of the novel, including the naming of people and places, to build the invented world.

In speculative fiction, the works of Le Guin and Tolkien, for example, showcase elaborate worlds, crafted languages and imaginative presentations that invite us to what Richard Mathews termed 'infinite possibility' in his book *Fantasy: The Liberation of Imagination* (2002). There is a large presence of language and sophistication in the created worlds inside the fictional realms of Le Guin's Earthsea books and Tolkien's *The Lord of the Rings* (1954). Both authors love languages, where Le Guin applies it as power in the Earthsea books, and knowledge of the language of magic, the language of dragons, the language of nature, the language of creation … is power. To philologist Tolkien, the culture and linguistics of Middle-earth are part of his investment in worldbuilding that compounds the credibility of his fantasy works as literature classics.

Ngũgĩ wa Thiong'o shows intimate knowledge of his own world, investing in an examination and comprehension of the Gĩkũyũ tradition, that guides his creation of a complex and believable imaginary world. It's a strange imaginary world but understanding its culture helps the reader who is unfamiliar with the Gĩkũyũ culture to see the world of the Gĩkũyũ people with fresh eyes.

One would wonder about the pitfalls of pronouncing unusual names and places emerging as obstacles to the reader. Orson Scott Card cautions on care in the invention of language: Can the human mouth pronounce it? (1990, p.56). Card states:

> Words or names that are mere collections of odd letters like xxyqhhp or h'psps't are doubly dumb, first because they constantly distract the reader and force him to withdraw from the story and think about the letters on the page, and second because even strange and difficult languages, when transliterated into the Roman alphabet, will follow Roman alphabetic conventions.
> (Card, 1990, p.56)

Ngũgĩ wa Thiong'o avoids these pitfalls because the Gĩkũyũ language is phonetically accessible, as are the names of the characters in *The Perfect Nine*. In a prologue that introduces the reader to the language, the author breaks down the main phonetics:

> … in Gĩkũyũ, the "ũ" is pronounced like the "o" in "boat"; the "ĩ" is pronounced like the "a" in "take" (p.ix)

In addition to language, the author invites the reader into the African world and its culture through place (thatched-roof huts, granaries full of harvest, kraals full of cows, goats and sheep); through clothing (brides in soft leather skirts trimmed at the edge with a multicolour of beads and shells, necklaces and copper rings around the women's necks); through food: (goat meat, sweet potatoes, yams, arrowroots, millet, sorghum, herbal wine); through song and dance (drums, flutes, whistles, claps, ululations); and through the power of oral storytelling (as days came and went, feasting in daytime, storytelling in the evening) before embarking on the ultimate quest.

The Perfect Nine is deeply cultural, emphasising the importance of naming in African tradition, the place of ceremony and the heart of kinship, bonded by blood or marriage—as one groom says to Gĩkũyũ and Mũmbi:

> "I want to talk to you, my father and my mother," he said,
> "For I cannot call you by any other name, given that
> You received me and accepted me as your son."
> (wa Thiong'o, 2020, p.200)

Through culture, Ngũgĩ wa Thiong'o builds on the basic concepts that run across the narrative, building history, developing the rules of the invented world, then dramatizing them, in order that the literary construction is not only accessible but fascinating to the reader.

Worldbuilding through nature

There's good nature and bad nature. Mũmbi speaks of the power of nature:

> Water is life for humans, animals, and plants.
> Water makes the mud out of which life is molded.
> The sun sends rays of heat into the muddy dough,
> And breathes the breath of life into the dough.
> The earth drinks the water and seeds sprout.
> (wa Thiong'o, 2020, p.188)

Together with her husband Gĩkũyũ and their daughters, she values the land of Mũkũrũweinĩ with its water, earth, air and sun, the place where man, woman, birds, worms, animals and creatures of the sea live as one with nature. She speaks to the suitors about the sacredness of land and nature:

> She told them that reverence for all life was one of the rules of Gĩkũyũ and Mũmbi.
> To harm plants and animals without good cause was to harm life.
> Never kill an animal unless in defense of self or to satisfy hunger.
> And if one uproots a tree, one must plant another to replace it.
> (wa Thiong'o, 2020, p.69)

But not all nature is good. The story uses hostile nature to foreshadow a survivor's story, a narrative of courage, not only in Gĩkũyũ and his wife Mũmbi, but in their daughters and their suitors. It is malevolent nature that spews harms on the way, like the red boulders Gĩkũyũ and Mũmbi dodged, the ones that chased them to the plains before they reached Mũkũrũweinĩ. Like the world that convulsed and erupted around them, ridges forming as the earth trembled, and tremors from the belly of the land forged gobbling valleys deep and wide. Like the rivers of fire, whose flames spurted skyward to devour hills and whose fumes incinerated the flora and fauna. There's darkness so deep, it makes the rest of the darkness look like day. It's a darkness shaped like a human, and echoes of sound herald the wander of spirits in the forest.

And once Gĩkũyũ and Mũmbi had cautiously delivered themselves to Mũkũrũweinĩ, their home country, their daughters and their suitors would also face nature's harms in the shape of hurricanes that carried men in the air like leaves, wind that shuddered as it plummeted dying humans onto the land, rivers that refused to be clean but were murky with bamboo and crocodiles, grass that sank and swallowed men, not to mention the thorns, nettles, nests of red ants, dusts of tsetse flies and the otherworldly creatures hindering the journey.

Through nature, Ngũgĩ wa Thiong'o builds and populates his invented world, and breathes into it subversive messages of sustainability, the power of nature and humanity's harmony, or disharmony, with the environment.

Worldbuilding through otherworldly creatures

An ogre was an ogre, no matter their names.
(wa Thiong'o, 2020, p.131)

Gĩkũyũ and Mũmbi, before they were safe in Mũkũrũweinĩ, encountered the dragon of the water that vomited white anger on the shore. Now their daughters and their suitors in their quests will meet more otherworldly creatures in the forests full of black and pregnant with ogres.

Ogres like the king whose magical hair on his tongue can heal Warigia, but which suitor has the courage, or cunning, to endeavour the hair's retrieval? Through the ogre of endless darkness, the ogre that fumes fire and fury, the ogres that morph into a hyena and the vulture, the reader gets to understand the hostile landscape, and comprehend characterisation and the perils of the treasure hunt, which endows more significance (and readerly gratification) to the narrative's climax and the denouement when they arrive.

And though beauty is in the eye of the beholder, the reader discovers with the daughters and their suitors that there are beauties that are inherently evil:

> Suddenly another wonder sprang up before us.
> I can't remember who first spotted him, but
> He was extremely well built, a beauty the color of chalk.
> The entire body, together with the clothes, was chalk white.
> His hair—long, straight, and soft-looking—fell on his back and shoulders.
> It was also chalky, whiter than the whiteness of an ostrich.
> But let the rays of the setting sun fall on his body and clothes,
> And they shone with more than the seven colors of the rainbow.
> And then he whistled at us.
> (wa Thiong'o, 2020, p.163–164)

Another white beauty emerges, and she is equally ravishing. As the daughters and their suitors find distraction in the white, long-haired newcomers, the daughter Wanjikũ comes to her senses and reprimands the rest for preferring all that glitters. Just then, a strong wind blows and reveals the beauty for the skeleton it is—an ogre of the white chalk, wearing masks of human body and hair. And there's a moral to the story about coveting that which you don't know, about an 'outer' that conceals the 'inner'.

Through otherworldly creatures in *The Perfect Nine*, Ngũgĩ wa Thiong'o successfully introduces vital tensions in the narrative, inward turmoils and outer conflicts that move the quest narrative forward.

In closing

Overall, in *The Perfect Nine*, Ngũgĩ wa Thiong'o creates a well-mapped literature of the strange, one that's accessible to the reader because of its elaborate worldbuilding in the creation mythology, culture, nature and otherworldly beings. His own understanding of the Gĩkũyũ people, and hosting the narration within the frameworks of Gĩkũyũ folklore and real-world traditions, helps to map an invented world that the reader understands. The author's investment in worldbuilding compounds the credibility of their fiction to the universal reader, in a work that invites the reader to enrich their curiosity on the mythologies and traditions of the Gĩkũyũ people, and African literature in general.

References

Campbell, J., 1949. *The Hero with a Thousand Faces*. New York: Pantheon.
—, 1990. *The Hero's Journey: Joseph Campbell on His Life and Work*. 3rd ed., ed P Cousineau. New York: Harper & Row.

Campbell, J. & Moyers, B., 1988. *The Power of Myth*. New York: Doubleday.

Card, O. S., 1990. *How to Write Science Fiction and Fantasy*. Ohio: Writer's Digest Books.

Carver, R., 1981. *A Storyteller's Shoptalk*. [online] Available at <https://www.nytimes.com/books/01/01/21/specials/carver-shoptalk.html> [Accessed 30 May 2020].

Csicsery-Ronay, Istvan Jr., 2004. *Who Framed Science Fiction*. [online] Available at <https://www.jstor.org/stable/i394218> [Accessed 30 May 2020].

Gĩkũyũ Centre for Cultural Studies 2020. *Gikuyu Origins*. [online] Available at <https://mukuyu.wordpress.com/tag/kikuyu-creation-myth/> [Accessed 30 May 2020].

Kariuki, E., 2019. *Kikuyu, Meru, Gumba and Chuka Myths of Origin*. [online] Available at <https://owlcation.com/social-sciences/Kikuyu-Other-myths-of-Origin> [Accessed 30 May 2020].

Mathews, R., 2002. *Fantasy: The Liberation of the Imagination*. London: Routledge.

Stockwell, P., 2000. *The Poetics of Science Fiction*. Harlow, UK: Longman.

Tolkien, J.R.R., 1954. *The Lord of the Rings*. London: George Allen & Unwin Ltd.

Vogler, C., 1998. *The Writer's Journey*. 3rd edn. Studio City, California: Michael Wiese.

wa Thiong'o, N., 1963. *The Black Hermit*. Kampala: Makerere University Press.
—, 1965. *The River Between*. London: Heinemann—African Writers Series.
—, 1977. *Petals of Blood*. London: Heinemann—African Writers Series.
—, 2006. *Wizard of the Crow*. London: Harvill Secker.
—, 2018. *Kenda Mũiyũru*. Nairobi: East African Educational Publishers Ltd.
—, 2020. *The Perfect Nine: The Epic of Gĩkũyũ and Mũmbi*. New York: The New Press.

Environmental Change as Catalyst for Worldbuilding in Ursula K. Le Guin's *Always Coming Home*

Octavia Cade

Abstract

Ursula K. Le Guin, in her novel *Always Coming Home*, constructs a future anthropological textbook describing the fictional Kesh people, one which contains records of their culture. That culture is post-apocalyptic, although within the histories of the surviving population no record of that apocalypse remains. Nonetheless, it is clear from the text that the disaster was environmental in nature, with tectonic change and rising sea levels changing the geography of the world. The Kesh, unmoored from their pre-apocalyptic history, and existing in a fundamentally different ecology, have developed a society adapted to their new environment. Le Guin therefore uses devastating environmental change as a catalyst for cultural change, and her interest in anthropology – derived from her father Alfred Louis Kroeber, who was an anthropologist himself – has resulted in a holistic approach to worldbuilding. The impact of apocalyptic change has been so immense that it reverberates through all aspects of Kesh life – including art, music, human reproduction, labour relations and housing – and by treating worldbuilding as an exercise in anthropology, Le Guin has created an entirely fictional culture that contains artefacts of modern life but is not defined by it. This worldbuilding, predicated as it is on a new way of interacting with a new environment, shines a light on the tensions and problematic relationships of human interactions with the natural world today.

*

If science fiction can be used as a lens by which contemporary society may be critiqued, then the alternate universe is possibly one of the most useful tools by which that critique is accomplished. Describing a world, familiar to the readers and yet different, allows those readers to compare and contrast the different aspects of their culture with the speculative mirror the alternate universe presents. Furthermore, if the instigating factor – the factor which prompts the change to a new world, and a new way of living – is something which can also occur in the contemporary world of the reader, then the alternate universe can also provide a potential future, and one which can either be worked towards or avoided.

Clearly, there are some instigating factors which cannot be recreated. The outcome of a past battle, for instance, or an earlier discovery of an influential technology such as electricity or steam... these scenarios can easily be explored within alternate universe science fiction, but they will always be entirely fictional. Instigating factors such as significant environmental change, on the other hand, can provide a more malleable – and more realistically plausible – narrative, on the grounds that these events can actually, or may still in the future, take place.

Always Coming Home, by Ursula K. Le Guin (first published in 1985), is an example of this latter kind of science fiction. The text is presented as a form of anthropological record, seemingly part textbook and part narrative; a particularly interesting choice given that "science-fiction as a genre provides opportunities for performing thought experiments in the field of anthropology, serving as a perfect testing ground for hypothetical scenarios that predict possible future(s) of human societies" (Jakimovska and Jakimovski, 2010, p.55). Similarly, Baker-Cristales argues that Le Guin, in texts like *Always Coming Home*, is carrying out "an anthropological thought experiment – what sorts of possibilities are there for human existence, thought, and social ordering?" (2012, p.24). These are questions asked, and answered, in a very specific setting – indeed, it is arguable that such questions, and such thought experiments, are incapable of being answered without a close understanding of their own particular setting.

The book opens with the sentence "The people in this book might be going to have lived a long, long time from now in Northern California" (Le Guin, 2001, p.xi). This gives a very clear setting for *Always Coming Home*, a setting that provides from the first a means of comparison to a specific existing location, both social and environmental. It is also clear, however, that this setting, for all the familiarity that "Northern California" may present, is simultaneously substantially different in its presentation.

The greatest part of that change is geological, resulting from the earthquakes that – in any reality – are part of life on what is known as the Cascadia Subduction Zone, the tectonic plate boundary that stretches from Northern California to Canada. This has led, in *Always Coming Home*, to a changed landscape, one substantially different from that experienced today. A landscape, in fact, that is so different that modern maps are no longer accurate: "Nobody knew how old the maps we had were [...] but they were out of date" (Le Guin, 2001, p.139). There have been "earthquakes and shifts along fault lines, vast subsidences and local elevations, all of which had, among other effects, left most of what we know as the Great Valley of California a shallow sea or salt-marsh, and brought the Gulf of California on up into Arizona and Nevada" (Le Guin, 2001, p.159). The change is hard to navigate, with the land

so buckled up by earthquakes and subsidences and so deeply
scored by faults and rifts that walking the length of it is like
crossing a forest by climbing up every tree you come to and
then back down. There was usually no way round. Sometimes
we could walk along the beaches, but in many places there
wasn't any beach – the mountains dropped sheer into the sea
(Le Guin, 2001, p.139).

That sea, made difficult to access, becomes a thing of otherness and distrust. This is a perception exacerbated by the remnants of industrial life dating from before the environmental apocalypse that so reshaped the world. Even though the apocalypse is generations in the past, the coastal environments of *Always Coming Home* are littered with the industrial by-products of pre-apocalypse, particularly the substance known as fumó. A glossary entry refers to fumó as "apparently a residue of industrial products or byproducts, perhaps of petroleum-based plastics, which occurs in small whitish grains or larger concretions, covering regions of the ocean surface and found on beaches and tidal flats, often to a depth of several feet; useless, indestructible, and poisonous when burning" (Le Guin, 2001, p.513).

This polluted environment, full of residual, unfamiliar, and unpleasant artefacts of life before apocalypse, is the home of organisms that are unsurprisingly distrusted, making their home as they do in a marginal and contaminated environment. Fish is a popular food, but the popularity is restricted to the "prized" freshwater fish (Le Guin, 2001, p.421). Oceanic fish, on the other hand, are "more often traded for than caught, since few people of the Valley wanted much to do with boats or deep water" (Le Guin, 2001, p.421). This is indicative of a society in which sailing, particularly, has been downgraded in importance, both as a means of acquiring food (by offshore fishing) and, implicitly, as a means of transport. Given the challenging terrain that exists in some of this new Northern California, terrain which can sometimes have "no way round", maritime transport might be thought to be, in places, a more efficient means of movement. It is clear from the text, however, that dislike for time spent on the ocean is common amongst at least some of the Kesh.

That dislike may result from an environment that is actually threatening as well as being merely perceived as threatening, both related as it is to the detritus of apocalypse and as a possible contributor to it. The narrator comments that the "Fisher Lodges of the Lower Valley sometimes gathered shellfish on the sea beaches, but the Pacific "red tides" plus residual pollution of the oceans made mussel-eating a risky business" (Le Guin, 2001, pp.421-422). Notable here is the existence of red tides, toxic algal blooms that can indeed harm both marine life and the organisms which feed on that life, as well as deplete oxygen levels within ocean waters. These blooms are notable due to what they imply about the physical environment. Algal blooms can have several (nonexclusive) causes. One of these is high nutrient content within the oceans, a concentration that usually results from chemical runoff such as that of the fertilisers used on intensively farmed lands. While the Kesh are certainly reliant on agriculture, the likelihood of their relatively small, low-tech population causing sufficient runoff to ensure frequent red tides is unlikely. A much more plausible cause for the tides is that of warming surface temperatures in the ocean, a phenomenon increasingly associated with climate change.

There are other indications of climate change, primarily recorded in the oral histories of the Kesh. The tale "Four Beginnings" is told by Cooper of the Red Adobe of Ounmalin, and is related as having been passed down to him by his uncle, who presumably heard it from older relatives of his own. As a narrative, it is ambiguous, telling of four different stages of human history. It is the second stage that speaks of climate change – of the destruction caused by the melting of ice, of sea level rise and mass flooding. While this alteration of climate could relate to a warming world such as we are currently experiencing, it might also be read as the end of the last ice age, and the changes wrought upon the landscape in the shift from glacial to interglacial periods. No matter the interpretation, the influence of climate on the post-apocalyptic environment of the Kesh is clearly of great importance – not only with the implied rising temperatures of the ocean, but with the expanse of arid and semi-arid environments within and surrounding Kesh lands.

This is only to be expected. If the apocalypse experienced by the people living generations before the Kesh was primarily geological, it is not to say that it was only geological. Contemporary trends in areas such as biodiversity, climate, and pollution, and the consequences thereof, would not necessarily disappear in the aftermath of significant tectonic change. In some cases, the effects of each are likely to be exacerbated. Increased biodiversity within an ecosystem, for instance, increases the resilience of that ecosystem following disturbance. An impoverished ecosystem, after an earthquake, may well struggle to recover and become even more marginal and unsustainable than it was prior to that earthquake.

The world that Le Guin has created, therefore, is substantially different to the Northern Californian environment that influenced its creation. That environment, suffering enormous damage after what must have been an extraordinarily powerful tectonic event, one that decimated human life within the region, is the catalyst for a new way of living. The worldbuilding that

Le Guin engages in is developed from that central event. While relics of the former world still hold some importance in the cultural development of the survivors, this is an importance that (naturally) decreases over time, as social, economic, and environmental adaptation to the new land takes priority, and eventually becomes embedded as the new normal for the surviving population.

The cultural evolution that results from this sudden, significant environmental change is one which has utopian overtones. This is a theme that Le Guin has explored in other texts. Jameson comments, of her novel *The Left Hand of Darkness*, that Le Guin uses techniques of reduction to simplify her narrative world, describing it as "based on a principle of systematic exclusion, a kind of surgical precision of empirical reality" (1975, p.223). The frigid planetary environment that characterises *The Left Hand of Darkness* is, Jameson says, primarily isolating: it is "a fantasy realization of some virtually total disengagement of the body from its environment or ecosystem" (1975, p.222). That disengagement from ecosystem is underlined by the minimal focus, in that novel, on plant and animal life. By ever narrowing the focus of interaction with the environment, Le Guin is able to explore "an experimental landscape in which our being-in-the-world is simplified to the extreme" (Jameson, 1975, p.222) and this isolation is then used as a tool by which to justify not only differences in culture, but a comparative analysis of that culture compared to that of the reader (and, of course, the writer).

That technique of reduction – a reduction based purely in the environment – is present in *Always Coming Home* as it is in *The Left Hand of Darkness*... albeit in a different way, and from a very different direction. Where the latter uses extreme climate as a way to narrow the focus on the social, economic, and cultural life within a specific ecosystem, *Always Coming Home* uses environmental disturbance to first reduce and then very deliberately broaden that focus. The reduction, here, is implicit. It is also, primarily, economic.

The enormous, apocalyptic environmental change of *Always Coming Home* is primarily historical. It is something that has occurred generations prior to the events of the novel, and, crucially, it is something that has cut off, almost at once, the ability of the pre-existing economic system to continue. There are a number of post-apocalyptic narratives that retain capitalism in some form, often extreme, and this has a tendency to skew the narrative towards further disruption. If diversity in a system encourages resilience after disturbance, then the monoculture of capitalism, in which the only goal is gain-at-all-costs, actively works against system resilience. Those who were poor, disadvantaged, and exploited prior to apocalypse, for example, frequently become even poorer, even more disadvantaged, and even more exploited after apocalypse. The first few pages of *Always Coming Home*, however, make it very clear that capitalism is no longer the norm within the community. Note the following passage:

> The great-grandmother of my grandmother was the first to live in our rooms, on the first floor, under the roof; when the family was big they needed the whole floor, but my grandmother was the only one of her generation, and so we lived in the two west rooms only. We could not give much. We had the use of ten wild olives and several other gathering trees on Sinshan Ridge and a seed-clearing on the east side of Wakyahum, and planted potatoes and corn and vegetables in one of the plots on the creek southeast of Adobe Hill, but we took much more corn and beans from the storehouses than we gave
> (Le Guin, 2001, p.7).

Life in the *post*-apocalyptic society of the Kesh is clearly very different. Pre-apocalypse, we can surmise, was a world very like our own. A dwelling may be voluntarily sold if it becomes too large for the family inhabiting it, but that family is not obliged to share while they are in possession of it. Here there is no indication that the dwelling is owned by any individual or family; instead it is communal property, and spaces within it are shared according to need. Neither is the distribution of food, in our contemporary world, a formally communal endeavour, but here the act of production is an act directed to the enrichment of the whole. Grain, fruits, and vegetables are contributed by individuals and families to the community storehouses and taken out again as needed. There is no indication, in the above passage, that the need for more or less space, or more or less food, is perceived as, for instance, greedy or shameful. It is clear that accumulation for accumulation's sake, when others are in need, is no longer considered appropriate.

That is a fundamental cultural, political, and economic shift away from the European, industrialised world of old Northern California, and it is a shift that clearly took place in a post-apocalyptic world where, initially, resources must have been scarce and the potential conflict to obtain them high. It would have been easy for a society devastated by environmental disturbance to fall further back into the cultural norms of a pre-existing capitalism, but Le Guin is not interested in showing this. Nor, it must be said, is she particularly interested in showing the transition from one system to another, revolutionary as it must have been. Instead, environmental conditions have been used to almost surgically reduce – as Jameson notes of *The Left Hand of Darkness* – the engagement of the body (whether the individual body or the body politic) with the economic ecosystem that might otherwise be expected to influence the direction of a culture. Environmental change, in *Always Coming Home*, acts as the catalyst for an almost total cultural schism.

How, then, returning to an earlier comment, can this be interpreted as potentially illustrating a utopian theme? Utopias, of course, have a long history within the literature of our world, and they are nearly always designed as a mirror to contemporary conditions. That mirror shows a potential future, or an alternate present, a place where people "might be going to have lived", as Le Guin puts it, in which some sort of change has improved the lives of (at least some of) the people living within the new society. Naturally, that improvement is subjective, and influenced by the biases and desires of the author; there are some utopias which would be anything but for those forced to live in them (usually these unfortunates differ in some significant way, such as race, gender, or religious belief, from the author). From the perspective of that author, however, the desired utopia is a progression in human development, an example of the perfectibility of human relations both with themselves and their environment.

From the perspective of Le Guin herself, *Always Coming Home* "is a kind of alternative to the way we live" (Le Guin, et al., 1991, p.61). Writing of utopias in her essay "A Non-Euclidean View of California as a Cold Place to Be" (collected in *Dancing at the Edge of the World*), she says that utopias should not be places that cling to and reinforce the European, masculinist ways of thought that have so denigrated perspectives not like their own. "Perhaps the utopist would do well to lose the plan, throw away the map" she says (Le Guin, 1989, p.98) and it is instructive to remember how maps, in *Always Coming Home*, have themselves literally become useless, unrepresentative of the altered world in which the Kesh are living.

Elements of *Always Coming Home* can certainly be read as utopian. While some people may argue that there are advantages to capitalism, for instance, it seems that the fundamental change in economic relations has removed the worst excesses and consequences of that ideology, limiting starvation and homelessness. It is unfortunate that, in this version of Northern California, cataclysm is necessary to finally address these issues, but addressed they have been, and the emphasis on community rather than individual property appears, in the Kesh culture, to good effect. Similarly, the apparent refusal to engage in the construction of advanced weaponry is another advantage of the change in economic system:

> To construct a tank or a bomber was so difficult and so unnecessary that it really cannot be spoken of in terms of the Valley economy. After all, the cost of making, maintaining, fueling, and operating such machines at the very height of the Industrial Age was incalculable, impoverishing the planet's substance forever and requiring the great majority of humankind to live in servitude and poverty
> (Le Guin, 2001, p.380).

The capitalist desire for gain above everything else leads to a competition for resources that soon becomes exploitative, in more ways than one. It is a competition that is not only environmentally unsustainable but socially and economically unsustainable as well, leading as it does to environmental degradation, poverty, and war. This refusal, too, has utopian overtones, implying as it does that humanity has progressed past the unchecked greed and violent aggression that are almost requirements of the capitalist system.

This is not to say, however, that *Always Coming Home* is a completely utopian portrait of the ideal. For all that the state of the physical environment, and the ruthless reduction of the (resulting, initial) economic environment have influenced utopian change, there are still aspects of Kesh society that do not approach the ideal. Violence is still a factor, with conflict erupting between different groups, such as that resulting from the antisocial behaviour of the Condor people: "Two years ago they killed eleven people and stole eight women and all the horses. They come every winter and take our food. If you try to fight them you had better have guns and bullets. They do" (Le Guin, 2001, p.378). Violence exists, even if on a smaller scale, but two factors are notable here.

The first is that even the Condors, who the author describes as "satirical" (Le Guin, et al., 1991, p.61), are not engaged in developing tanks or bombers. They may be exploitative and aggressive, but even they have limits; the target of the satire, then, is more horrifyingly ridiculous than the mirror. The second factor is that the Condor people differ significantly from those around them. They are noted as being "unusually self-isolated; their form of communication with other peoples was through aggression, domination, exploitation, and enforced acculturation. In this respect they were at a distinct disadvantage among the introverted but cooperative peoples native to the region" (Le Guin, 2001, p.379). If this sounds as if the Condor represent the remnant survival of unchecked capitalism within Northern California it may well be true, yet they are a minority who cannot effectively challenge the cultural majority. Interestingly, their difference is perceived by the rest as sickness. "We have been fighting a war with these sick people for two lifetimes" (Le Guin, 2001, p.378), it is observed. Two axioms have developed, amongst the Kesh, for this sort of ill health. "Very sick people tend to die of their sickness" is one, and "Destruction destroys itself" is the other (Le Guin, 2001, p.380). One might argue that, if this is the case, and if the Kesh analysis of sickness holds, then the environmental cataclysm that destroyed the former Northern California was a simple reflection of the health of its inhabitants. (That, however, is flirting perhaps too much with metaphor, and assigning distinctly too much agency to tectonic plates.)

This view of sickness is one that, as the anthropological observer of the Kesh relates, upends previously held definitions and perspectives. "What we call strength it calls sickness; what we call success it calls death" (Le Guin, 2001, p.380). Thus, even the instances of non-ideal behaviour within the text can be used as examples of utopian criticism, and environmental change prompts yet another example of revolutionary, progressive worldbuilding within the text.

The effects of pre-apocalyptic impacts on environment and ecology, however, continue to linger. If pre-apocalyptic economic systems have been largely removed from the text, reduced almost to nothing outside of the culture of the Condors, then remnants of the physical systems have proved equally poisonous. The impacts of industrial pollution on the marine environment have already been mentioned, but there are impacts, too, on the Kesh themselves. Genetic changes have led to lower life expectancies, an increase in congenital diseases, and a low birth rate – all things that the anthropological observer describes as "disastrous" (Le Guin, 2001, p.380), before going on to check herself. Her querying of that conclusion is something which might be echoed by the reader. An increase in severe congenital diseases is certainly difficult to find advantageous, but a low birth rate following environmental disaster, in which resources would have been difficult to access and exploit, might certainly be described that way. In the rebuilding of a society, the reimagining of a world out of a struggling and marginal ecosystem, a high birth rate might result in a level of consumption that is simply unsustainable.

More interesting to the observer, however, and presumably to the reader, who are themselves consuming the utopian possibilities of *Always Coming Home*, is the question of progress. More specifically, the *criticism* of progress: what it is, and how much value it has. Is it possible that natural selection has become social selection? So the observer asks, anyway:

> In leaving progress to the machines, in letting technology go forward on its own terms and selecting from it, with what seems to us excessive caution, modesty, or restraint, the limited though completely adequate implements of their cultures, is it possible that in thus opting not to move "forward" or not only "forward," these people did in fact succeed in living in human history, with energy, liberty, and grace?
> (Le Guin, 2001, pp.380-381).

This, perhaps, is the fundamental question of the text, and it is a question that results inexorably from apocalyptic, cataclysmic environmental change. Previous relationships with the land, with environment and ecology, are abruptly severed, and the opportunity to create new relationships is offered. Le Guin's anthropologist narrator observes the bad as well as the good, in an effort, one presumes, to avoid idealising a way of life beyond its deserts. (Contemporary impulses to return to "a simpler time", as the phrase goes, are often guilty of this.) Yet, in *Always Coming Home*, the idea of potential remains, the belief that even the most challenging of environmental and social conditions can provide motivation to build a world, and a society, more suited to the land which supports it.

References

Baker-Cristales, B., 2012. Poiesis of possibility: the ethnographic sensibilities of Ursula K. Le Guin. *Anthropology and Humanism*, 37(1), pp.15-26.

Jakimovska, I. & Jakimovski, D., 2010. Text as laboratory: science fiction literature as anthropological thought experiment. *Anthropology Magazine*, 10(2), pp.53-63.

Jameson, F., 1975. World-reduction in Le Guin: the emergence of utopian narrative. *Science Fiction Studies*, vol. II, n. 3, pp.221-230.

Le Guin, U.K., 1989. *Dancing at the edge of the world: thoughts on words, women, places.* New York: Grove Press.
—, 2001. *Always Coming Home*. Berkeley: University of California Press.

Le Guin, U.K., Barton, T., Chodos-Irvine, M. & Hersh, G., 1991. The making of Always Coming Home. *Mythlore: A Journal of JRR Tolkien, CS Lewis, Charles Williams, and Mythopoeic Literature*, 17(3), pp. 56-63.

Tolkien: When worlds are built within dreams

Enrico Spadaro

Abstract

In his study about fantastic literature, *La Narrazione fantastica*, the Italian scholar Remo Ceserani (1933-2016) analyses the elements that constitute the fantastic world. In his opinion, the fantastic always depends on reality and the passage from the realistic world to the fantastic one happens thanks to a "mediating object".
In J.R.R. Tolkien's work, the Secondary World, as the author defines it in *On Fairy-stories*, is mostly shaped throughout language, given that Tolkien was a philologist and his tales had been written "to provide a world for the languages", as he states in his letter no. 165.
Although languages are the prime mediating object that builds Tolkien's Secondary World, there is another element which lets protagonists and readers enter this fantastic world. This is "dreams". As a matter of fact, in the unfinished tale *The Lost Road*, the protagonist has recurrent dreams, sometimes defined as "linguistic dreams", where visions of a far world appear and which eventually lead him directly to the island of Númenor. The fantastic world of Middle-earth progressively takes shape in front of the English protagonist Alboin Errol and the passage from the primary to the Secondary World is complete. Moreover, an autobiographical element is also present here, since the Professor constantly had nightmares about a drowning island, which is finally the destiny he gives to Númenor.
Although in *On Fairy-stories*, dreams are merely quoted, this paper aims at showing how the oneiric component plays an important role in the constitution of Tolkien's fantasy worlds: not only can it be found in *The Lost Road* or in its sequel *The Notion Club Papers*, but even in *The Lord of the Rings*, concerning the feelings, the sensations, and the perceptions of some characters such as Frodo, and in some

fundamental names as *Olorin* or *Lorien*. Where do these oneiric worlds stem from? Can dreams really be considered as a "mediating object" in Tolkien's creation process? And what is then left when awakening occurs?

Introduction

John Ronald Reuel Tolkien's invented world *Arda* is a complex world, a fantastic world where many other fantastic worlds are developed, explored, and built within. It is the setting of his mythology and of his two novels published in his lifetime, *The Hobbit* (1937) and *The Lord of the Rings* (1954-55). The latter, according to his author, may be defined as a great fairy story and has now undoubtedly become one of the masterpieces of fantasy literature.

Tolkien elucidated his theory on fantasy literature in his well-known essay *On Fairy-stories*, firstly composed to be delivered in a 1939 lecture and then published in 1947 in *Essays Presented to Charles Williams*. In its pages, Tolkien highlights the importance of fantasy and the fact that a fairy tale is only accomplished if its author makes the reader experience a Secondary World, where the "inner consistency of reality" may be felt (Tolkien, 1983 p.138). The fantastic world that is so built must be consistent and comply with the rules of the real world. In his study about the fantastic, *La Narrazione fantastica* (1983), the Italian scholar Remo Ceserani (1933-2016) also analyses the elements that constitute the fantastic world and affirms that the fantastic always depends on reality. In his opinion the passage from the realistic world to the fantastic one occurs thanks to a "mediating object" (Ceserani, 1983, p.220): a concrete artefact or a concept which let fantasy spread throughout the narration.

When it comes to Tolkien, language cannot but be considered as the prime mediating object in the constitution of his Secondary World, since his stories were initially conceived to give his artificial language an appropriate background. However, another mediating object, which is more evident in some of Tolkien's unfinished stories and subtly hidden in his novels, might be here taken into consideration.

Oneiric worlds I

> And the Dreams. They came and went. But lately they had been getting more frequent, and more—absorbing. But still tantalizingly linguistic. No tale, no remembered pictures; only the feeling that he had seen things and heard things that he wanted to see, very much, and would give much to see and hear again—and these fragments of words, sentences, verses. (Tolkien, 1987, p.49).

So reads a passage from the unfinished tale *The Lost Road* that Tolkien wrote in the second half of the 1930s and was published by Christopher Tolkien in the fifth book of the *History of Middle-earth, The Lost Road and Other Writings* (1987). He and C.S. Lewis had agreed to write respectively about time-travel and space-travel, and Tolkien initially conceived the tale of an English contemporary man, Alboin Errol, who, as an historian and language passionate, had to travel back in time throughout the legends of northern and western Europe until reaching the island of Númenor.[1] Tolkien wrote only four chapters, the first two set in contemporary England and two *Númenórean*

---

[1]. This is indeed the first allusion to Númenor and Christopher Tolkien included in the fifth book of the *HoMe* the very first extant versions of the legend of the Drowning of Númenor, both entitled *The Fall of Númenor* (pp.11-38). In the third part of the ninth book of the *HoMe*, *Sauron Defeated* (1992), Christopher Tolkien included the third version of *The Fall of Númenor*, and the text of another tale about the island of Númenor, *The Drowning of Anadûnê* (pp.331-441). All these texts merge in what is the definitive version contained in *The Silmarillion*, which is entitled *Akallabêth* (p.248).

chapters where the characters of Elendil and his son Herendil appear, as counterparts of the English protagonists, Alboin and his son Audoin.

From the beginning, dreams are one of the main features characterising the life of Alboin: in the first scene of the first chapter, when he is but a boy, his father Oswin is looking for him, and once he has found him, he says: "Well, you must be deaf or dreaming" (Tolkien, 1987, p.40), since his son was not answering his calls. The same scene is reproduced in the *Númenórean* chapters, when Erendil asks his son: "Of what art thou dreaming, Herendil, that thy ears hear not?" (Tolkien, 1987, p.65).

At night, thanks to dreams, artificial languages seize Alboin's mind and show to him fragments in an unknown idiom, where words such as *Sauron*, *nūmenorē*, and *atalante* appear for the first time in Tolkien's *Legendarium*. Here is but an extract of a vivid passage that comes to the protagonist at morning:

> *ar sauron tule nahamna ... lantier turkildi*
> and ? came ? ... they-fell ?
> *unuhuine ... tarkalion ohtakare valannar ...*
> under-Shadow ... ? war-made on-Powers ...
> *herunumen ilu terhante ... iluvataren ... eari*
> Lord-of-West world broke ... of-Iluvatar ... seas
> *ullier kilyanna ... Númenore ataltane ...*
> poured in-Chasm ... Númenor down-fell ...
> (Tolkien, 1987, p. 51)

It seems as if, thanks to the medium of language and dreams, a new world is shaping, and finally, at the end of the second chapter, a vision of Elendil is introduced. The mysterious Númenórean character summons Alboin to start his journey back in time. The myth of the Land of Gift and its destruction invades Alboin's spirit, haunts him, creates vivid images in which a story and a new world is being built. The "Dreams", which are then written in capital letters, open the door to a different world, a fantastic world; they are the instrument which lets characters travel in time and discover new realities: it is not a case that Christopher Tolkien wrote *A Dream in Time* as a subheading for the tale.

Dreams are not a simple allegorical feature, but they happen to be an authentic bridge to unexplored thoughts and conceptions, which transmit to the mind something subtler than mere visions. In *The Lost Road* (Tolkien, 1987), dreams and reality are confused and blended, combined, and mixed up, so that there is no more limit between rationality and subconscious. One of Tolkien's inspirations may undoubtedly be an author dearly beloved by the Inklings: George MacDonald. In his works *Phantastes* (1858) and *Lilith* (1895), he produced a kind of "ultra-reality" where his characters experienced fairy adventures in dreamlike worlds.

In *The Lost Road* (Tolkien, 1987), dreams are dealt with in two different ways: at the beginning, in the first part of the tale, dreams are felt as simple oneiric conditions and characters may tell what they have dreamt of the previous night. Then, without giving any further notice, any boundary between dreams and wakefulness is blurred and then disappears. Initially, Alboin is simply dreaming and then reporting his dreams to his father, but then he himself becomes Elendil: the two characters are united in one and the new world of Númenor unveils. "Have you ever had a dream, Neo, that you were so sure was real? […] How would you know the difference between the dream world and the real world?" – asks Morpheus to Neo in the famous film *Matrix* (1999). Places and landscapes are developed and shown to the reader as if the tale were taking place in a kind of dreamed reality.

In *The Lost Road* (Tolkien, 1987), dreams are turned into the frame and the mechanism of the story: they open the road to the Secondary World and let the protagonists move in time, backwards or forwards. This is what is explicitly shown in the respective titles of the first chapter "A Step Forward. Young Alboin" (Tolkien, 1987, p.39) and in what should have been the third, according to Tolkien's unachieved project, "A Step Backward. Ælfwine and Eadwine" (Tolkien, 1987, p.86). These two titles were jotted down only after the composition of the two chapters, as states Christopher Tolkien in his commentary, and the repetition of the term "step" might suggest that the *leitmotiv* of dreams is to be identified as a clear path the protagonists are travelling along. Moreover, in the second chapter, when Alboin falls asleep while sitting in his armchair, the narrator does not directly say he is starting to dream, but that he is passing "out of the waking world" (Tolkien, 1987, p.52). The fact that Tolkien explicitly mentions "world", a term often recurring in his conception of fantasy and fairy stories, is remarkable. The contemporary reality and the new dreamed one, the isle of Númenor, become one only thing, combined both materially and textually, since several elements are parallelly shown up between them, such as the "Eagles of the Lord of the West", which both Alboin and Elendil see over in the sky.

The state of incompletion of the Númenórean chapters and the drafts and the notes concerning the unwritten chapters make it hard to define precisely the actual time characters would spend in the other realities and worlds they would visit. Tolkien's project outlines only the well-known figure of Ælfwine, "elf-friend", where the name Elendil stems from, representing the unifying conscience that perform on the literary plan the dream where myth and history are combined. It is likely that Tolkien was about to exploit the same narrative strategy C.S. Lewis would adopt in the writing of his famous seven-novel series of *The Chronicles of Narnia*. In the first volume, *The Lion, the Witch and the Wardrobe* (1950), when the four protagonists return back to England, after several years spent in Narnia, time has not passed since their departure and they end up again in the same situation and age as they had left. Similarly, it may be supposed that such time gap, between departure and return, would concern also Alboin and Audoin in *The Lost Road* (Tolkien, 1987), as if they had simply dreamt during their travel in time.

However, the plan for such an immense and fascinating tale was soon abandoned, as Tolkien was fully absorbed in what would become his first literary success, that is *The Hobbit* (1937) and then the demand for a sequel. Although publishers Allen & Unwin, whom Tolkien sent the manuscript of *The Lost Road* (1987) to, said that it contained "passages of beautiful descriptive prose", they did not take into consideration a possible publication, since they remarked the tale was but a "hopeless publication". (Tolkien Gateway, 2021)

Oneiric worlds II

The "new Hobbit" was being conceived at the end of the 1930s, but the long gestation of Tolkien's magnum opus did not divert his author from his ideas about dreams, languages and new worlds. Between 18th December 1944 and 21st July 1946 – these were the dates when Tolkien wrote Letter no. 92 to his son Christopher and Letter no. 105 to his publisher Stanley Unwin respectively – Tolkien worked on a new attempt at writing a time-travel history, entitled *The Notion Club Papers*, published in 1992 in the ninth volume of the *History of Middle-earth, Sauron Defeated*.

Although like most of Tolkien's works the tale was not completed, there is a great quantity of writing, both manuscript and typescript, where many interesting and intriguing elements can be found. The initial idea concerning travelling back in time clearly recalls *The Lost Road* (Tolkien, 1987), but here the frame and the setting change: although it is not utterly suppressed as it will be seen in the second part of the tale, the simple father-son relationship – which maybe hinted at the duos Tolkien-Christopher and Bilbo-Frodo – is now turned into a literary Oxonian club in the 1980s, whose connection to the Inklings cannot but be evident. As a matter of fact, a list of club members precedes the beginning of the story and in the very first draft Tolkien associated the names with his real literary companions:

> Beneath *Ramer* he wrote "Self", but struck it out, then "CSL" and "To", these also being struck out. Beneath *Latimer* he wrote "T", beneath *Franks* "CSL", beneath *Loudham*[2] "HVD" (Hugo Dyson), and beneath *Dolbear* "Havard"
> (Tolkien, 1992, p.150).

Although the list was enlarged, and these explicit references disappeared in the following manuscripts, allusions and homages to his friends may still be felt while reading the reports of the Notion Club. The story is in fact set in contemporary Oxford, where blurred indications are given about university life, examinations, and terms that show a latent autobiographical element, which, though almost never explicitly expressed by the author, is always present in Tolkien's works. This is not the scope of this paper, but autobiography is undoubtedly a large theme that deserves further analysis as far as Tolkien's literary career is concerned.

---

2. Then changed into Lowdham in the following drafts.

The Notion Club Papers (Tolkien, 1992) is divided into two parts, "The Ramblings of Michael Ramer: *Out of the Talkative Planet*" and "The Strange Case of Arundel Lowdham", which significantly differ from one another. Dreams lie at the core of the accounts of the two characters who are experiencing them. On the one hand, Ramer's mind is experimenting with dreams, exploring the possibility that the mind may travel through space or time independent of the boy, regardless of what is occurring in the present; on the other hand, Lowdham clearly mentions the emergence of a new language, the Adunaic, and the matter of Númenor overtly intrudes the story and features it.

The first part may be compared to a kind of science fiction tale: "I want to travel in Space and Time myself [...] I want contact of worlds, confrontation of the alien" (Tolkien, 1992, p.169). These worlds, which do possess their own laws, should be integrated into the story, and characters journeying through them should be incarnated within them. The means to achieve this sort of incarnation cannot but be dreams: "As in *The Lost Road*, the incarnated mind dreams itself, and its reality" – states Verlyn Flieger in her essay *A Question of Time* (Flieger, 2001, p.134). It is a new exploration of dreaming, which is similar to Coleridge's feelings when, after a nightmarish night, he composed *Kubla Khan* (1797, published in 1816), which recalls the theories of the engineer John William Dunne (1875-1949). In his *An Experiment with Time* (1927), Dunne shows that from data collected while dreaming and from their interpretation, a kind of premonition may be detected in every individual, especially when the subject is experiencing a change in his/her daily life, for instance travelling or moving to another place. According to Dunne, there could be dreams which refer both to the present and to the future with evident consequences on individual's life. Tolkien and Lewis had read Dunne's work, since many notes and commentaries may be found in Tolkien's edition of *An Experiment with Time*: if Dunne is the theory, *The Lost Road* and *The Notion Club Papers* may be intended as its literary practice.

"I have long been interested in dreams, especially in their story-and-scene-making, and in their relation to waking fiction" (Tolkien, 1992, p.175) – says Ramer, and again: "The mind can be in more than one place at a given time" (Tolkien, 1992, p.177). When Ramer describes his dreams, he wants to depict the beauty he sees in them, and to give a vivid picture of all the places he is enjoying. What's more, when compared to Alboin's passages out of the waking world in *The Lost Road* (Tolkien, 1987), Ramer is aware of his dreams and he tries to activate them and live them:

> Imagine an enormously long, vivid, and absorbing dream being shattered […] like falling out of one world into another where you had once been but had forgotten it. […] I was awake in bed, and I fell wide asleep: as suddenly and violently […]: I dived slap through several levels and a whirl of shapes and scenes into a connected and remembered sequence
> (Tolkien, 1992, p.184).

Compared to his predecessor, Ramer's dreams are more conscious, more concrete and vivid, as if Tolkien had really grasped the true essence of the oneiric component: if in *The Lost Road* (1987) it was simply sketching a new dreamed world, now it is analytically and deeply shaping such world, and this will effectively be seen in the second part of *The Notion Club Papers* (1992).

The consciously analytical and descriptive dream-pictures Ramer accounts are progressively replaced by the linguistic echoes that appear in Lowdham's mind in the second part.

Languages, which at the beginning are simply fragmented, strongly make their entries. Lowdham reports passages in what he recognises as "Avallonian", which may recall Alboin's "Beleriandic" in *The Lost Road* (Tolkien, 1987), in Anglo-Saxon – remarkably the sentence "*westra lage wegas rehtas, wraikwas nu isti*" (Tolkien, 1992, p.243)[3] – and above all in "Adunaic". This is clearly the language of Númenor, and Christopher Tolkien included *Lowdham's Report on the Adunaic Language* as the very last part of the ninth volume of the *History of Middle-earth*, following *The Drowning of Anadûnê* (Tolkien, 1992, p.413). The isle that has been given to Earendil's heirs is once again the main topic of the story: Lowdham may be easily identified with Alboin Errol and even with Tolkien himself, as it will be shown in the following lines.

On the account of Night 65, Thursday, May 8th, 1987, songs are sung, neologisms introduced and languages, stories, and myths discussed upon, when "suddenly Lowdham spoke in a changed voice, clear and ominous, words in an unknown tongue [...] *Behold the Eagles of the Lords of the West! They are coming over Nūmenōr!*" (Tolkien, 1992, p.231). This was quite the same sentence uttered by Alboin and then by Elendil in *The Lost Road* (1987): Tolkien is actually once again exploiting the same motif. And when Lowdham mentions his father Edwin, he quotes an Anglo-Saxon verse his father used to speak about, which is almost the same as the lines Alboin evokes in his dreams. "Ælfwine the Fartravelled son of Éadwine" (Tolkien, 1992, p.244) reappears, and this is only one of the signs of the overtly replicated father-son relation that Tolkien had developed in *The Lost Road* (1987). Lowdham's full name is Alwin Arundel Lowdham, which perfectly fits the

---

3. In *The Lost Road*, Alboin spoke "*Westra lage wegas rehtas, nu isti sa wraithas* [...] *a straight road lay westward, now it is bent*" (p.47).

name thread of the structure of the dream stories: from Oswin Errol to Alboin and to Audoin and from Edwin to Alwin, the old English name Ælfwine is always present. And if Éadwine means friend of fortune, Ælfwine is obviously "elf-friend", which directly evokes the figure of Earendel (Eärendil), the half-Elf half-Man who sailed to Valinor and contributed to the rescue of the Children of Ilúvatar against Morgoth, playing the role of a kind of Messiah in Tolkien's *Legendarium* at the end of the First Age. As it can be read in *The Lost Tales*, Ælfwine was an English ancient mariner, and actually Christopher Tolkien adds and comments:

> From the beginning of this history [The History of Middle-Earth] the story of the Englishman Ælfwine, also called Eriol, who links by his strange voyage the vanished world of the elves with the lives of later men has constantly appeared (Tolkien, 1992, p.279).

But a note from his father Christopher found next to the manuscript of *The Notion Club Papers* says: "Do the Atlantis story and abandon Eriol-Saga […]" (Tolkien, 1992, p.281): what may it imply? That, if initially the Notion Club had only to discuss about the Eriol-Saga, which is likely to be the mythology Tolkien was constantly developing about England, now this was rejected in favour of the overwhelming topic of Atlantis, that is Númenor. Strikingly, when Ramer hears the name "Númenor" he intervenes by saying that this is his name for Atlantis in his dreams, and when asked about the finding of that peculiar name, Lowdham answers: "Oh I don't know […] It comes to me, now and again. Just on the edge of things […]" (Tolkien, 1992, p.232). This seems to recall Tolkien's own way of developing a tale, as he states in his letters when writing about the foundation of his works: "To me a name comes first and the story follows" (Tolkien, 1981, Letter no. 165). Moreover, it is another clue concerning the association between Lowdham and our author himself, to which for instance it could also be added the reference to the famous lines from the Anglo-Saxon poem *Crist*, "*Éala Éarendel, engla beorhtost/ofer middangeard monnum sended!*" (Tolkien, 1992, p.236). These words give Lowdham "a curious thrill", which is exactly the same effect they had on Tolkien, who drew inspiration from them when he wrote the very first germ of his *Legendarium* in the 1914 poem *The Voyage of Eärendel the Evening Star* (Tolkien, 1984, pp.267-269).

If we turn back to dreams, it should be highlighted the fact that similar images and names may appear in different people's visions, as it occurs to Ramer and Lowdham about Númenor or even to Boromir and his brother Faramir when they both dream of a voice speaking of Imladris, which finally would lead the elder brother to Rivendell in *The Fellowship of the Ring* (Tolkien, 2004, I, ii, p.320). If Imladris, which is at first an unknown land to Boromir and Faramir, is shaping within their dreams, so it is Númenor in Ramer's and Lowdham's respective visions. Moreover, the association of names, kindred, and ancestry seems to show that Lowdham is dreaming a kind of deeper development of Alboin's dreams in *The Lost Road* (Tolkien, 1987). However, there is no figure such as Elendil that summons the protagonist to the new worldbuilding within dreams: similarly, to the first part of *The Notion Club Papers* (Tolkien, 1992) waking and oneiric experiences are intertwined, as if languages, names, and pictures burst into Lowdham's consciousness in a kind of Proustian way. As Verlyn Flieger remarks: "Whereas the Errols were to move into the past as Alboin fell quietly asleep in his chair […], the comparable episode in *The Notion Club Papers* has the past come storming directly into the present" (Flieger, 2001, p.134). This happens in Night 67, when the Avallonian and Adunaic languages Lowdham dreams of, report the terrible downfall of an ancient kingdom: the story of the *Atalante* is being built and it is so absorbing that characters are transferred to other times and other consciousnesses. Guildford, who is the fictional reporter of the papers, describes Jeremy and Lowdham as being in the world of Númenor, discussing about *Zigūr* (that is Sauron), the attack on Tol Eressëa (here called *Avallōni*) and the power of Eru. Boundaries between worlds are totally blurred, since the two speaking men call each other *Nimruzīr* and *Abrazān*, and finally, while they are "hanging over the side of a ship" (Tolkien, 1992, p.251), which is but the edge of the window of Ramer's college room, a terrible storm bursts out and inundates all of Oxford. Tolkien clearly exploits this stratagem to evoke the drowning of Númenor so that the Secondary World he is building in his dreams is directly connected to the Primary World. Most surprisingly, in 1987, the year when *The Notion Club Papers* (Tolkien, 1992) are set, a real storm occurred which ferociously caused severe damage between northern France and southern England in the night of 15th-16th October (RMS, 2007). Tolkien writes "June 12th 1987" (Tolkien, 1992, p.252), so his prevision was wrong only by four months; but a question arises then: how could our author foretell such an event? Had he perchance dreamt of it?

In the following meetings, the Club members still discuss about Avallonian and Adunaic languages, and Tolkien relates the concepts of the drowned land to Celtic mythology, with a lengthy focus on *immrama*, the legendary voyages of Irish pilgrims which were also part of *The Lost Road* (Tolkien, 1987, p.85). As in his former attempt at a world-travelling tale, Tolkien introduces Anglo-Saxon legends, such as the story of

King Sheave (Tolkien, 1992, p.273); however, the framework of the narrative remains unclear. More tales were supposed to be told, but after Night 70 only a blank page and some jotted notes can be found since Tolkien suddenly halted the writing of *The Notion Club Papers* (1992).

"Atlantis complex"

The Lost Road (Tolkien, 1987) and *The Notion Club Papers* (Tolkien, 1992) have been rightly considered as time-travel tales and are deeply analysed in Flieger's work *A Question of Time* (2001). What is remarkable is that both unfinished tales are accompanied by the texts concerning the island of Númenor, *The Fall of Númenor* and *The Drowing of Anadûnê* respectively. The notes Christopher Tolkien found, "Work backwards to Númenor and make that last" (Tolkien, 1987, p.85) and "Do the Atlantis story" (Tolkien, 1992, p.281), clearly reveal the relevance Tolkien wanted to give to the Númenórean conception. This inevitably leads to a striking aspect of Tolkien's life that significantly affected his literary subcreation. As Chistopher pointed out in his introduction to *The Lost Road* (Tolkien, 1987, p.10) and as it is confirmed in some of Tolkien's letters, the professor suffered from what he defined an "Atlantis complex". A terrible nightmare haunted and tormented his soul: in a letter to W.H. Auden he talks about a huge wave that submerges and inexorably destroys everything:

> […] for I have what some might call an Atlantis complex. Possibly inherited, though my parents died too young for me to know such things about them, and too young to transfer such things by words. Inherited from me (I suppose) by one only of my children, though I did not know that about my son

until recently, and he did not know it about me. I mean the terrible recurrent dream (beginning with memory) of the Great Wave, towering up, and coming in ineluctably over the trees and green fields. (I bequeathed it to Faramir.) I don't think I have had it since I wrote the "Downfall of Númenor" as the last of the legends of the First and Second Age
(Tolkien, 1981, Letter no. 163).

As Dunne had underlined the possible transmission of dreams and memories between members of the same family, so Tolkien states about his dream, which is imparted to his son Christopher (Roncari, 2005). The drowning nightmare is finally exorcised once the story of Númenor begins to be put into writing. All these elements are explicitly present in *The Lost Road* (Tolkien, 1987) and characterise the father-son duo Alboin-Audoin; later on, Lowdham and his dead father Edwin, who was a mariner and left him pieces in Anglo-Saxon, testify to the evocative and narrative power of dreams, as well as the autobiographical component in Tolkien's writing.

As a matter of fact, the conception of Númenor and all the events concerning its destruction arise in Tolkien's dreams and it may well be affirmed that this part of his Secondary World is built within his dreams, and then developed within the dreams of his fictional alter egos Alboin and Lowdham. Dreams work on the imagination of the writer and his characters so that they boost the narration and its evolution. This is not uncommon in the history of English literature, since an author that has often been compared to Tolkien because of his theories on "fancy" and "imagination" experienced almost the same dreaming instances. As John Garth points out in his *The Worlds of J.R.R. Tolkien* (2020), S.T. Coleridge, once he woke up from a turbulent dream, composed the visionary poem *Kubla Kahn* (1816), but he was suddenly interrupted by a person from Porlock and only a fragment of this poem has been left to posterity. Tolkien's two oneiric unfinished tales are in fact related to Porlock, because *The Lost Road* (Tolkien, 1987) originated while he was sojourning in this area with his fellows Lewis and Barfield and one of its incomplete chapters concerning Ælfwine was supposed to be set in Porlock. Moreover, the same scene is to be replicated in *The Notion Club Papers* (Tolkien, 1992), when Lowdham and Ramer "dream themselves into the minds of Anglo-Saxons at the time of the Danish attacks – with Lowdham as the minstrel Ælfwine" (Garth, 2020, p.75).

Although dreams prove to be an effective mediating object in the building of worlds, in his famous theoretical manifesto, the essay *On Fairy-stories*, Tolkien showed an ambivalent attitude towards their power of creation:

> It is true that Dream is not unconnected with Faërie. In dreams strange powers of the mind may be unlocked. In some of them a man may for a space wield the power of Faërie, that power which, even as it conceives the story, causes it to take living form and colour before the eyes. A real dream may indeed sometimes be a fairy-story of almost elvish ease and skill – while it is being dreamed. But if a waking writer tells you that his tale is only a thing imagines in his sleep, he cheats deliberately the primal desire at the heart of Faërie: the realisation, independent of the conceiving mind, of imagined wonder
> (Tolkien, 1983, p.116).

Coda: Frodo and the evolution of dreams

Between the writing of *The Lost Road* (1987) and *The Notion Club Papers* (1992), Tolkien started composing *The Lord of the Rings*, and the three works are undoubtedly interrelated, especially as far as the conception of time and the treating of dreams are concerned. As we have seen in the case of Boromir and Faramir, all the main characters are affected by the power of dreams, and there are even places that imply oneiric features – Lórien is one of them, since the root "loro" means "to slumber" and time flows differently in this elvish realm. However, Frodo's visions appear to be fashioned on the previous experiences of Alboin, Elendil, Ælfwine, and then Lowdham. Similarly to his predecessors, the hobbit is able to travel and to conceive far and unknown worlds in his dreams but he is the only one that finally reaches these worlds and achieves his journey in the Blessed Realm of Valinor. Frodo is the final point where the previous world travelers merge together, from a literal, psychological and spiritual point of view.

When walking with him, his friends Merry, Pippin, and Sam dream, but their visions are merely narrative embellishments; on the other hand, Frodo's oneiric experiences always hide subtle messages and premonitions. While sleeping in Crickhollow, before leaving for the Old Forest, Frodo seems to foresee his doom. He hears noise from afar, which he realises being the sea that he has never seen before, and finally a lonely tower appears and insistently attracts him (Tolkien, 2004, I.I, p.152). The mystery will be solved only at the end of the novel when Frodo departs for Valinor and it is clear that it was a premonitory dream. The impressions Frodo feels in his dream are so vivid and accurately described that they include auditive, olfactory, and visual sensations so that the reader may conceive the dream vision as a journey to another place and another time, as it occurs in the pages of *The Lost Road*.

Although Tolkien underlined his peculiar resemblance to a hobbit, he always denied autobiographical reflections in his novels. Without any further analysis concerning the implications and influences of Tolkien's life and his contemporary world on the *Legendarium*, it could be affirmed that every character our author depicts – especially the protagonists of his stories – reflects aspects of his life. This may be also inferred when it comes to the characters that have been dealt with so far: the Errol family, the main members of the Notion Club, as well as Frodo are to be included in this list. The three works concerning them – *The Lost Road, The Lord of the Rings, and The Notion Club Papers* – might form a pattern when themes and arguments are generated and developed. This also involves the relevance dreams assume in the evolution of the respective plots.

If the *The Lost Road* is a dream in time where the world of Númenor is initially shaped, *The Notion Club Papers* is affected by the drafting of Tolkien's main novel: in *The Return of the Shadow* (1988), being the sixth book of *The History of Middle-earth*, the efforts and the enormous work our author put into shaping Frodo's dream passages may be appreciated. This testifies to the evolution of dream conceptions and explains how the way to reach the oneiric world of Númenor has changed. As well as languages – the first and foremost mediating object in Tolkien's mythmaking that never stopped to be modified, constituted and outlined – so dreams followed an evolution pattern that affects the worlds that are built within them.

References

AA. VV., 2003. *Dizionario dell'universo di J.R.R. Tolkien*. Milano: Bompiani.

Arduini, R. et al. eds., 2015. *Tolkien e i classici*. Roma: Effatà Editrice.

Carpenter, H., 1977. *J.R.R. Tolkien: A Biography*. London: George Allen and Unwin.

Curry, P., 2004. *Defending Middle-Earth. Tolkien: Myth and Modernity*. New York: Houghton Mifflin.

Drabble M.(ed.)., 1985. *The Oxford Companion to English Literature*. Oxford: Oxford University Press.

Drout, M.D.C., 2007. *J.R.R. Tolkien Encyclopedia. Scholarship and critical assessment*. New York: Taylor & Francis.

Fimi D., 2009. *Tolkien, Race and Cultural History*. New York: Palgrave.

Flieger, V., 2001. *A Question of Time. J.R.R. Tolkien's Road to Faërie*. Kent State Univ Press.

Garth, J., 2003. *Tolkien and the Great War: The Threshold of Middle-earth*. London: Harper Collins.
—, 2020. *The Worlds of J.R.R. Tolkien*. Princeton: Princeton University Press.

Gulisano, P., 2001. *Tolkien. Il mito e la Grazia*. Milano: Ancora.

Giuliano, S., 2013. *J.R.R. Tolkien. Tradizione e modernità nel Signore degli Anelli*. Milano: Bietti.

Hammond, W.G., 1993. *J.R.R. Tolkien: A Descriptive Bibliography*. Winchester: Oak Knoll Books.

RMS, 2007. *The Great Storm of 1987: 20-Year Retrospective, RMS Special Report.* [pdf] Available at: <http://forms2.rms.com/rs/729-DJX-565/images/ws_1987_great_storm_20_retrospective.pdf> [Accessed 8 July 2020].

Roncari, B., 2005. *I Sogni.* [pdf] Available at: <http://www.endore.it/Arretrati/8/Rubriche/MinasTirith.pdf> [Accessed 15 July 2020].

Tolkien, J.R.R., 1977. *The Silmarillion*. London: Allen and Unwin.
—, 1980. *Unfinished Tales*. London: Allen and Unwin.
—, 1981. *The Letters of J.R.R. Tolkien*. London: Allen and Unwin.
—, 1983. *The Monster and the Critics and Other Essays*. Tolkien, C. ed. London: Allen and Unwin,
—, 1987. *The Lost Road and Other Writings*. History of Middle-earth vol. V. Tolkien, C. ed. London: Harper Collins.
—, 1988. *The Return of the Shadow*. History of Middle-earth vol. VI. Tolkien, C. ed. London: Harper Collins.
—, 1992. *Sauron Defeated*. History of Middle-earth vol. IX. Tolkien, C. ed. London: Harper Collins.
—, 2004. *The Lord of the Rings.* 50th Anniversary Edition. London: Harper Collins.
—, 2007. *The Children of Húrin*.Boston-New York: Houghton Mifflin Harcourt.
—, 2015. *The Hobbit*. London: Harper Collins.
—, 2015b. *The Story of Kullervo*. London: Harper Collins.
—, 2018. *The Fall of Gondolin*. Boston-New York: Houghton Mifflin Harcourt.

Tolkien Gateway, 2021. *The Notion Club Papers*. [Online] Available at: <http://tolkiengateway.net/wiki/Notion_Club_Papers> [Accessed 6 May 2020].

Tolkien Italia. [online] Available at: <https://tolkienitalia.net>

The Tolkien Society. [Online] Available at: <https://www.tolkiensociety.org>

Patrick Mcgrath's Ghastly New York: The Perfect Decaying Cityscape for Restless Minds

Tatiana Fajardo

Abstract

This paper analyses the depiction of New York in Patrick Mcgrath's *Ghost Town: Tales of Manhattan Then and Now*, a collection of three stories which illustrate critical periods in the history of the city: the American War of Independence and its aftermath in the first tale, "The Year of the Gibbet"; the mid-eighteen fifties and the Civil War in the story "Julius"; and, finally, the consequences of 9/11 in "Ground Zero". With his dark prose, McGrath portrays characters haunted by several terrible events occurring in the metropolis, and thus this article will not only focus on the city itself, but also on McGrath's worldbuilding, through the social, political and even artistic environments of the periods he presents. Similarities with early American Gothic pieces by the likes of Edgar Allan Poe and Washington Irving will emerge, and the analysis will explain the connections between literary works by other writers and McGrath's tales, following Mikhail Bakhtin's concepts of "monologism", "dialogism", "heteroglossia", "answerability", and "chronotope". Freud's concept of the "uncanny" and Julia Kristeva's "abjection" will also be analysed.

Introduction

Patrick Mcgrath's *Ghost Town: Tales of Manhattan Then and Now* (2006) presents three tales in different historical periods of the city. All the events chosen by the author depict a dark moment in the city's history: the War of Independence in "The

Year of the Gibbet", the Civil War in the background of "Julius", and the aftermath of 9/11 in "Ground Zero". Interestingly, the writer opts for the term "town" when referring to the huge, powerful metropolis, since the first story he composes explains the origins of the location. Moreover, McGrath's ghost stories serve to connect the past with the present, as his then and now suggest. The horrors of 9/11, with which readers are familiar, are echoed in previous periods in history.

This article will explain the employment of the city of New York in McGrath's tales. Having said that, it is important to remark that, as the writer painstakingly highlights the social and political atmosphere in which his characters dwell, this text will also analyse these features in depth. Moreover, in the story "Julius", art plays an important role, and this study will explain its relevance to the understanding of McGrath's plot.

In order to examine all the stories, Mikhail Bakhtin's theories of heteroglossia, dialogism and chronotope will be considered, as well as a brief development of Freud's uncanny and Julia Kristeva's abjection.

"The Year of the Gibbet": The Ghost of a Mother Haunting her Moribund Son

Patrick McGrath's first story narrates the final moments of a man, Edmund, infected with the Pest in New York in 1832. On his deathbed, he pens about some of the tragic events that changed his life forever; in particular, the public hanging of his mother by the British Lord John Hyde in 1777. The trauma he suffers due to his guilt over his mother's death follows him in the ghostly city. McGrath cleverly equates Edmund's feelings to the rotting cityscape he dwells in: "New York has become a place not so much of death as of the *terror* of death" (McGrath,

2006, p.1). The changes in the once prosperous city are explained by the narrator: "New York is finished as a seaport, so vulnerable are we to disease, being a crossroads for all over the world" (McGrath, 2006, p.2). Nevertheless, while a lot of the population flee hunger, poverty and disease, Edmund remarks, "better by far stay in one's own place, and there prepare for the end" (2006, p.2). He continues to emphasise that the date is the Fourth of July, a key day for American Independence.

As the aim of this article is to depict concepts developed by Mikhail Bakhtin in the Neo-Gothic stories of McGrath, the first idea which will be analysed is the "chronotope", a term which Bakhtin borrows from Albert Einstein's theory of relativity, and which is translated from the Greek *chronos* and *topos* as "time-space". It is defined as the "interconnectedness of temporal and spatial relationships that are artistically expressed in literature" (Bakhtin, 1981, p. 84). Since McGrath chooses Manhattan as the setting for his stories and expands on the history of the city in three different moments, Bakhtin's concept is clearly exemplified.

This setting is not new in McGrath's writing; he had already published three tales in his collection, *Blood and Water and Other Stories* (1988): "The Angel", "Lush Triumphant" and "Hand of a Wanker", thus creating what he considers to be his "Manhattan Gothic" (personal correspondence, McGrath, 2020). Nevertheless, the three tales McGrath brings together in *Ghost Town* share a common feature: they all take place before or during a war. Agnieszka Soltysik Monnet and Steffen Hantke state that "the Gothic was born, and it thrived in its infancy, in times of war. From the atrocities of the French Revolution to the ravages of the Seven Years War… the battles of civil and national wars provided a steady background noise to the development of the genre" (2016, p.xi). Thinkers such as Edmund Burke, so influential in the theory of the Gothic, or E.T.A Hoffmann, who had to relocate due to Napoleon's armies, are some examples of how war affected the genre. As a consequence, one of the key characteristics in Gothic fiction is transgression against social norms. In McGrath's narratives, the concept of "decay" also emerges and, as Sue Zlosnik claims, "abjection within the Gothic text frequently signifies both fear concerning the breakdown of culturally constructed boundaries of identity at a particular historical moment, and an attempt to shore them up" (2011, p.7).

In "The Year of the Gibbet", the protagonist's mother is a patriot, and after her husband dies due to a fever caught while fighting against the redcoats, she is left alone with her three children in a New York decimated by the 1776 fire which consumed hundreds of buildings. McGrath's skills in worldbuilding lie in his depiction of a ravaged city full of liminal spaces and moments of the day: "We made a sorry sight, I am sure, at dawn, the crowd tramping homeward but without homes to go to. Where once stood houses and orchards there was no more than a smoking tract of black earth with here and there fragments of chimneys and parts of walls" (2006, p.14). The remaining New Yorkers attempt to survive by creating shacks and cabins in what will later be named "Canvas Town", behind the ruins of Trinity Church, which Edmund's mother considers to be "the first step in building ourselves a nation." (2006, p.20) The country that will become one the most potent in the world was created from the ruins and the sickness of its people. Nicholas Royle states that "the uncanny has to do with a strangeness of framing and borders, an experience in liminality" (2003, p.2).

McGrath's stories blur not only the landscapes, but also the characters he portrays, and the time. When Edmund is writing about his memories, he describes his mother as "obstinate and blunt-spoken, and fiercely protective of her own, a big, handsome woman with broad shoulders and a thrusting chin, her neck a column of flesh the color of marble—" (McGrath, 2006, p.8). The protagonist then continues to mention that he has her skull, which he keeps on the table (McGrath, 2006, p.8). The confusion between the living and the dead haunts Edmund as he recalls always seeing the ghost of his mother at twilight: "I was alert to all movement in the gloom, each footfall in the empty streets, each flickering shape in the glow of a campfire in the places made desolate by war" (McGrath, 2006, p.60). Edmund even takes his sister Lizzie with him, as she also wishes to see the ghost of their mother, but she does not share his hallucinations.

While Edmund's mother is portrayed with masculine traits, her enemy, Lord Hyde, is presented as effeminate. Liminality, in this case between feminine and masculine, is demonstrated once more. Edmund says that Hyde's "skin was white as chalk and his lips were scarlet and he wore a plumed silver helmet and a pale blue coat edged with gold… he *rode* like a lady, and on his plump face played a haughty smile as he glanced down at the cheering townspeople" (McGrath, 2006, p.11). Later in the story, Hyde provokes Edmund's mother and she exclaims, "You painted whore! [...] You king's trumpet!" (McGrath, 2006, p.18). As a result, Hyde seeks revenge, and when he discovers that she is a spy helping General Washington against the British, he murders her himself.

The guilt Edmund feels for his mother's death haunts him for the rest of his existence. He and his sister Lizzie would accompany their mother under the pretence of travelling to Newark to visit relations, while in reality their mother was helping in the plot against the British. Edmund's inability to lie when answering an official about what illness their grandmother suffers from that requires their frequent visits, triggers his mother's arrest and consequent hanging. The ghost of his mother thus begins to haunt him as a symbol of the repressed guilt he suffers.

One of Mikhail Bakhtin's main concepts is "heteroglossia"; that is, "*another's speech in another's language*, serving to express authorial intention but in a refracted way... the direct intention of the character who is speaking and the refracted intention of the author" (Bakhtin, 1981, p.324). McGrath sagely portrays the devastating effects war has on citizens through Edmund's narrative, when the protagonist claims that "half a century has passed since the Year of the Gibbet, and the war has been transformed in the minds of my countrymen such that it now resembles nothing so much as the glorious enterprise of a small host of heroes and martyrs sustained by the idea of Liberty" (McGrath, 2006, p.61), thus omitting the starving and sick population who have been struggling to survive.

While recalling his mother's death, Edmund states that "the soldiers, all but two, had marched back to the house, that the body of my mama was lifted into [the coffin] and the lid nailed down" (McGrath, 2006, p.56). Edmund continues to explain how even now he can still hear the "Tap-tap-TAP" (McGrath, 2006, p.56) of the hammers and imagines his mother "tapping inside it" (McGrath, 2006, p.57). McGrath echoes some of Edgar Allan Poe's stories, such as "The Fall of the House of Usher" (1839) or "The Premature Burial" (1844), when composing this fragment of his tale. The writer is well read in Gothic fiction, and his term "The New Gothic", defined in collaboration with Bradford Morrow in a 1991 anthology of the same name, focuses precisely on the importance Poe had on the Gothic, pointing out how "with Poe the Gothic turns inward, and starts rigorously to explore extreme states of psychological disturbance" (McGrath, 1991, p.xi). Poe blurred the boundaries between the known and the unknown in "The Premature Burial": "The boundaries which divide Life and Death are at best shadowy and vague. Who shall say where the one ends and the other begins?" (1844). Similarly, Poe's readers can witness Roderick Usher's mental breakdown when he believes that he has buried his sister alive in "The Fall of the House of Usher": *"We have put her living in the tomb!... I now* tell you that I heard her first feeble movements in the hollow coffin" (Poe, 1998, pp.64-65). In his worldbuilding in "The Year of the Gibbet", McGrath, like Poe before him, accentuates the psychological states of his characters after suffering a traumatic event.

McGrath thus employs what Bakhtin defines as "dialogism", the study of "life and behaviour of discourse in a contradictory and multi-languaged world" (Bakhtin, 1981, p.275). McGraths's tale maintains its individuality while also referring to previous narratives. He places his text in a "dialogue" through the influence he obtains from other Gothic stories, a feature he continues depicting in his second story, "Julius".

"Julius": The Mad Artist in Love

McGrath's second story moves from the New York of the Revolutionary War to 1950 when a woman, Alice, imagines her family background from 1835 onwards. She fantasises about the rise and fall of her wealthy family led by the strict and domineering businessman Noah van Horn. The story narrates how Noah succeeds in running cotton out of Georgia to London, and how, after fathering three daughters, he finally has the son he so much desires as a descendant for his mercantile kingdom, despite the death of his wife while giving birth.

On this occasion, the first mention of New York which McGrath pens echoes the hopes of Noah van Horn: "Often he spoke of the day when New York would surpass even London as the greatest port and marketplace in the world, and he said it with the confidence of a man who could expect to pocket a large share of the profits when that day came" (McGrath, 2006, p.65). In this story, McGrath's worldbuilding is demonstrated in his clear distinction between the greed of the businessmen, embodied by Noah and his protégé and son-in-law Max Rinder, who wanted to create a new enterprise in the city, and the artists: bohemian characters such as Jerome Brook Franklin or Noah's son Julius. These latter characters believe in the ideas of the American poet and philosopher Ralph Waldo Emerson and "Transcendentalism", following the connection humans can have with nature: "There I feel that nothing can befall me in life—no disgrace, no calamity (leaving my eyes), which nature cannot repair…" (McGrath, 2006, p.75)

These artists trusted that a young nation, such as the United States was at that point, needed to have its own art, independent of Europe, and they were truly inspired by the works of painters such as Thomas Cole and his depiction of the American Sublime. According to Bakhtin, "when a human being is in art, he is not in life, and conversely. There is no unity between them and no inner interpretation within the unity of an individual person." (Bakhtin, 1990) Bakhtin defines "answerability" as the personal experience an individual reflects in a piece of art, and vice-versa: "I have to answer with my own life for what I have experienced and understood in art, so that everything I have experienced and understood would not remain ineffectual in my life" (Bakhtin, 1990). When Julius attends the artistic lessons of Jerome Brook Franklin, the narrator's grandfather, he is an utterly inexperienced boy who repeats Franklin's ideas as if they were his own.

The plot's key moment is set in the appearance of Franklin's model, Annie Kelly, who Julius immediately falls in love with. Noah van Horn disapproves of the relationship between his son and the girl because she is Irish: "He (Noah) would employ them (Irishmen), but allow one of their women to draw close to his children, to befriend his daughters and walk out with his son—it must be stopped, and the sooner the better" (McGrath, 2006, p.116). Noah's racism towards Irishmen is present from the beginning of the tale, as he moves his family to Waverley Place because he considers Manhattan to be "increasingly susceptible to the diseases which according to him came in through the port with the Irish and found fertile breeding grounds in the narrow filthy streets and fetid courtyards where they lived" (McGrath, 2006, p.65). Nevertheless, Noah's racism is selective as he does not hesitate to ask his assistant and future head of the family, Rinder, who is of Bavarian background, to get rid of Annie Kelly.

While continuing with Bakhtin's concept of "chronotope" and how McGrath chooses to illustrate the life of a nineteenth century family in New York, it is significant to remark how the author also portrays Freud's concept of the "uncanny", which was briefly mentioned in the previous section. Freud claims this about the "uncanny": "[the 'unhomely'] is what was once familiar ['homely', 'homey']. The negative prefix *un-* is the indicator of repression" (1919, p.151). Repression is clearly demonstrated through Noah, when he indirectly blames Julius for his wife's death, and also by way of Julius himself, whose beatings at the hands of his father when he was a child, astonishingly enough, were rapidly forgotten.

Nonetheless, when Annie disappears, Julius's behaviour becomes violent; his sisters even witness how he transforms into a "creature" who begins "*chanting* at them, blasphemy and obscenity!" (McGrath, 2006, p.133). McGrath cleverly links Freud's "uncanny" with Julia Kristeva's concept of "abjection", a "something" which we are not able to "recognize" (Kristeva, 1982, p.2). Where, in "The Year of the Gibbet", the reader can find the mourning of a lost mother, in "Julius" we are presented with a boy who does not know his mother, and the feminine figures he is mainly influenced by are his sister Charlotte, who encourages him to paint, and then Annie, whom he wishes to have a romantic relationship with. When Annie disappears, Julius tells the butler, Quentin, that he had spent time out looking for his *mother* (emphasis as per McGrath, p.130).

Julius attacks Jerome Brook Franklin, thinking he has murdered Annie Kelly, and Rinder does "what wealthy New York families have always done when insanity erupts and scandalous behaviour ensues which has at all costs to be kept out of the press: he sent him to a private asylum" (McGrath, 2006, p.138); in this case, near the Hudson Valley, in the Catskills. McGrath chose this location, among other ideas, because he owned a book called *The Unknown Night* (2003) by Glyn Vincent "about an American artist called Ralph Blakelock, who spent 15 years locked up in a mental institution in upstate New York... Julius of course missed the building of the Brooklyn Bridge—so I was able to describe his astonishment, years later, when he first saw it" (personal correspondence, McGrath, 2020).

Interestingly, McGrath reuses Bakhtin's idea of dialogism in this story, as he echoes two tales from a couple of the most important American authors of the nineteenth century: Washington Irving and, once more, Edgar Allan Poe.

Julius spends 20 years in the Asylum, unaware of the civil war taking place in his country and the 1863 Riots, and how they are affecting his family, especially his father's businesses related to cotton planters and slavery in the South. When he goes back home after twenty years in the centre, he observes the changes present in the metropolis: when expressing his impression of the abovementioned Brooklyn Bridge, the narrator says that "he was so astonished he could not move for several minutes" (McGrath, 2006, p.163). The fact that Julius misses some major events in the history of his country echoes Washington Irving's "Rip Van Winkle" (1819). Irving writes:

> It was some time before he could get into the regular track of gossip, or could be made to comprehend the strange events that had taken place during his torpor. How that there had been a revolutionary war,—that the country had thrown off the yoke of old England,—and that, instead of being a subject of his Majesty George the Third, he was now a free citizen of the United States.

Nonetheless, the reader may wonder, why is it a Gothic story? McGrath depicts his characters as ghosts, especially at the end. The narrator, who is imagining the events, echoes an unseen ghost who narrates the situations Julius and his family experience, while the van Horn family themselves "are all dead now, and what survives of them are the phantoms, merely— the daguerreotypes, the photographs, the paintings" (McGrath, 2006, pp.172-173). Similarly to the aforementioned story, "The Fall of the House of Usher" (1839), by Edgar Allan Poe, McGrath depicts the fall of a wealthy family and how its terrible secret destroys their welfare. While Poe illustrates how an unnamed narrator portrays two siblings and how the man, Roderick, buries his sister Madeline alive, Noah van Horn's descendants do not recover from the tragedy which troubles Julius. Rinder, the main protagonist in Annie Kelly's disappearance, is confined to a wheelchair by the end of the story, and "the room truly belonged to the man in the painting (Rinder) and not the withered leaf, the homunculus he had become" (McGrath, 2006, p.155). The glorious days are gone, and Alice's mother herself suffers from nostalgia: "She would sit in the gloom of our little apartment on a winter afternoon… and gaze out… where she lived the last years of her life in a state of shabby gentility contemplating the glory that was once the House of van Horn" (McGrath, 2006, p.165).

It can be considered that McGrath employs what Mikhail Bakhtin names the "chronotope of the threshold", which is "connected with the breaking point in life, the moment, the decision that changes a life" (Bakhtin, in Richardson, 2002, p.21). While the van Horns separate from each other, as only Hester and Julius remain in the family home, New York expands and this can be read as "the warning sign of an era of the isolated individuals in the big city—the 'ghost city'" (Kuo, 2007, p.67). McGrath equates a family's increasingly isolated members to the general situation of an expanding city and how its developing power creates a sense of solitude in its citizens.

McGrath's last story, "Ground Zero", continues this feeling of isolation in a town hurt by the aftermath of the 9/11 attacks, as the last section of this article will explain.

"Ground Zero": A Broken City after a Terrorist Attack

"Ground Zero" is the tale of a psychiatrist and her patient, Danny Silver, a lawyer whom she has been treating for seven years. The plot is set after the attacks of 9/11 and it perfectly captures how New Yorkers experienced the traumatic event and its aftermath. While all the previous stories alienate their foreign characters, with conflicts such as the British against the Americans or the interests of a wealthy family endangered by an Irish girl, this last story emphasises the division amongst Americans after the attacks. McGrath thus moves his worldbuilding from a city attempting to survive in his first tale, and its financial development in "Julius", to the devastation of a city which embodies capitalist power. On this occasion, the psychiatrist does not experience the 9/11 attack directly, as she is out of the city, and is focused on her patient Danny, who begins a romantic relationship with a Chinese artist and prostitute, Kim Lee, shortly after having a sexual encounter with her through an escort service. While, at first, Danny's psychiatrist defines her as "a woman he had hired for sex" (McGrath, 2006, p.186), by the end of the story, she constantly describes the artist as "his Chinese prostitute" (McGrath, 2006, pp.212, 237). Additionally, there is a moment in the narrative when Dan and his psychiatrist talk about Kim, and she says: "You didn't tell me she was Chinese. What's her name?". To which an irritated Dan replies: "She's called Kim Lee. And she's as American as you or me though I shouldn't have thought that needed saying!" (McGrath, 2006, p.207). As such, in his tale, McGrath accentuates the racism witnessed in the city after the attack by intertwining the personal situation of his characters with the social and political settings.

"Othering" individuals is one of the main characteristics of Gothic fiction and, as Kristin M. Wilson states, following Judith Halberstam's analysis, "Gothic fiction gave nineteenth-century readers the excitement of reading about perverse physical activity while situating the Other (sexually, racially, etc.) in the foreign body of the monster" (Wilson, 1996, p.131). Narratives such as Robert Louis Stevenson's *The Strange Case of Dr Jekyll and Mr Hyde* (1886) or Bram Stoker's *Dracula* (1897) depict the socially unacceptable behaviour of Hyde or the vampire Dracula by portraying them as monsters. However, more modern Gothic writings, such as the ones by McGrath, represent how some characters employ "a discourse of racist representation" (Wilson, 1996, p.131), as they feel a threat to their notions of racial purity (Wilson, 1996, p.131). Although Wilson is referring to contemporary horror films, McGrath highlights the same "Othering" in his stories, therefore employing, once more, Bakhtin's "dialogism" in his connection to previous Gothic pieces.

One of the main features introduced by McGrath into the text is the reaction of New Yorkers to the attacks. Danny, a lawyer specialised in Civil Rights, is horrified with the consequences he observes: "Dan tells me (the psychiatrist) what John Ashcroft's people are up to, the ethnic profiling, the rounding up of as many men as they can find of Near Eastern or North African descent. The suspension of due process, the wholesale pullback of traditional American freedoms—" (McGrath, 2006, p.212). Nonetheless, the narrator, when she hears his statement, reflects: "I do not tell him this but I am beginning to think that John Ashcroft is right" (McGrath, 2006, p.212). McGrath thus depicts the different views citizens can express, emphasising a heteroglossia or multivoicedness (plurality of speech) in his writing. Bakhtin clearly defines the epic genre as monologic, with an "utter separateness of past and present" (Graham, 2000, p.89). Graham claims that "tradition, for Bakhtin, both preserves the closed nature of epic and ensures that it remains unchanged in its movement through history" (Graham, 2000, p.88). The "closed nature" of the epic refers to its distance in time and place to the moment the readers/audience are reading or listening to the tale, and the defence of an idealised concept of nation. McGrath, consequently, in all the stories he presents in his book, chooses "dialogism" and displays a diverse range of scenarios in the city, not only the monologic setting.

McGrath's last story was actually the one which gave the author the idea of developing the other two tales explained so far, as the writer himself explains:

> "Ground Zero" was the first, and grew out of my experience walking late at night around the ruins of the towers just a couple of days after the attack. I described it in a nonfiction piece for the *Dublin Review*, and then decided to incorporate it into a story. I then went to my publisher, at the time it was Bloomsbury, and proposed a book of three stories, all about New York but set at different periods
> (Personal correspondence, McGrath, 2020).

In this story, the city is divided in their attempts to continue with the hectic daily lifestyle, but "the further south he (Dan) got the more unreal the city became. There were soldiers in the streets, and cops everywhere. National Guardsmen. Emergency vehicles, road blocks, searches. Smoke was rising from the fallen towers and the air smelled very bad" (McGrath, 2006, p.187). The psychiatrist voices the uncanny effect the city has on her, saying, "all that had once been familiar was strange to me now" (McGrath, 2006, p.195).

The supernatural aspect of the tale is experienced by Kim Lee, as she sees the ghost of her dead boyfriend, Jay, who died on the 104th floor of the first tower that was attacked. The day after the tragic event, she believes she sees him again in Grand Central and confesses to Dan that "she would never forget the expression on his face... A terrible quiet sad anger, and it was directed not at the men who had murdered him, but at her" (McGrath, 2006, p.184). Later on in the story, Dan learns that Kim had an affair with Jay's father, Paul Minkoff. Dan explains to the psychiatrist how the affair continued for a while until Jay discovered it. According to the narrator, Dan reckons that Lee is attracted to powerful men (McGrath, 2006, p.227) and later on Dan states that perhaps fathers hate sons because "they're threatened by them. They arouse the fear of death in them. They resent a potential which no longer exists for them" (McGrath, 2006, p.237). While Dan attempts to accept Kim's transgression, the narrator perceives the evil in her as "a woman who could take pleasure in the admission that she was excited at the prospect of betraying her lover with his own father" (McGrath, 2006, p.228). Fathers are considered as competitors in this text, yet mother figures, or the lack thereof, reappear, as in the previous tales. Dan's mother died, and the psychiatrist's ignorance towards her patient's pain and suffering is significant since she considers him to be "like a son" (McGrath, 2006, p.175). Her incapacity to understand the feelings he is dealing with creates friction between them and, at the end of the narrative, Dan decides to stop his therapy with her and continue his relationship with Lee.

McGrath once more links the personal situation of his characters to the city. When the narrator tells of how Jay discovers Lee's affair with his father, the story moves from that personal torment to New York's affected area: "Ground Zero has now shrunk to the extent that I can stay within two or three blocks of the ruins on all but the west side of the site" (McGrath, 2006, p.239). As mentioned above, the narrator maintains her obsession with Lee as, when she stares at a headless and limbless mannequin in a shop window selling underwear, her first thought is to link it to the Asian woman, claiming that the "sexualized provocative variety" would be "patronized by the likes of her" (McGrath, 2006, p.239). The objectification of Dan's girlfriend is accentuated when the psychiatrist's next thoughts are about how "Bush has signed the Patriot Act" and "Ashcroft has pushed through a change in prison regulations which will allow federal agents to listen in on defendants' conversations with their lawyers" (McGrath, 2006, p.240), a fact which obviously would affect Dan's work. The connections between personal and societal events are constant in the narrator's mind, and though she claims that she is confident that Dan will go back to her when he has trouble with Lee, the implied perception for readers is that she is in need of closure to continue with her life.

As John Sheng Kuo notes, McGrath, through his story, depicts how "the ghostly image of the Twin Towers will not be banished" and that it is impossible to bury "or disguise that historical terror which haunts the American national identity" (Kuo, 2007, pp.71-72). Actually, one of the main features of the story is how the reaction of some Americans to the attack, against the most symbolic building of the capitalist power which the United States represents, triggers doubt as to what freedom and community truly mean. Once more, McGrath gives us a narrator who has not lived through the events she describes, a woman who imagines both what suffering the attacks could have caused and, especially, what experiences other people could have had in their romantic relationships. In the same way as Alice, in "Julius", she moves like a ghost inventing moments she has never witnessed and reflecting upon them without having the opportunity to present real conclusions to her hypotheses.

Conclusion

Patrick McGrath's portrayal of New York city in his collection of stories, *Ghost Town: Tales of Manhattan Then and Now*, (2006) depicts the evolution of the city in three key moments in its history: the Revolutionary War of the 18th century, the development of its industry during the 19th century and, finally, its temporary collapse after the 2001 attacks. McGrath could easily have chosen a method of depicting the rise, evolution, and fall of the capitalist system embodied by the metropolis, yet his stories "The Year of the Gibbet", "Julius" and "Ground Zero" expose the light and shadow of each period. This "dialogic" approach, following the Bakhtinian concept explained above, questions the identity and freedom of a country founded on the need for independence from the British kingdom, but also with contradictory desires for liberty and dominance over other nations which gave rise to the haunting past so often illustrated in American Gothic fiction. As has been shown throughout this article, in his tales McGrath does not only describe the city itself, but also engages a form of worldbuilding in which the social and political events, as well as the psychological breakdown of his characters, help us understand the diverse moments of the metropolis he depicts.

Through some of Bakhtin's concepts, such as "heteroglossia", "answerability" and, in particular, the "chronotope", McGrath's depiction of Manhattan can be explained. Furthermore, the "uncanny" and the "abject", so commonly employed when analysing Gothic narratives, have been explored, with the aim of shedding light on the neo-Gothic stories of McGrath.

References

Bakhtin, M.M., & Holquist, M., 1981. *The Dialogic Imagination: Four Essays*. Austin: University of Texas Press.

Freud, S., 1919. *The Uncanny*. [pdf] Available at: <http://www.english.upenn.edu/~cavitch/pdf-library/Freud_Uncanny.pdf> [Accessed 10 October 2020].

Graham, C. in Brown, B.A., Conway, C., Gambol, R., Kalter, S., Ruberto, L. E., Taraborrelli, T.F., Wesling, D., eds., 2000. *Bakhtin and the Nation*. Lewisburg: Bucknell University Press.

Hantke, S. and Monnet, A.S., eds., 2016. *War Gothic in Literature and Culture*. New York: Routledge.

Holquist, M., Bakhtin, M. M., 1990. *Art and Answerability*. [Kindle Version] Available at: <http://www.amazon.es> [Accessed 10 September 2020].

Irving, W. 2019. "Rip Van Winkle". [online] Available at: <http://www.gutenberg.org/files/60976/60976-h/60976-h.htm> [Accessed 25th October 2020]

Kristeva, J., 1982. *Powers of Horror*. [pdf] Available at: <http://users.clas.ufl.edu/burt/touchyfeelingsmaliciousobjects/Kristevapowersofhorrorabjection.pdf> [Accessed 25 October 2020].

Kuo, J. S., 2007. *9/11 as American Gothic: Terror and Historical Darkness in Patrick McGrath's Ghost Town in Concentric: Literary and Cultural Studies 33.1* [pdf] Available at: <http://www.concentric-literature.url.tw/issues/The%20Gothic%20Revisited/3.pdf> [Accessed 25 September 2020].

McGrath, P., 1988. *Blood and Water and Other Stories*. New York: Simon and Schuster.

—, 2006. *Ghost Town: Tales of Manhattan Then and Now*. London: Bloomsbury Publishing Plc.

—, 2020. Personal correspondence with Tatiana Fajardo, September 30, 2020.

McGrath, P., and Morrow, B. eds.,1991. *The Picador Book of the New Gothic*. New York: Random House.

Poe, E.A., 1998. *Selected Tales*. Oxford: Oxford University Press.
—, "The Premature Burial". [online] Available at: <https://www.gutenberg.org/files/2148/2148-h/2148-h.htm#chap2.16> [Accessed 20 October 2020].
—, "The Fall of the House of Usher". [online] Available at: <https://www.gutenberg.org/files/2148/2148-h/2148-h.htm#chap2.16> [Accessed 20 October 2020].

Richardson, B., ed., 2002. *Narrative Dynamics: Essays on Time, Plot, Closure, and Frames*. Columbus: Ohio State University Press.

Royle, N., 2003. *The Uncanny*. Manchester: Manchester University Press.

Wilson, K. M., 1996. *Cross-Cultural Othering Through Metamorphosis*. [pdf] Available at: <https://escholarship.org/content/qt4j15m6ww/qt4j15m6ww.pdf> [Accessed 20 October 2020].

Zlosnik, S., 2011. *Patrick McGrath*. Cardiff: University of Wales Press.

The Book of Copper and the Anvil of Death: William Blake's Gothic Creation Myth

Claire Burgess

Abstract

William Blake, a poet and artist known as a radical, a madman, or a genius, is not often considered to be a mythmaker or a worldbuilder, despite the fact that Blake's later works – especially his major poems and visual art between "America, A Prophecy" (1793) and "Jerusalem" (1820) – delve deeply into the creation of an imagined fallen universe that mirrors this one but is not *precisely* our own. Blake's forged universe is one that is in many ways blacker and more hideous, and ruled by indifferent tyrants that oppress and maim while creating life in the same stroke. Indeed, the dreadful narrative of the primary worldbuilding tool for this universe, i.e. his creation myth, relies upon a classic Gothic thread: a hubristic seeker of arcane and profane knowledge creating something monstrous. "The Book of Copper and the Anvil of Death: William Blake's Gothic Creation Myth" explores the nature of this knowledge through visual analysis of Blake's illustrations, then inspects the main players within the creation myth, Urizen and Los, as possessors of this divinely-bestowed, powerful knowledge that Blake also believed himself to have... and which, in true Gothic fashion, springs from the grave. In this manner, this paper will demonstrate that Blake's engagement with the Gothic genre goes well beyond his predilection for graveyard imagery, and that the substance of William Blake's creation myth lies upon Gothic bones.

*

William Blake's forged, fallen universe is one that is in many ways blacker and more cruel than our own, and ruled by indifferent tyrants that oppress and maim while creating life in the same stroke. With an analysis of Blake's creation myth for this universe, and a brief exploration into the hideous result, this paper will establish that the narrative web Blake spins, like those of Goethe and Shelley, relies upon a hubristic seeker of arcane and profane knowledge creating something monstrous. To show this, this paper will trace Blake's use of the art of language as he demonstrates himself to be in possession of supernatural powers of creation in one of the three areas of artistic production that are normally shut off to those within the fallen world; the arts that require special intervention in order to be properly perceived. These arts are language, visual art, and song:

> But in Eternity the Four Arts: Poetry, Painting, Music,
> And Architecture which is Science: are the Four Faces of Man.
> Not so in Time and Space: there Three are shut out...
> "Jerusalem" (Erdman, 1988, 10)[1]

This paper will also include samples from Blake's poetry and artworks that prove that he bestowed this wisdom and these powers upon his two major players in the creation myth: Urizen and Los. After this, the paper will demonstrate that the source of this knowledge within the narrative is, in true Gothic fashion, the grave. Finally, the paper will turn to the abominable result of Urizen and Los's machinations: fallen man and its home in the Mundane Shell, who are both monstrous in their very nature.

---

[1]. Unless otherwise noted, all text samples in this thesis will include plate numbers corresponding to those found in David V. Erdman's *The Complete Poetry and Prose of William Blake* (1988) for easy reference, as plate arrangement and numbering can vary edition by edition.

*

Blake has created a pattern in his worldbuilding poetry that is both a rubric for perception and a multifaceted, ever-changing mythological system. Characteristically for a man as unique as William Blake, this system, while absolutely reminiscent in basic archetypal ways to Biblical mythology and Classical myths, is also very much not just vertical changes made to traditions that came before it. As the character Los states in "Jerusalem":

> I must Create a System, or be enslav'd by another Mans
> I will not Reason & Compare: my business is to Create.
> (Erdman, 1988, 10).

Blake's cosmology is a form of imaginative thinking that, rather paradoxically, uses literal versions of imaginative forms in order to demonstrate essential human truths. His goal was to uncover the mythological universe of the human imagination, rather than projecting it on an objective God or similar analogy of external order (Frye, 1976, p.109). This was no silly pastime, nor was it an accomplished series of Pygmalion retellings or reconfigurations of Olympian psyches; as Northrop Frye said (1976, p.112), Blake understood the underlying archetypal structures of myth and narrative better than anyone in literature. It is with this knowledge that he was able to collect what he truly believed to be the secrets of the universe, which are unlocked by opening the doors of perception with Blake as a guide to the process. This is done with a thoroughness that is oftentimes baffling, because in order to demonstrate the essential truths of the universe and of the evolved creatures within it, quite a lot of ground needs to be covered. This is why Blake found the need to retell his creation myth a handful of times in different poems.

Blake's myth takes a number of structural cues from the German mystic Jacob Boehme. Boehme, in his work *Aurora*, analysed the makeup of the human psyche, placing Imagination at the center of man's potentially infinite powers, and attacking "reason" as its opposite and its enemy. He likewise believed that the Bible was symbolically of great value, and that it expressed some of the deepest truths of the human soul, though the Church was blind and despicable (Damon, 2013, pp.39-41). It is no wonder, then, that he was very influential for William Blake (Stevenson, 2007, p.253). In Boehme's version of the story of creation, three elements are of note: 1) creation and the fall occur simultaneously, 2) this takes place due to an eternal being's high degree of introspection, and 3) the Fall occurs in two stages, the second being the creation of Eve as a division from the side of Adam. Blake follows those three characteristics closely, but changes a few things: 1) Eternity consists of an entire society of eternal beings with infinite power (this is reformulated in "Four Zoas"), 2) the act of creation is sparked by the physical formation of Urizen himself, who was expelled from Eternity by the other immortals for his tyrannical aspirations, and 3) Blake has two major creators at work, including Los (Stevenson, 2007, p.234).

Blake refers to his creation story, and as the characters of Urizen and Los, countless times throughout his poetry, as he continued to cultivate his points of view on creation, existence, unity, and monstrousness over the course of his life. However, the complete narrative of the creation myth proper takes place in three poems. The first is "The (First) Book of Urizen", which is the first of three books in what Blake called his Bible of Hell. "Urizen" tells the story of creation as outlined above. Urizen, angered at his failure to take tyrannical control of the immortals, isolates himself in exile from his peers, where he hardens into the fixed form of man in seven stages (these stages, of course, recalling the number of days that God took to create Earth in the Bible). Los, the blacksmith with his anvils of death (Blake, 1804–1820, p.675), is sent to observe this process, which leads him to become equally forgetful of Eternity and equally obsessively introspective. In the end, he aids Urizen in his transformation by lending permanence to the forms Urizen morphs into. Los then splinters in two – he becomes both Los and a female Emanation named Enitharmon, with whom he makes a child named Orc. The Fall is completed with the chaining of Orc with links formed from jealousy. The remainder of the narrative tells of Urizen's explorations of the dark world he has created, where he witnesses the creation of the four elements, which are called his children, a parade of creatures, and then finally humanity. All of the things in this world are restricted under his Net of Religion, and the poem ends with humanity fleeing him in an Exodus from Egypt.

The second and third books of this infernal Bible of Hell were "The Book of Ahania" (1795) and "The Book of Los". "Ahania", though originally conceived to be the second of Urizen's books, was retitled, and occupies itself with a reinterpretation of the events of *Exodus*. "Los" is a retelling of "Urizen" from Los's point of view, and the narrative is cast in such a way that it shows a much greater level of similarity with Genesis, which may have been the reason for the retelling. The only change is that the six-day endeavor to give form to Urizen is omitted, and readers are simply privy to the tale of Los binding the sun to Urizen's spine. However, much more attention is given to Los aiding in creating the rest of the disorganised universe that he finds himself trapped in, and it is here that the seven-day structure appears once more.

He makes fire, water, earth (at which point, he himself gains physical form), the cosmos, and then, finally, Adam. Blake was dissatisfied with the way that the Bible of Hell turned out, which is why he scrapped it and either retold the stories once more or took segments of it to insert into "Four Zoas".

"Four Zoas", though unfinished, is still a much longer poem than either "Urizen" or "Los", as it ambitiously attempts to place all of Blake's myths within one larger work. Therefore, within the first section of the work is found a reformulation of the creation myth with a few changes, such as the introduction of The Universal Man, who has now replaced the society of Eternals that was in the original version of the myth (he is later called Albion in "Jerusalem"). The elements of the Man's psyche are seen in human form in four figures called "Zoas". The Man falls sick when the Zoas begin to war against each other, which can be seen as an allegory of the conflict of the various parts of the soul, such as passion and reason. The conflict begins because Urizen and his fellow Zoa, Luvah, want control over the sick and sleeping Universal Man. Urizen is characterised slightly differently here, and his motivations for seeking order and control now come from a fear of an abyss that opens before him during the course of the action.

*

When trying to make sense of the worldbuilding of William Blake, and to apply a simple answer to the question "What does any of this really mean?" in his mythology, it is hard not to feel disoriented. Scholars and poets have long tried to lay patterns of thinking atop his structures, and this paper is no exception. For while many of Blake's poems betray a slightly muddled, ever-evolving execution of ideas, there is something in them that the reader seems to understand innately. As one Blake scholar put it, among all of the categories scholars try to place Blake in, "there was also that category of what was not known, but understood" (Warner, 1984, p.xvii). It is exactly that hard-to-define but readily-felt sensation that puts these later poems in the same category as *Dracula* or *Frankenstein*. While Blake is certainly not a Gothic writer strictly speaking, this particular feeling characteristic of his poetry is a Gothic one.

The scholar David Punter has in recent decades expanded what the definition of the Gothic is, and it was to his writings that this paper owes a great debt, for it is with this exploration in mind that Blake's mythical-literary patterns became evident. Punter puts forward the premise that three principal symbolic figures run through Gothic works. He calls these figures "the wanderer", "the vampire", and "the seeker after forbidden knowledge" (Punter, 1996, p.87). This statement is the bedrock upon which this paper rests. While there are indeed examples of the first two of these figures in Blake's poetry, "the seeker after forbidden knowledge" is the one that best identifies the figures found in Blake's creation myths, and it is on these figures that this paper will focus. Ultimately, when speaking about the supernaturally-gifted and creatively-minded seeker after forbidden knowledge, one is speaking of a trio of enmeshed figures both within and without the poetry: Urizen, Los, and Blake himself. All three figures seek and find arcane knowledge in a doomed attempt to create life, and the resulting monstrous universe and human form is their terrible reward.

The primary art that William Blake believed himself to possess – and that he bestowed upon Urizen and Los for their own creative act – is the power of divinely-granted language. Blake firmly believed that language and writing were gifts from the beyond, or perhaps from the mythic past, which makes writing itself a kind of arcane knowledge.

This idea is hardly original to Blake. During the mediaeval period, and even earlier, holy books explaining the creation of the universe become representative of the divine presence, and the divine presence itself becomes located within the book; the book's textuality, within this divine context, no longer merely conveyed the word of God, and it was no longer mere metaphor (Bloom, 1987, pp.90-91). Therefore, according to mediaeval writers, if the holy book is the literal God as well as the literal word of God, it is easy for that metaphor to shift laterally and expand to encompass the entirety of the world that is created by God. Hugh of St. Victor, a twelfth century writer, said:

> For this whole visible world is a book written by the finger of God, that is, created by divine power; and individual creatures are as figures therein not devised by human will but instituted by divine authority to show forth the wisdom of the invisible things of God
> (Bloom, 1987, p.92)

In his work 'The World and the Book', Gabriel Josipovici explains that to Christianity, this equivalence between the physical world and the holy book was literal and pressing: "never has there been such faith in the phenomenal. What guarantees this faith is the incarnation, for it is the eruption into time of the eternal, into space of the infinite" (Bloom, 1987, p.92). The idea that the earthly realm is itself the word of God in the form of a holy book was ground-breaking, and fundamental to understanding the full parameters of Blake's overarching metaphor, along with its slippery relationship with literal reality to the mediaeval point of view. When Blake wrote a book, he was creating a world.

While the above paragraph may seem initially to be a

misguided attempt to ascribe religious sentiment to the notoriously antireligious Blake, it is important to remember that his works are fully saturated in Biblical imagery and context, and that while he believed truly that there is no Natural Religion, he also mined wisdom from within the pages of holy books. He locates the divine reception of this gift in the Biblical place of Sinai in the passage below, in which he also – through the deletion of two words in the first line – implies that heaven is something that can be read, just as a book:

> Reader! Of books! Of heaven.
> And of that God from whom
> Who in mysterious Sinais awful cave
> To Man the wondrous art of writing gave.
> "Jerusalem" (Erdman, 1988, 3)

Words are the magical building blocks of Blake's *Universe stupendous*, and the multiplicity of potency here is that when this gift is applied to the characters within this universe, such as Urizen and Los, Blake is using words to create a semi-divine creature within a literary universe that in turn uses words to create the physical realm within a universe. It is almost dizzying to contemplate.

A significant amount of time is spent fleshing out the importance of the written word with Urizen (who is, creatively speaking, the Apollo to Los's Dionysos) in particular, as he is the maker and keeper of the books of laws governing the four departments of life, each made of a metal: science in gold, love in silver, war in iron, and sociology in brass. He describes the making of these books in the passage below; it is a terrible process of sin and solitude. One particularly remarkable part of this passage is located in the first line of the sixth stanza, where the word "metals" is broken up into "me" and "tals", which is intentional, as the entire word could have fit upon the line if he had wanted it to do so (Wolfson, 2003, p.67). Clearly, Blake intended for Urizen to be saying that he made the books of himself. One can see again that the creator of the book and the book itself are considered to be one and the same.

> 6. Here alone I in books formd of me-tals
> Have written the secrets of wisdom
> The secrets of dark contemplation
> By fightings and conflicts dire,
> With terrible monsters Sin-bred:
> Which the bosoms of all inhabit;
> Seven deadly Sins of the soul.
> 7. Lo! I unfold my darkness: and on
> This rock, place with strong hand the Book
> Of eternal brass, written in my solitude.
> 8. Laws of peace, of love, of unity:
> Of pity, compassion, forgiveness.
> Let each chuse one habitation:
> His ancient infinite mansion:
> One command, one joy one desire,
> One curse, one weight, one measure
> One King, one God, one Law."
> "The (First) Book of Urizen"
> (Erdman, 1988, 4).

Urizen is literally the embodiment of the written word in the form of the book. Since the written word in the form of Urizen is expressly law, he can be described as a creator god that personifies a concept outlined by Michel Foucault:

> Consequently the father separates, that is, he is the one who protects when, in his proclamation of the Law, he links space,

rules, and language within a single and major experience. At a stroke, he creates the distance along which will develop the scansion of presences and absences, the speech whose initial form is based on constraints and finally, gives rise to the structure of language but also to the exclusion and symbolic transformation of repressed material.
(1977, p.81)

With this in mind, one is reminded that not only is Urizen the written word, he also is the creator of the restraints that govern it. He is grammar, rhyme scheme, stanza, and verse, and as such he is the embodiment of all of the rules of writing that Blake so enjoyed breaking. Urizen as word and Urizen as law is necessary to the poetic universe here, just as it is necessary to any Gothic narrative. Without law, there can exist no transgression, desire, or excess in the way that defines Gothic fiction (Botting, 1999, p.26), along with the monstrous and fallen universe that Urizen creates. Drawing attention to the limits of language and existence only emphasises when those limits are shattered. Laws aided in the creation of the universe, and they also created a confinement against which the created beings could strain.

*

Of course, given Blake's predilection toward the extreme, it should not surprise us to find the emphasis on the importance of the written word is compounded even further in his worldbuilding with the utilisation of polysemous language. This concept was derived from two theologians that had an immense impact on Blake: Jacob Boehme and Emanuel Swedenborg. Swedenborg, who was interested in clearing away the traditional trappings of religion from the simple truth of God and Christ, had perhaps more influence on Blake than any other single thinker; Blake was, in fact, an active member of his church (Davies, 1966, pp.31-35). Both Boehme and Swedenborg placed an inordinate amount of importance on language: Boehme stated that "language is the agent of man's likeness to God", and for Swedenborg, every word constitutes a literal meaning and an "internal" one which consists of a spiritual meaning that is inaccessible to human intelligence (Hilton, 1983, p.14). Thanks to Swedenborg, Blake believed that the infinite is present in finite words, and he aims to entirely dissolve linguistic and artistic boundaries.

A pertinent example of this polysemy can be found in the word "grave", which, in Blake's poetry, can function as the adjectival "serious", the nominal "burial place", or the action word for "to carve" either separately or all at once (Hilton, 1983, p.19). This is a critical word for Blake, as the comprehension of humanity's own mortality lies at the core of his creation myth and is the source of all arcane truths. The understanding of death and the confrontation of the grave entails a transformation of the mind's understanding of itself and its relation to the physical universe. Blake, Urizen, and Los are all men who have come to grips with the nature of the grave, as this paper will explore further shortly, and it is from this sombre contemplation of both burial places and of engraving that these creators of universes discover the secrets necessary for the making of worlds. There are innumerable mentions of graves bursting, shrieking, and frightening the characters, but there is one activity that stems from the grave in Blake's narratives that is particularly evocative and critical in understanding just how death and creativity are linked: resurrection.

In figure 1, from "America", a recurring visual motif can be seen that will come up once more later in this paper.

Fig 1: "America: A Prophecy" (Erdman, 1988, 6)[2]

A male figure is perched upon a sepulchre as though he has just sprouted from it. He gazes upwards, and his eyes strain to perceive the infinite heavens.

The text below him describes the scene:

The grave is burst, the spices shed, the linen wrappèd up;
The bones of death, the cov'ring clay, the sinews shrunk and dry'd
Reviving shake, inspiring move, breathing, awakening,
Spring like redeemèd captives, when their bonds and bars are burst.
"America: A Prophecy" (Erdman, 1988, 6).

---

[2]. All images in this paper are in the public domain, and taken with thanks from the Yale Center for British Art, available at: <https://britishart.yale.edu>

This figure is indeed arising from a burst grave, his embalming accoutrements having been shed, his flesh returning to his withered bones. Life and death are so intertwined as to be confused in terms of timeline. Life not only leads to death, but they are one and the same; life cannot take place without death both preceding it and following it. Graves, like sleep, are things to be risen from. The action word "spring" in this section is both a verb and a symbol: spring the season, too, is the very concept of rebirth distilled.

The second meaning of the word "grave" is one that obviously carries much weight when considering these illuminated works: the act of digging into a hard surface to leave a pattern behind. These graves left behind by Blake's acids or engraving tools are also to be risen from; the ideas embodied by the words one reads or the images one considers are brought to life in the reader's own mind (Hilton, 1983, p.21). Words, then, function something like seeds, which is a commonly referenced Biblical metaphor: the seed is the word of God. The word-seeds bear much fruit in the reader's imagination, especially in the hands of literal creator gods such as Urizen and Los. It is with these seeds that the entirety of creation can grow into being. The grave is both the word used to describe the act of making a work of art such as America, and it is the source of the knowledge that enables their actual creation within Blake's mind. The acquisition of the knowledge and the creation of the forms are one and the same, just as is the reporting of this activity to the reader. This is seen in the brief quotation from Jerusalem here that this is the case:

> The Visions of Eternity, by reason of narrowed perceptions,
> Are become weak Visions of Time & Space, fix'd into furrows of death…
> "Jerusalem" (Erdman, 1988, 49).

The "furrows of death" here, of course, refer to both meanings of the word "grave." In context, this quotation is simply referring to the doomed nature of creation, which is blinded and crippled in this fallen world, trapped by mortality and physicality. However, it also refers to the impaired nature of the creative act itself, which is undertaken by Blake, of course, but also Urizen: Figure 2 shows the demiurge with a pen in one hand and in the other, an engraving tool.

Fig 2: The (First) Book of Urizen (Erdman, 1988, 1).

Before him is, significantly, a tombstone. The inky divots burned into the copper plates upon which these stories are told are but shadows of the eternal truths they are meant to represent, just as humanity's created bodies are lacking in perception. The etched and engraved poem is the setting for transformation and rebirth, however flawed.

*

When it came to finding the great truths of this universe in order to, in turn, use them to create his own universe on the page, Blake was much more aligned with the thinking of Gothic revivalists than with the great minds of the Enlightenment. Gothic writers wanted to shape their craft into something that could imagine the unimaginable, and turn their works into a distorted magnifying glass that would show people a truth otherwise inaccessible (Frye, 1974, pp.97-98). It is in using the creative act to make non-realistic inventions that, Blake believed, brought his works closer to ones that could be characterised as divine (Abrams, 1953, p.275). Blake, Urizen, and Los all look to create form from maddening terror and critical error, and to create flesh and bones out of darkness.

Edward Young's "The Complaint: or, Night-Thoughts on Life, Death, & Immortality" (1742-1745), an example of graveyard poetry, was illustrated by Blake in the year 1794 or 1795[3], which is a number of years after Blake was an active poet, and a few years after he penned The Bible of Hell. Therefore, it is hard to say with any certainty whether Blake actually read this poem before penning the first versions of his creation story. However, it indubitably influenced "The Four Zoas", as they have mirroring structures that break the narrative up into nine sections, each called "nights", and there are enough similarities

---

3. Available at: <http://www.blakearchive.org/work/but330>.

between "Night Thoughts" and the rest of Blake's creation story concerning the personification of Urizen and Los that it is clear that Blake is at least participating in the same tradition as Young was, even in his earliest explorations into his cosmology. "Night Thoughts" is a tale of the soul of the poet who releases himself from material matters and invokes the powers of darkness to assist his visionary voyage in exploration of the entire universe (Punter, 1996, pp.34-35). Within the poem, Young advises that focusing on death is the way to attain exquisite anguish, and it is in terror that he locates a hubristic aspiration towards divinity; the claim of self-divinity is central here – pain, anguish, death, and horror can bring a person towards ultimate comprehension and divine power (Punter, 1996, pp.35-39). Wisdom of the highest and most inaccessible kind, according to Young, is only found in darkness, despair, and in death. Blake most certainly took this concept to heart.

Death, in Blake's poetry, is not an abstract concept, but rather a physical place. This can be understood chiefly by visual analysis of figure 3, which incorporates visual motifs that are actually dispersed throughout Blake's poetry (Makdisi, n.d., pp.110-132). Figure 3, created in 1805, is the final iteration of the motifs, which takes two figures previously portrayed as isolated elements and combines them into one composition. This paper has in fact already reproduced the stargazing young man at the top in figure 1 from "America", and devoted readers of Blake will also encounter the hunched and bearded man entering Death's Door many times and in many different illustrated manuscripts. Clearly, these two figures hold great importance for Blake. Furthermore, we come to understand that these two figures were always linked in Blake's mind, as well (Makdisi, n.d., p.121).

If one takes what one knows about the potency of the grave

as a function of Blake's craft of engraving and apply it to this image, one arrives at an interesting observation. The bearded man is being literally engraved in two senses: Blake is etching him into a copper plate, and the old man is interring himself into a sepulchre. A cause and effect on two levels is seen, then: within the framing of the image proper, the seed of the engraved image is leading to a new creation springing from the earth above him, and we as viewers, in turn, bring the entire process as Blake imagined it to life in the viewer's mind as he or she looks at the image. When one adds to this the fact that Urizen himself is only ever represented like this – with long, trailing white beard and pale robes – one could make an argument for an even further dimension. Perhaps what is represented here is Urizen again at the threshold of death, being swept forward by either a gust of air or by a brash compulsion to reach the extremes of the universe in order to create and control. Above him is man, in all his fallen but heaven-bent glory – the flesh-bound and holy result of Urizen's machinations as abetted by Los. This is not an outlandish theory, especially given that the end result of the saga of this motif is that it served as an illustration of Robert Blair's "The Grave", yet another example of graveyard poetry. Blake's illustrations of the poem concerned themselves chiefly with the parting of the soul and body, which is a chief concern of Blake's, and the ultimate fate of the universe in the creation myth in his own cosmology.[4] With all of this evidence before us, I would argue that the dark expanse of despair into which Urizen and Los enter before they begin to create the Mundane Shell is this very realm of death as described by graveyard poets. It is there in the grave – both in terms of the etching into the copper plate and the resting place – that they seek and find the arcane truths from which spring the cosmos and humanity.

---

4. Available at: <http://www.blakearchive.org/work/bb435O>

Fig. 3: *Death's Door*, printed by Luigi Schiavonetti, 1765–1810, after Blake's design.

*

With the graven word and the sacred wisdom gained from plumbing the depths of the grave, the world and its inhabitants are thus created in much the same way that it occurs in the Bible: "And the Word was made flesh, and dwelt among us" (John: 1:14). Blake, Urizen, and Los all take part in the creation of this flesh-bound poetic universe, and in terms of both the poems themselves and the universe they describe, the results are not precisely what the creators had imagined. These three men's joint attempt to rationalise experience into a homogenous system results in its precise opposite – a world of terror and chaos that will not obey the laws set forth.

The creatures dwelling within the Mundane Shell in the poetry are monsters in multiple senses of the word. The first relates to the way one views humanity visually, and this does not refer simply to creatures that are ugly – though there is plenty of that within the poetry and illustrations, as well. It is more complicated than that, and more compelling when viewed within the framework of harnessing the power of the language arts. Peter Brooks (1993, p.218) defines monstrosity as something born both from nature and from something beyond it; it is something that calls into question what vision itself means, the language we use to classify what we see, and the means by which we can even judge or control the phenomenal world at all.

> What, then, in unprincipled nature, is a monster? A monster is that outcome or product of curiosity or epistemophilia pushed to an extreme that results – as in the story of Oedipus – in confusion, blindness, and exile. A monster is that which cannot be placed in any of the taxonomic schemes devised by the human mind to understand and to order nature. It exceeds the very basis of classification, language itself: it is an excess of signification, a strange byproduct or leftover of the process of making meaning. It is an imaginary being who comes to life in language, and once having done so, cannot be eliminated from language. Even if we want to claim that "monster," like some of the words used by Felix and Agatha [in *Frankenstein*] – "dearest", "unhappy" – has no referent, it has a signified, a conceptual meaning, a place in our knowledge of ourselves. The novel insistently thematizes issues of language and rhetoric because the symbolic order of the visual, specular, and imaginary relations, in which he is demonstrably a monster. The symbolic order compensates for a deficient nature: it promises escape from a condition of 'to-be-looked-at-ness.'

A monster is a body created by the imagination that exists in order to be regarded and wordlessly shuddered at – one that transgresses all conceived barriers and that cannot be wrapped up tidily or conceptualised with language. Monstrosity is the Gothic encapsulated: easily felt but difficult to describe. Truly, language alone is not enough to encapsulate the monstrous, nor are our eyes alone enough to comprehend it.

Blake is the seminal poet of the fallen, shattered body that is both human and dehumanised, and the blindness characteristic of the conceptual core of monstrosity as described above is part and parcel of the very idea Blake has of the closed doors of perception. The fallen nature of humankind and physical impurity are enough to call into question language and how we use it to describe the world and ourselves. We are monstrous spectacles in our very nature:

> Ah! Weak & wide astray! Oh shut in narrow doleful form!
> Creeping in reptile flesh upon the bosom of the ground:
> The Eye of Man, a little narrow orb, closd up & dark.
> Scarcely beholding the Great Light; conversing with the ground.
> The Ear, a little shell, in small volutions shutting out
> True Harmonies, & comprehending great, as very small:
> The Nostrils, bent down to the earth & clos'd with senseless flesh.
> That odours cannot them expand, nor joy in them exult:
> The Tongue, a little moisture fills, a little food it cloys.
> A little sound it utters, & its cries are faintly heard.
> "Jerusalem" (Erdman, 1988, 49).

The "reptile flesh" of humanity not only ties us symbolically to the earth, but is also responsible literally for the shutting up of the doors of perception. Part of humanity's monstrousness is its physical deformities, most assuredly, but it is also its wormlike blindness. In other words, humanity is indeed monstrous because it is something before which one can do nothing but wordlessly gawk, as Brooks defines it, but included in that monstrousness is also our inability to comprehend it. Monstrousness in Blake's poetry is an unending, horrific vortex that is reminiscent, in fact, of the black realm of death from which it was created. The fallen universe created by Urizen and Los is a place of dreadful distortion and disease, and not only for those dwelling within it. What follows this creation are countless tales of monstrous humanity that call into question both mankind's limits of perception and our ability to verbalise what we take in.

*

As Clive Bloom (1987, p.34) states:

> Gothic horror [...] is about that which should not be, whose comprehension is the end of sanity and the opening of the abyss, in which cursed state of knowledge of the forbidden becomes manifest, the veil is withdrawn and the fabric of the material universe falls to dust.

If there is one thing that defines Blake as an artist, it is this characteristic that he has in common with the entirety of the Gothic genre. It is, in short, the attempt to portray in art the absolute darkest and most horrible side of the sublime to convey:

> The roaring of lions, the howling of wolves, the raging
> of the stormy sea, and the destructive sword...
> portions of eternity too great for the eye of man.
> "The Marriage of Heaven and Hell" (Erdman, 1988, 8)

This is best understood, as this paper argues, by exploring the creation myth that set in motion the world built, and the wondrous powers the poet has in common with his two creator gods: Urizen and Los. This paper's examination has walked the long and tortuous path through Blake's creation myth from skull to spine to bowels in order to show that by harnessing and compounding the multitudinous powers of the art of divine language, Blake, Urizen, and Los all attempt to extend the reach of man, whether mortal or eternal, to create something that transgressed and shattered all boundaries as previously conceived. These seekers after forbidden knowledge were driven by abominable hubris to push against and define every limit they encountered in order to create something that was ultimately a karmic punishment for their ambition: a monstrous poetic world.

References

Abrams, M.H., 1953. *The Mirror and the Lamp: Romantic Theory and the Critical Edition*. London: Oxford University Press.

Blake, W., 1804–1820. "Jerusalem". In: W.H. Stevenson, ed. 2007. *Blake: The Complete Poems*. 3rd ed. New York, NY: Routledge, pp.648-890.

Bloom, C., 1987. *The 'Occult' Experience and the New Criticism: Daemonism, Sexuality and the Hidden in Literature*. Sussex: Harvester Press.

Botting, F., 1999. The Gothic production of the unconscious. In: G. Byron and D. Punter ed. 1999. *Spectral Readings: Towards a Gothic Geography*. Basingstoke: Macmillan Press, pp.11-26.

Brooks, P., 1993. *Body Work: Objects of Desire in Modern Narrative*. London: Harvard University Press.

Damon, S. F., 2013. *A Blake Dictionary: The Ideas and Symbols of William Blake*. Hanover, NH: Dartmouth College Press.

Davies, J.G., 1966. *The Theology of William Blake*. Hamden, CT: Archon Books.

The University of North Carolina at Chapel Hill and the University of Rochester, 1996. [online] Available at: <http://www.blakearchive.org> [Accessed 31 October 2020].

Erdman, D.V., 1988. *The Complete Poetry & Prose of William Blake*. New York, NY: Anchor Books.

Foucault, M., and Bouchard, D.F., 1977. *Language, Counter-Memory, Practice: Selected Essays and Interviews by Michel Foucault*. Translated from French by D.F. Bouchard and S. Simon. Ithaca, NY: Cornell University Press.

Frye, N., 1974. *Fearful Symmetry*. 4th ed. Princeton, N.J.: Princeton University Press.
—, 1976. *Spiritus Mundi: Essays on Literature, Myth, and Society*. Bloomington, IN: Indiana University Press.

Hammond, G. and Busch, A., 2012. *The English Bible, King James Version: Volume Two, The New Testament and the Apocrypha*. New York, NY: W.W. Norton & Company.

Hilton, N., 1983. *Literal Imagination: Blake's Vision of Words*. Berkeley, CA: University of California Press.

Makdisi, S., n.d.. The political aesthetic of Blake's images. In: M. Eaves ed. 2003. *The Cambridge Companion to William Blake*. Cambridge: Cambridge University Press, pp.110-132.

Punter, D., 1996. *The Literature of Terror: A History of Gothic Fictions from 1765 to the present day. Volume 1: The Gothic Tradition*. London: Pearson Education Limited.

Stevenson, W.H., 2007. *Blake: The Complete Poems*. Abingdon-on-Thames: Routledge.

Warner, J.A., 1984. *Blake and the Language of Art*. Montreal: McGill-Queen's University Press.

Wolfson, S.J., n.d.. *Blake's language in poetic form*. In: M. Eaves ed. 2003. The Cambridge Companion to William Blake. Cambridge: Cambridge University Press, pp.63-84.

Canada's Fantasy Worlds: Exploring Worldbuilding in Urban Fantasy

Ellen Forget

Abstract

Worldbuilding has always been an important piece of writing fantasy, and urban authors have an interesting challenge – to keep readers engaged in a fantasy world seemingly set on the Earth we already know. The challenge therein comes from needing to make the fantastical elements introduced to the world plausible and, most of all, *believable* to the reader who is already familiar with the overall setting. Some authors do this by having their stories set in a fictional place on our Earth and others choose to use existing cities, highlighting important landmarks as parts of their story. This paper focuses on questions of style and worldbuilding technique for authors writing urban fantasy set in various parts of Canada.

Introduction

Urban fantasy is a relatively new term to describe a subgenre of fantasy literature that is set on a recognisable Earth, either in modern times (contemporary urban fantasy) or in past eras (historical urban fantasy). Works of urban fantasy combine our real world with elements of the fantastic to create a world recognisable in setting, but unreal or magical in narrative. The most common fantastical elements authors use to create their urban fantasy works are those that are considered supernatural or paranormal; these types of fantasy elements work well within an urban setting because the existence of demons, faeries, or shapeshifters can often be more easily explained through faith/belief or unknown underworld narratives than the existence of humanoid beings such as dwarves or orcs, or more invasive nonhumanoid beings such as dragons or tauntauns. Many urban fantasy stories utilise the masquerade or invisible to normals trope, which means average human characters are unaware of the existence of the supernatural elements within their world – often very early in the narrative the main character will discover the supernatural world within their own, leading to whatever plot then follows. Popular examples of this include the *Vampire Diaries* novels (1991-2014) by L. J. Smith (also a TV series) and *Supernatural* (2005-2020). Some urban fantasy stories lean more into the *urban* rather than the *fantasy* into what Colin Harvey calls a liminal fantasy, "in which the narrative *feels* fantastical but in which the fantastical is implied rather than overtly dealt with" (2015, p.44). An example of a liminal urban fantasy would be the first book in Kelley Armstrong's Cainsville series (2014); the first book in this series hints at fantastical elements that are finally revealed at the end of the book, and the subsequent books start to explain what's revealed at the end of *Omens*.

As a subgenre, urban fantasy works with "the rhetorics of both fantasy and the literature of the urban, occasionally as pure bricolage but more interestingly as a form of artistic resistance to what recent writers have seen as the exhaustion of traditional modes of the fantastic" (Irvine 2012, p.202). The traditional modes Irvine references here would include forms of high fantasy, which is often what people first think of when they think of the fantasy genre – *The Lord of the Rings* (Tolkien, 1954) is the classic example of traditional high fantasy. High fantasy typically comes in long books and series, rivalling the science fiction subgenre space opera in length, character count, and detail. In contrast, urban fantasy books are often shorter, more often come in stand alone novels than other fantasy subgenres (although many are in series), and include a much smaller cast of characters who all deal with the main conflict more directly. While urban fantasy is often considered a newer subgenre, we can look to books such as Mary Shelley's *Frankenstein* (1818) and Bram Stoker's *Dracula* (1897) as early examples of including fantastical humanoid characters in a world otherwise like our own. These two novels are inspirations for many of the popular urban fantasy series, particularly those with zombie (or the animated dead) and vampire characters.

This paper discusses urban fantasy worldbuilding techniques used by Canadian authors who chose to set their novels in locations across Canada – from Vancouver to Halifax, and everything in between. Some of these authors chose to have their works set in a specific Canadian location – Melanson's *Terminal City* (2016) and *Winter's End* (2017) in Vancouver or Chadwick Ginther's *Graveyard Mind* (2018) in Winnipeg – and others chose to use vague locations – Pat Flewwelling's Helix trilogy (2014-2019) references being in Canada[1] and Cherie Dimaline's *Empire of Wild* (2019) set in a town near the Georgian Bay. By setting their stories on our Earth, and specifically in Canada, these authors defined a set of rules for their narrative's world. Each book and each author use that to their advantage in different ways to tell their story and create their vision of the world.

---

1. In a personal correspondence, Flewwelling mentioned that the series is set near Algonquin Park in Ontario, but there is no specific mention of this location in the books. In chapter three of *Helix: Blight of Exiles*, the main character, Ishmael, guesses that he is in Canada in a conversation with another character. The second book is specifically set in Ontario and the third in Halifax.

Supernatural Canada

Not all urban fantasy is set in a known city or place on Earth. Some authors choose to use the generic setting of Earth – or an unnamed planet remarkably similar to Earth – or a city/town/farm setting that appears to be on Earth as we know it. The benefit to this, as Stephen L. Gillett explains it, is that the "reader can bring to the story a vast background of experience; after all, we *live* on [Earth]" (1995, p.3). With a generic Earthlike setting, every reader can bring their personal experience of living on Earth to their reading of the book; the question then becomes why would some authors choose to use a specific setting if only a small number of their potential readers would be familiar with that city? As Dowd et al say in their worldbuilding chapter of *Storytelling Across Worlds*, "The physical layout of the city as well as more general contexts affect your storytelling" (2013, p.44); when using a real-world location as a setting, authors have to be careful about the details they use, as those familiar with that geographical area will be able to spot inconsistencies and errors, but those details of the city are available for them to use. Using a real city can offer the author inspiration and the landscape of that city can affect how they – and, ultimately, help them – tell their story.

Dowd et al say,

> Worlds have their own set of physical and metaphysical rules and mythologies that govern the characters and the environment. Some may mirror or actually be on Earth ... The 'rules' of the world however must be stated or dramatized early in the story ... and remain consistent for the audience to believe the story. A complex World must be built
> (2013, p.43).

Readers will already be at least generally familiar with some of the rules governing our complex Earth – gravity, oxygen, the physiology of humans and common animals – and the challenge then comes in how the fantastical elements of the story *break* those rules in a way that is believable, yet unique and unexpected.

When asked why he decided to set his novels in Canada, Trevor Melanson answered: "Canadians are used to seeing their settings and stories Americanized. But America shouldn't be the world's default, so I went with the country that I lived in and that I knew best" (personal correspondence). Melanson's books *Terminal City* (2016) and *Winter's End* (2017) are set in a fictional version of Vancouver, British Columbia; in the books, the city setting is called Terminal City, and those familiar with Vancouver will know that this is one of the city's nicknames, given for its location and terminal port on the west coast of Canada. Not every reader of these novels will have lived in or visited Vancouver, so they may not get *every* reference – even some Vancouverites will miss some pieces – but the specific setting adds particular benefits to the narrative – in this case, *rain*.

Climate and weather play a large role in worldbuilding in any fantasy story because it is a natural phenomenon that can drastically affect the narrative of your story and it is often a tool for magical manipulation. A rainstorm the night before a planned invasion could delay the fight, a hot climate can lead characters to dehydration, a tornado can whisk a character away to an unknown land. Even people unfamiliar with *Game of Thrones* (Martin, 1996) know the "winter is coming" reference because it's so vital to the overall story. The city of Vancouver is commonly referred to as *Raincouver* because of its wet climate, and Melanson uses that effectively in his fantasy narrative. He first hints at the importance of rain in the dedication for Terminal City: "For Vancouver. You're most beautiful in the rain, no matter what anyone says." Throughout the book there are other minor references to rain, including this note from the mayor of Terminal City:

> I don't mind the rain. It comes down a lot in Terminal City, that's for sure, but let me ask you this: is there any city out there more beautiful than Terminal? When the sun comes out, and even when it doesn't, this city shines. The rain keeps it clean, keeps it shimmering, keeps our pocket of the world perfect. At the end of the day, even a rainy one like this, there's no place I'd rather call home.
> (2016, p.12)

Each reference to rain helps build the image of Terminal City as a complete world in itself, a world with changing weather and inconveniences as real as the Vancouver I know. But good worldbuilding does not simply build the setting in which the characters act, it needs to also add to the narrative – it needs to *affect* the story or characters in some way. Rain accomplishes this in *Terminal City* by triggering the final confrontation between the main character, Mason Cross, and the antagonist, Rowland. Mason looks out his window one day and sees rain – but not just any rain, he sees *blood rain* pouring from the sky, signalling that Rowland was alive and in Terminal City waiting for him (2016, p.159). This event could have been a trigger regardless of rain being mentioned previously, but the foreshadowing accomplished with each brief mention of the weather adds to the ambiance of Terminal City and the engagement with the world Melanson created within this fictional Vancouver.

Rain and Melanson's dedication are not the only clues to show that the Terminal City in *Terminal City* (2016) is Vancouver; recognisable landmarks are another benefit and constant to keep in mind when a story is set in a real place. On page 150 of *Terminal City* there is mention of the Granville Bridge collapsing – while the Granville Bridge in Vancouver has never collapsed, it is a real bridge and known to anyone who is familiar with the area. On the other side of Canada, Chris Patrick Carolan set his debut novel *The Nightshade Cabal* (2020) in the province of Nova Scotia. Carolan's novel is an historical urban fantasy, set in 1880s Halifax. It's a lot more difficult to find recognisable landmarks from 140 years ago, but *The Nightshade Cabal* starts with a scene in the Theatre Royal, a theatre that still exists in Halifax today.[2]

When using an existing city, authors have the benefit of finding and using particular landmarks and architecture that already exists within that city, rather than having to fictionalise towers, parks, and bridges. Most authors are not architects or city planners, so coming up with a city map that makes sense to knowledgeable readers can require a significant amount of research and planning; alternatively, that research time and energy can be spent looking at existing maps and planning the story around existing structures. Throughout *Terminal City* (Melanson, 2016) and *The Nightshade Cabal* (Carolan, 2020) there are references to existing street corners, parks, buildings, and bridges. To readers unfamiliar with those cities, these structures could just as easily be fictional in their minds, but to readers who know the city, they are key landmarks they recognise and identify with for added value. Many readers in

---

[2]. The Theatre Royal that existed in the 1880s and the one that exists now are different buildings, but the new theatre sits on the same site as the one that was there in that time.

that first group will look up a map of the city to plot out where major events happen – it is as engaging as high fantasy novels that include a map of the fictional setting in the publication.

Using a generic city setting on Earth for urban fantasy can seem like the safe option to reduce the risk of alienating the reader if they are unfamiliar with a specific city, but readers will be just as unfamiliar with a fictional city. The benefits of using the details of real cities with existing structure, architecture, and climate can certainly outweigh any perceived risk of unfamiliarity. I felt just as connected to Carolan's 1880s Halifax – a city I've never visited, even in modern times – as I did to Melanson's Vancouver – the city where I lived for most of my life – because Carolan used the setting of Halifax to build a bigger fantastical world.

Elements of the Paranormal

There are many ways an author can bring magic and elements of the fantastic into their stories, and one way is by introducing characters that are magical in nature. In other subgenres of fantasy, there is virtually no limit to the types of beings or creatures that appear in the story. In some genres, particularly high fantasy and science fantasy, there can be hundreds of fantastical beings or creatures in any world or universe. In urban fantasy, however, authors are limited to using only the types of beings that can be reasonably explained in some manner, either through a faith or belief system (for demons, angels, and other types of heaven versus hell type fantasies) or through true historical events and traditional stories (witches, vampires, lycanthropes, and other humanoid characters are usually explained this way). Authors will typically choose one of these explanations to rely on throughout their story – whether it is a short story, a series of novels, or a transmedia property – otherwise, they risk readers being confused about the source of the magic or fantastic elements. Dowd et al explain that "The cultural history of our own planet provides plenty of starting points for building new cultures, but it also means that there's research to be done if we're setting our story within an existing one" (2013, p.44). Answers to how the supernatural can exist within the real world and particularly the explanation of how most humans are unaware of this existence require thoughtful planning to maintain consistency and continuity, which can also include extensive research when using historical and culture-based explanations. The world (and its characters) "ultimately has to be rooted in something familiar, or something that can be extrapolated into something familiar, or audiences spend too much time trying to make sense of every little thing and become distracted from the story" (Dowd et al 2013, p.54).

Among the most common types of fantastic characters in urban fantasy are vampires, shapeshifters, and various magic users, which can include witches, wizards, necromancers, and those with psychic powers such as kineticists. Mason Cross, the main character in Melanson's books, is described as being a necromancer, as he deals with death magic. Mason crosses over to the spirit realm multiple times throughout the two novels and draws power from the spirit realm to perform his magic; at one point, he dies, is sent to the spirit realm, and then returned back to life on Earth. Carolan's main character is described as a *techno*mancer, a term that is used to describe his use of magic with and on various types of technology and mechanics. These different types of magic help to enhance the reader's view of the narrative's world. In *Terminal City* (Melanson, 2016), the reader can expect a lot of dark magic to occur, characters will probably die and come back to life with minimal explanation as to how it happened, and there will likely be some sort of final battle between the main character and the antagonist. Similarly, with the technomancer in *The Nightshade Cabal* (Carolan, 2020), we can expect a more steampunk type story that focuses on technology and mechanics rather than life and death magic. The reader can guess or assume all of these aspects of the world simply based on the fact that necromancers or technomancers exist within it.

Another common supernatural element used in urban fantasy is that of the shapeshifter. The most popular shapeshifter is the lycanthrope or werewolf (a human who can turn into a wolf, whether by the full moon or some other trigger), but shapeshifters can take other forms as well. Flewwelling's Helix series (2014-2019) includes a group with a variety of shapeshifters. Ishmael, the main character, shapeshifts to a cat and other characters are "Bears, foxes, wolf hounds ... *gorillas*" and there is a "whole spectrum of 'werewolf' too – everything from four-legged and tailed, like the Padre, all the way up to 'nothing but peach fuzz, point teeth and black fingernails'" (2014, p.96). This wide cast of shapeshifters was necessary to create the plot point that ultimately required the characters to be isolated on an island together with no way to escape. These characters also help shape the world we see in Helix, because their power, strength, and form have direct impacts on the island's geography, flora, and fauna – particularly in the forest. Without these characters being in the forms that they are, the landscape of the story's world would be entirely different. Alternatively, the classic werewolf can also exist within urban fantasy, as seen in Axel Howerton's *Furr* (2016), an urban fantasy set between the provinces of Alberta and British Columbia wherein the main character, Jimmy Finn, is unaware that he is turning into a werewolf. In this case, the shapeshifter is reacting to the world around him, rather than shaping it as in Flewwelling's Helix series.

Cherie Dimaline's bestselling and award-winning novels *The Marrow Thieves* (2017) and *Empire of Wild* (2019) are inspired and informed by traditional Métis stories, particularly regarding the Rogarou, which is similar to a classic werewolf but with some significant differences that are unique to the traditional Métis story. In an interview with Publishing Perspectives, Dimaline says, "It's imperative when we tell stories in an Indigenous context that we're in connection to the nation(s) that we're speaking of – or speaking on behalf of – even in fiction" and that "Many of our stories are ceremony, history, teachings, and cannot be mishandled" (2017). Dimaline's work speaks to what Dowd et al say about including cultural history in our stories: "We must dig deep enough into the backstory of these cultures to understand their mythology, religious and spiritual beliefs, values, alliances and enemies and how they have developed over time and across the physical geography of the world" (2013, p.44). The traditional stories of the Métis Dimaline includes in her novels are captivating and can be compared to an urban fantasy context as *Empire of Wild* (2019) specifically is set in modern day Ontario with elements of magic and the fantastic; however, the background of traditional Indigenous stories must be acknowledged – Dimaline's books are captivating because she, a Métis author, knows the history of the stories she uses in her fictional narratives.

The Reveal

One of the most common themes in urban fantasy is having the reader be introduced to the main character when they – like most of the rest of the world – are completely unaware of the supernatural presence in their city, country, world, or universe. TV Tropes calls this the masquerade or the invisible to normals trope, as the paranormal beings will often masquerade in the world as humans or be invisible to them. Then an event happens that makes the main character suspicious that something *isn't quite right*, but they just can't figure out exactly what, which eventually leads to a slow reveal of the supernatural. This can happen through the character figuring it out on their own, but being unsure of their discovery until someone (or something) confirms it with them directly, or another character will beg for their help with something supernatural, but the character will be unwilling to believe their claims are true until they see or experience it for themselves. The reveal is a vital part of worldbuilding because it tells the reader how the main character(s) will interact with the supernatural part of their world and it shows the world to the reader through the characters' eyes, even if the story is not written in first person. Sometimes the reader discovers the supernatural along with the main character (as exampled in Kelley Armstrong's *Omens* (2014)) and other times the reveal is made to the reader before the main character figures it out.

Tyner Gillies's Resolution Cove books (2012-2015) take the latter approach, revealing details of the supernatural world and the demons within to the reader before the main character, Constable Quinn Sullivan, realises what's happening in his little town in British Columbia. On the first page of *The Watch* (2012) we see Quinn shooting at a suspect, seemingly hitting him square in the chest multiple times yet the suspect is completely unaffected by it. A reader who knows the genre of the book will already be suspecting there's something supernatural at play here, but Quinn assumes that he was somehow missing every shot because there is no way the suspect would still be standing otherwise. From the very first page, the reader knows more about the story's world than the main character. This theme continues throughout the book as the narrative Quinn follows slowly reveals more oddities and details that can only be explained by the supernatural. The reader sees the world – natural and supernatural – being built around Quinn, largely without his knowledge until the very end when he finally sees the demon he has been hunting all along. This slow reveal of the supernatural world shows the reader the subtleties that can contain supernatural secrets and the true motivations of the character fighting a force bigger than they can imagine. In this case, we see Quinn's desire to solve the mystery and protect his town – especially his new girlfriend, Carrie – regardless of the potential cost; he is not quite willing to believe in anything for the sake of the fight, but he gets there eventually.

In chapter two of *The Watch* (2012), we meet Autumn Donnelly, another new resident of Resolution Cove and the character who ultimately reveals the truth to Quinn after giving him hints he refuses to believe; she tells him that there is a connection he doesn't see between the string of violent acts occurring in the small town, and tells him not to let his "police training, or common disbelief, completely rule [his] thinking in this" (2012, p.32) and that there is a reason he was the one to respond to each of these incidents, which he scoffs at, refusing to believe a woman who claims she can sense the feelings and emotions of others, which he refers to as "mumbo-jumbo" (2012, p.214). Quinn's disbelief remains throughout most of the book, until he finally says to Autumn, "I don't know if I'm ready to believe everything … But I'm ready to listen" (2012, p.213). Autumn Donnelly is an example of worldbuilding through characterisation – the reader might be picking up on some of the clues in the narrative about what is going on, but

Autumn's conversations with Quinn confirm those suspicions.

The general population of humans in Gillies's fantastic Resolution Cove will never learn of the supernatural presence that threatens their wellbeing, but we do see multiple reveals of the magic in this world. In order to help Quinn through the narrative of the second book, *Dark Resolution* (2015), Autumn tells Carrie, Quinn's girlfriend, what *really* happened when Quinn nearly died during the events of *The Watch* (2012). This reveal allows these secondary characters to play a larger role in the overall story by having them actively participate in the resolution to this second book, which also hints at Carrie's role growing into a more active secondary character in the third book, which has yet to be published.

While some urban fantasy authors choose to work with the slow reveal, Chadwick Ginther does the opposite with his Winnipeg-based underworld story *Graveyard Mind* (2018). In the first chapter we meet Winter Murray in a graveyard covering death cult Karl's corpse as he begs her not to until she is interrupted by a vampire, at which point she claims she thought she was not on his territory but on McCoy's – an "animated skeleton with a penchant for wearing dead men's clothes" (2018, back cover). Similar to Carolan's technomancer main character, Winter is a supernatural being herself – a necromancer and a chimera – so the story starts with her already aware of Winnipeg's supernatural underworld, and an active participant in it, whether she likes it or not. However, most human residents of Winnipeg are unaware of the underworld they live so close to, and it is part of Winter's job to keep it that way – a common part of the invisible to normals trope so often used in urban fantasy narratives.

Through this quick reveal, the reader knows that Winter is well accustomed to the existence of various supernatural beings, which tells us a lot about her overall character: she is a keeper of these supernatural secrets, she will not be surprised when *odd* things start to happen in Winnipeg, and she can help solve whatever mystery is occurring in the city. Another benefit to the quick reveal tactic that Ginther uses is that it accomplishes a large piece of worldbuilding in the first few pages: the reader is immediately aware of the existence of humanoid beings and, in this case, the underworld that exists in parallel to the real city of Winnipeg.

Conclusion

Authors of urban fantasy have an interesting worldbuilding challenge compared to authors of high fantasy; the latter creates an entirely fictional world in which they make all the rules and can bend our understanding of physics to fit the needs of their plot or characters. Settings in urban fantasy, however, set on Earth or an Earthlike planet, already have an established set of rules that readers will know and understand, and any fantasy element brought into that world breaks those rules and requires a believable explanation as to how these fantastical beings or magic can exist when most of the population is completely unaware of it. Authors need to know how and when to break or bend those rules and bring in researched elements of history and faith to explain the unexplainable to their readers as well as the characters discovering magic for the first time.

The subgenre of urban fantasy appears to be steadily growing in popularity, aided by well-funded TV productions such as *Vampire Diaries* (1991-2014), *Supernatural* (2005-2020), and *Lucifer* (2016-present). In Canada specifically, most publishers who publish science fiction and fantasy have a few urban fantasy titles on their list, most of which are series, which speaks to the existing readership and publisher support for these types of titles.[3] This growing popularity means that the market will likely start to see greater varieties of themes, tropes, and characters being used in urban fantasy. Varieties of urban fantasy exist in settings all around the Earth, and in fictional settings on planets that appear to be Earth as we know it. This paper outlined the most common existing themes seen in urban fantasy with specific examples of usage from Canadian authors who chose to set their stories in Canadian cities. As Melanson says, Canadians are used to seeing American settings for most of the media we consume, which means Canadian authors are motivated to set their stories in Canada whenever possible to increase representation of Canada and Canadian stories in the overall media landscape. Writing urban fantasy – fantastical, magical stories set on Earth as we know it – is one way authors of speculative fiction genres can participate in the CanLit canon and contribute stories set all across our vast country.

---

[3]. Books referenced in this paper come from a variety of publishers in Canada, including: Tyche Books, Dark Dragon Publishing, and Random House Canada, among others.

References

Armstrong, K., 2014. *Omens, Cainsville*. Vintage Canada.

Carolan, C.P., 2020. *The Nightshade Cabal*. The Parliament House.

Dimaline, C., 2019. *Empire of Wild*. Penguin Random House Canada.
—, 2017. *The Marrow Thieves*. Cormorant Books, Ontario.

Douglas, C., 2017. *Indigenous Writers in Canada: Interview with Author Cherie Dimaline* [online]. Available at: <https://publishingperspectives.com/2017/11/indigenous-writers-canada-interview-author-cherie-dimaline/> [Accessed 29 November 20].

Dowd, T., Niederman, M., Fry, M., Steiff, J., 2013. *Storytelling Across Worlds: Transmedia for Creatives and Producers*. Taylor & Francis.

Flewwelling, P., 2014. *Blight of Exiles, Helix*. Tyche Books, Alberta.

Gillett, S.L., 1995. *World-Building: A Writer's Guide to Constructing Star Systems and Life-supporting Planets, Science Fiction Writing*. Writer's Digest Books, Cincinnati.

Gillies, T., 2015. *Dark Resolution*. Dark Dragon Publishing, Toronto.
—, 2012. The Watch. Dark Dragon Publishing, Toronto.

Ginther, C., 2018. *Graveyard mind*. ChiZine Publications, Peterborough.

Harvey, C., 2015. *Fantastic Transmedia: Narrative, Play and Memory Across Science Fiction and Fantasy Storyworlds*. Palgrave Macmillan.

Howerton, A., 2016. *Furr*. Tyche Books, Alberta.

Irvine, A.C., 2012. *Urban Fantasy, in: The Cambridge Companion to Fantasy Literature*. Cambridge University Press, pp.200–13.

Melanson, T., 2017. Winter's End. Edge Science Fiction and Fantasy Publishing, Calgary.
—, 2016. *Terminal City*. Edge Science Fiction and Fantasy Publishing, Calgary.

TV Tropes, n.d. *Invisible to Normals.* [online]. Available at: <https://

tvtropes.org/pmwiki/pmwiki.php/Main/InvisibleToNormals> [Accessed 29 November 20a).

TV Tropes, n.d. *Masquerade* [online]. Available at: <https://tvtropes.org/pmwiki/pmwiki.php/Main/Masquerade> [Accessed 29 November 20b].

Above the Level of the Everyday: The Estranging and Familiar Worlds of Simon Stålenhag

Kevin Cooney

Abstract

Science fiction draws the participant into worlds strange and new, but sometimes familiar and intimate. While many theories seek to explain or define the genre cognitively or emotionally, I believe the artist is at the nexus of Bertolt Brecht's *Verfremdung*—the defamiliarisation effect—where the viewer is detached from the familiar only to be reconnected in a provocative new way. Swedish digital artist Simon Stålenhag subverts naturalist or landscape painting by inserting advanced technology into the fictionalised environment of the 2015 art-book *Tales from the Loop*. Stålenhag portrays the familiar places or objects of everyday life only to disrupt them with disorientating juxtapositions or injections of seemingly incongruous objects. Through naturalistic worldbuilding, science fiction is freed from the shackles of techno-fetishism or sterile detachment, demanding the viewer rethink the world they know in ambitious, strange ways. In a sense, Stålenhag is science fiction's first naturalist painter.

*

The world built by Simon Stålenhag, exemplified by his first art-book *Tales from the Loop* (2015), was born from a fertile imagination and an artist's love and appreciation for nature, a 'mundane' kind of nature that grows along roads, fringes woodlands, and skirts suburban subdivisions. Through the real, accessible world at the intersection of human culture and nature,

Stålenhag paints landscapes unlike any other. Building a world with recognisable flora and fauna, Stålenhag emphasises natural locations, and as Maurice Levy observed, "It is well known that the truly fantastic exists only where the impossible can make an irruption, through time and space, into an objectively familiar locale" (Levy, 1988, pp.36–37). Stålenhag grows his strange technologies from a world familiar to him, captured in photographs and fictionalised in his digital paintings. His robots and flying barges, strange discarded machines, and rusting structures engross and enthral specifically because the wider world is rooted in reality. This foundation in recognisable forests, grassy fields, or even lonely suburban streets bathed in phosphorous yellow light is not just a canvas on which the world is painted but also a familiar character from which the fantastic erupts.

Starting as a crowd-funded narrative art-book, *Tales from the Loop* (Stålenhag, 2015) later spawned a tabletop Role Playing Game and inspired an Amazon series of the same name. The book tells the story of a fictional Particle Accelerator in eastern Sweden. Constructed at the height of the Cold War, Stålenhag's fictional "Loop" spawns technological marvels, as well as strange ruptures in the fabric of space-time. We see the technological leap's effects on the Swedish countryside through a series of fictionalised narratives based on Stålenhag's own life and experiences. Stålenhag anchors most illustrations with an undulating sweeping landscape. These swathes of grass, tundra, or pavement add accessible solidity to the illustration, resulting in viewer immersion. The photo-reference technique is reminiscent of holiday snaps of small vistas or narrow landscapes caught outside the back door or from a passing car, a visual style evoking the kind of photography taken in the pre-camera phone age. In the *Tales from the Loop* (2015) book, Stålenhag captures an authenticity many of us know, have seen, or experienced. His meticulous, energetic painting style does not paint away a sense of truthfulness; instead, it captures the world in a brief visual flash of colours and shapes of nature and machine. What leaps out is the world's naturalistic style punctuated or contrasted by the strange mechanical devices spawned from the "Loop". Stålenhag's two-legged machines and centrifugal hulks pepper a visually strange Sweden; yet culturally and environmentally, for the most part, the countryside and landscapes are the same. Stålenhag captures a realism, stealing images of his life and past in Sweden, without the burden of a dictatorial or prescriptive melancholy that much of modern retro-futurism bears. There is emotion in Stålenhag's original art-book, stories of first loves and fascinations with machines, but what the book does most effectively is embracing estrangement. To fully wrap one's arms around estranging themes, one needs to be fundamentally authentic in their worldbuilding.

The study of estrangement in science fiction has grown over the decades, but it is Bertolt Brecht's theatrical theory which most closely aligns estrangement with the work of Stålenhag. Fundamentally, through Brecht's Verfremdung, "the individual's relationship to reality is renegotiated" (Jestrovic, 2006, p.26). The German playwright saw estrangement as "not simply the breaking of illusion [...] it does not mean 'alienating' the spectator [...] It is a matter of detachment, of reorientation" (Willet, 1957, p.177). With its natural world of the Swedish countryside and roadside, the original Stålenhag book, the Loop's story, its strange machines, body-swaps, and the occasional dinosaur, estrange, but never alienate, the viewer. Reorientating the viewer's ideas of what science fiction can be, *Tales from The Loop* (2015) estranges the reader from a convincingly rendered world that always remains inaccessible.

According to Willet (1957), Brecht's stage productions were facilitated by the realistic visualisation and interpretation of sets. To fully estrange the viewer, to understand the themes or emotions embedded in the playwright's script, the world around the fictional characters needed to be authentic in distilled and uncluttered ways. The smallest detail of the scene or vista should be thought through and portrayed or removed for clarity. The authenticity needed for estrangement is expressed in this minutia:

> Every item that matters to the play is as authentic and tangible as it can be made, and all else is merely indicated: a real door, a real fence, a real street-lamp, standing solid and fit for use on an otherwise empty stage
> (Willet, 1957, p.157).

This Brechtian idea of a "real" fence or door is directly extendable to Stålenhag's Swedish countryside. The natural landscape is cherished and needed by him: "I need a real place to get that authenticity I'm after" (Nostalgi & Nördkultur, 2017). The natural world, its colours, shapes, beauty, and imperfections, are required to orientate the viewer before estranging them. Stålenhag's ability to render a world as both recognisable and strange originates from his lifelong interest in the natural world. He captures the landscapes of Sweden, a love of dinosaurs (which also populate the artist's fantastic Loop world), and abandoned or antiquated machines. Recognition of the real clearly motivates the artist; a natural landscape, peppered with machines, is universally appealing, and an intimately Swedish expression of place.

Although considered a futurist artist and storyteller, Stålenhag consistently credits three naturalist painters as inspiration. While many genre artists cite illustrators like Syd Mead or Ron Cobb, Stålenhag instead references wildlife and landscape painters Lars Jonsson, Bruno Liljefors, and Gunnar Brusewitz. In a way, Stålenhag's work could be considered naturalist science fiction. Liljefors, upon returning from the forest, "paints an unusual landscape which struck him that day," then lays it aside and returns to it after finding an animal, "which will fit into the completed background perfectly" (Blauvelt, 1926, p.506). This process could easily be reinterpreted into Stålenhag's 21st-century methodology. The *Tales from the Loop* (Stålenhag, 2015) art-book relies on the landscape as known and captured by centuries of artists but reconfigures the natural world through mechanical punctuation. Liljefors might compose a snowy field and Stålenhag a grassy roadside; they diverge when the composite image shows a naturalistic moose shunned in favour of lonely sentient machines. Stålenhag's ever-present camera exemplifies his commitment to finding his real-world motifs: "It makes a very big difference for me […] that makes it much more credible when you knew all these details, where things are located, and how everything is connected. And that makes this world and the storytelling in it feel more authentic and interrelated" (Nostalgi & Nördkultur, 2017). As a naturalist science fiction creator, Stålenhag utilises landscapes that embody a particularly Swedish view of the human cultural relationship with the environment. According to Eriksson and Arnell (2016, p.33), "the presence of idyllic grasslands is a necessary component of the romanticised traditional Swedish landscape […] their existence tells a captivating tale of human development, and how it gave form to the Swedish cultural landscape"; the best example of a uniquely Swedish landscape is the inäga. The fields and meadows painted by Stålenhag are similar to the Swedish inäga, or farmer-managed meadow.

Stålenhag's use of inäga-like spaces is best demonstrated in the *Tales from the Loop* illustration, "The Remote Glove". Two fair-haired boys manipulate a bipedal robot via an oversized electronic glove wired to a hard-shelled orange and white backpack. We see the boys from behind as the two-legged machine trots towards a distant police vehicle, a 1980s Swedish police Volkswagen van. Stålenhag credits "The Remote Glove" as the single work that spread via social media and propelled him to deals with Hollywood. The work perfectly captures him and his technique of estrangement through placemaking in the real world.

Importantly, Stålenhag's *Tales from the Loop* (2015) book takes place squarely in an authentic version of the 1980s. Stålenhag's publisher, Free League, asked the artist to utilise the decade more fully: "If you put it five years ahead into the future, for example, then people start to think, 'Okay, but then this has to happen'. If you instead say that it's set in this period everyone has lived in […] then you can instead play with the idea that alternate events occurred" (Nostalgi & Nördkultur, 2017). Tellingly, it is "this period everyone has lived" which facilitates a better, more easily recognised story that does not suffer at all from lack of nuance or imagination. On the contrary, Stålenhag's use of a familiar decade and natural environment means he is free to devote creative energy to the estranging punctuations in this alternative world. In part, the artist's fantastic mechanical elements work because of their basis on real machines, like a tractor: "I think that subconsciously creates a feeling of recognition, that it's something real" (Nostalgi & Nördkultur, 2017). Rather than becoming mired in the turgid narrative of generations of hard science fiction, Stålenhag freely embraces the real and unreal concurrently. These mecha are attention-getters not because they trod alien worlds but because they walk through fields at the roadsides of Sweden or Minnesota. Stålenhag's anachronistic machines in the landscape embody Tim Creswell's "*anachorism*" or "things in the wrong place" (2015, p.166). Through their weight, solidity, and normality in a familiar or authentic place, they tether the narrative through a form of "anachorism".

Stålenhag's place-making or worldbuilding combines landscape, mechanisation, and decline. Industry is the levering, estranging element in Stålenhag's future-past but it does not overly dictate the narrative. In *Tales from the Loop* (Stålenhag, 2015), the robots or massive energy-generating towers dominate the horizon but do not distract; they estrange, but do not alienate. The book's power remains the product of the human narrative's interface with landscape and industrial products and by-products. What contributes to the dialogue of estrangement is the viewer's engagement with a fictionalised nature via personal referencing of the field or marsh with such places in their own lives and experiences; along with the vivid, reality-grounded machines of Stålenhag's art-book. Stålenhag's naturalistic settings, fused with the levitating machines spawned by the Loop's weird-physics technology, make the "familiar seem unfamiliar to us, but this experience of estrangement can only impinge creatively on the real world we already know" (Fredericks, 1982, p.48). Perhaps this is why Stålenhag's world is often considered a sad place, because it dares to imagine a future-past which embraces the everyday melancholy and wonder of the natural world.

Traits of "anxiety, loneliness, melancholy" (Dixon, 2016, cited in Jakob Stougaard-Nielsen, 2020, p.165) are often applied to Scandinavian art and sometimes attached to Stålenhag's landscapes as forms of the melancholy or dystopic.

"Bleak" or "lonely" landscapes exist in naturalist art, whether that be in Sweden or the Italian Alps. Notably, as Stålenhag's work has grown, he has expanded geographically to a fictional California, distancing his world physically from the familiar and personal grounds of Scandinavia. Far from cold and raw, his faux Golden State is arid, dusty, and austere, the antithesis of his Swedish-rooted first work. Yet, he still evokes praise and feelings of anxiety, loneliness, and melancholy. What Stålenhag does so very subtly and effortlessly is worldbuilding that is not at all dystopian, but more realistic and possibly even utopian. Decay and misery are present in the *Tales from the Loop* (2015) book, but there has been much the same present in the world for generations, particularly after the dawn of the industrial revolution. No, writers and reviewers of Stålenhag's work who focus only on the rust and decay overlook, or are desensitised, to the natural world intertwined and knitted throughout the miles of machines and cables. These are not alien planets or cold, sterile white-panelled spaceship interiors; they are solidly present in the world as experienced and viewed by Stålenhag (with obvious artistic licence). To describe his oeuvre as dystopian would be to conflate a few paintings with the entirety of his work. Indeed, rusted androids or abandoned machines imply a sorry state, but there is also unrealised utopian energy, and forward propulsion is embedded in Stålenhag's worlds.

Stålenhag utilises maps to accompany his naturalist views of Sweden, further drawing the reader into his real-world-turned-strange. The Loop stretches out over islands and underwater, clearly laid out in Stålenhag's fictionalised map that orientates the reader, while concurrently estranging and inspiring. In his painted world, we see reverberations of Yi-Fu Tuan's perception that a map depicts reality, but it is of little use, for it cannot stimulate action, unless it has, in some sense, Utopia on it. One of the proper and moral uses of fantasy is to envisage the good—a possible world that does justice not only to human yearnings but to human potential. (Tuan, 1990, p.443)

Real ponds are littered with fictionalised technological detritus while equally, now, the landscape hosts "wild" robots, cybernetic boars, and dinosaurs. These devices and creatures interact with, either directly or distantly, the humans working, living, and travelling across the fictionalised map, which portrays tangible places. The frequently nameless characters, who are also often faceless, stop in fields to repair machines or sneak into culverts to relieve themselves as machines rumble past on roads traversing the Loop-world map. Children navigate the Loop map with open minds, while adults move on. As Stålenhag notes, "The kids are the ones playing in this landscape, asking questions. The grown-ups just pass it on their way to work" (Kickstarter, 2015). Human stories are written across the Loop map, yet in Stålenhag's own words, we find the definition of space versus place. Stålenhag's 1980s future does not rely solely on anachronistic machines, but on physical spaces translated into place. Tim Cresswell, in *Place: An Introduction*, paraphrases Tuan's belief that "space" is movement and "place" represents pauses (Tuan, 1977 cited in Creswell, 2015); we see the space-versus-place dynamic in the perceptions of children compared to adults in Stålenhag's work. Adults in the Loop book forget about roadside views or ignore the wooded glens and the mysteries they conceal; instead, they exist solely to move through Tuan's "space". Stålenhag's protagonists–children and teenagers– however, occupy Tuan's "place", as they pause to question, examine, and play with the machines and junk strewn throughout "Loop" Sweden. That pause captures a fictionalised moment in time that becomes, or embodies, "place". Place becomes a version of the world that is simultaneously fanciful and authentic.

Stålenhag's art-book places the viewer into a quasi-realistic and authentic relationship with the known world. As a constant balance between hope and despair, life cannot thrive imaginatively in bleached utopian images, as it equally cannot buoy humankind if it is mired in a dark, grimy, violent dystopia. Neither is the lived or experienced world that humanity knows. Like Stålenhag's fictional Loop technology, humans, machines, culture, and nature are linked by a sometimes whiplash-like relationship of joy and prosperity, or despair and poverty. Fundimentally, Stålenhag understands this by rooting his early stories in visually accessible places. He expands the reader's perception of the world from real to unreal, guiding the viewer towards a future filled with incredible potential and heartache. Simply put, the art-book captures the fantastic potential and reality of human existence. Every technological leap throughout history changes, manipulates, or reconfigures the landscape. Stålenhag places the next great technological leap into a world both familiar and estranging. Through the injection of machines and discarded technologies into naturalistic, comforting environments, he crafts worlds which challenge the perception that mundanity should be the standard of our everyday lives, and inspire the viewer to find comfort and hope in his robots among the roots.

References

Blauvelt, H., 1926. Bruno Liljefors — Greatest of Wild Life Painters. *The American Magazine of Art*, 17 (10), pp.505-512.

Cresswell, T., 2015. *Place: An Introduction*. Chichester: John Wiley & Sons Ltd.

Eriksson, O. and Arnell, M., 2016. How Did Infields Shape the Scandinavian Cultural Landscape? *RCC Perspectives*, [e-journal], 5, pp.33-40. Available at: <http://www.jstor.org/stable/26241401> [Accessed 30 October, 2020].

Fredericks, C., 1982. *The Future of Eternity: Mythologies of Science Fiction and Fantasy*. Bloomington: Indiana University Press.

Jestrovic, J., 2006. *Theatre of Estrangement: Theory, Practice, Ideology*. Toronto: University of Toronto Press.

Kickstarter, 2015. *Simon Stålenhag's Tales from the Loop Kickstarter Campaign*. [online] Available at: <https://www.kickstarter.com/projects/cabinetentertainment/simon-stalenhags-tales-from-the-loop/description> [Accessed: 10 October 2020].

Levy, M., 1988. *Lovecraft: A Study in the Fantastic*. Detroit: Wayne State University Press.

Nostalgi & Nördkultur, 2017. *Interview with Simon Stålenhag*. [online] Available at: <https://youtu.be/kZFRsXQsDcU> [Accessed 1 October 2020].

Stålenhag, S., 2015. *Tales from the Loop*. Culver City: Design Studio Press.

Stougaard-Nielsen, J., 2020. Nordic Nature: From Romantic Nationalism to the Anthropocene. In: Stougaard-Nielsen J. & Lindskog A., eds., *Introduction to Nordic Cultures*. London: UCL Press. pp.165-180. https://doi.org/10.2307/j.ctv13xprms.

Tuan, Y., 1990. Realism and Fantasy in Art, History, and Geography. *Annals of the Association of American Geographers*, [e-journal], 80 (3), pp.435-446. Available at: <www.jstor.org/stable/2563622> [Accessed 30 October 2020].

Willet, J., 1957. *The Theatre of Bertolt Brecht: A Study from Eight Aspects*. London: Methuen & Co.

The Nordic Countries in Worldbuilding: *Frozen* and *Frozen II*

Jyrki Korpua

Abstract

Frozen and *Frozen II* are two extremely successful animated movies that take place in a fantasy world. The world of the movies has connections to traditions of fairy stories and fantasy, and to the geography of the actual Nordic countries, but also to the livelihood of the real-world indigenous Sámi people. In particular, *Frozen II* was conscious and appreciative of dealing with the real-world connections to Sámi culture.

This article discusses the worldbuilding of the films from the point of view of fantastic milieus and surroundings. In focus here is the central milieu of Arendelle, the Enchanted Forest inhabited by the indigenous people of the north, and the mythical Ahtohallan; the "ultima thule", the farthest northern location of the fantasy world. In the movies, the 19th century Nordic milieu of Arendelle is placed in contrast to their neighbouring tribe of Northuldra, which represents a Sámi sort of way of living.

In focus here also is the textual part of the worldbuilding. For example, both movies were credited as being inspired by Hans Christian Andersen's fairy tale "The Snow Queen" ("Snedronningen", 1844). The central theme of both *Frozen* movies is the bond between two sisters, Elsa and Anna, who are princesses and later queens of the kingdom of Arendelle. The fantasy milieus are located outside the city of Arendelle, which is a more realistic place, but the magic inside the city originates from Elsa, the elder sister, who has magical powers. She is able to utilise cold and ice in similar ways to Andersen's title character of the Snow Queen, or the White Witch, Jadis, in C. S. Lewis's *Narnia* series; another character inspired by Andersen's Snow Queen.

This chapter discusses how fantastical milieus, references, and elements deriving from the livelihood of the Sámi people are central to the worldbuilding and the creation of the fictional world, in the *Frozen* franchise.

*

Frozen (2013) and its sequel *Frozen II* (2019), both produced by Walt Disney Studios and directed by Chris Buck and Jennifer Lee, are among the most popular movies of the 21st century (see Konnikova, 2014). *Frozen II*, with its more than $1.3 billion of global box office takings, is the highest-grossing animated movie ever (Rubin, 2020).

These movies mix fantasy and fairy tale into stories that are aimed at child audiences but which, because of their dual meanings, are also suitable for adult viewers. The dual meaning, or dual audience, here indicates how the story is suitable for adults and children alike, and might be interpreted and understood regardless of the viewer's age (see Beckett, 1999; Zipes, 1983). These are movies which, beneath their simple and quite straightforward fantasy narratives, also deal with important human problems like gender equality, orphaning and prejudice, in *Frozen*, and in particular the exploitation of indigenous people, in *Frozen II*.

Fantastic stories about princesses have always been important for Walt Disney Studios, but the *Frozen* movies also show us that princesses can be active, independent, and heroic. Elsa and Anna represent the powerful new generation of Disney princesses, casting the main male character, the ice salesman Kristoff, as a gentle, harmless, helpful—and slightly embarrassing—boyfriend. Then there is the role of deceitful antagonist, like Prince Hans in the first movie; or the comic role of a fairy tale "sidekick", like Olaf the Snowman. Of course, the actual gender of the last character is largely unimportant or necessary to know, although we can assume from the name, title, and pronoun used in the movies that Olaf is a "he", and a "snowman" (*Frozen*).

Elsa and Anna continue the tradition of female main characters in Disney movies, likes the classic heroines Snow White and Cinderella, or the next generation of slightly more active heroines, though still in need of emancipation, like Ariel in *The Little Mermaid* (1989), Belle in 1991's *Beauty and the Beast*, and Pocahontas in the movie of the same title, in 1995. This evolved into more competent and functional female characters through *Mulan* (1995), and Rapunzel in *Tangled* (2010). Still, it has been pointed out that Elsa and Anna are exceptional, as they display the kind of active agency that no past Disney princesses had (see Feder, 2014; Kowalski & Bhalla, 2018). Elsa and Anna are, like classic Disney princesses, privileged upper-class children and princesses of their kingdom. They are "white, rich and shockingly thin", as Feder (2014) puts it. Then again, they venture off on dangerous quests on their own. *Frozen* is also the first Disney movie where the princess, now a queen, makes a negative decision and an error that horribly affects everyone around her. Elsa freezes her kingdom and escapes the scene, leaving her subjects devastated. In both *Frozen* movies, the fantasy world is saved through acts of sisterly love, not because of the actions of a male prince or other suitor. In *Frozen*, it is in fact Anna who overcomes natural barriers like ice storms, avalanches, and even a magical eternal winter to save her sister (Warner, 2014, p.104). In both movies, Elsa and Anna are central to the narrative, while their actions are also essential for the wellbeing of their world.

Elsa and Anna are indisputably connected to their surroundings, and are part of the fantastic environment of the movies. Elsa, because of her powers, can even actively alter and change her own surroundings, as she does when she freezes Arendelle, or when she creates her own ice palace and ice castle in *Frozen*. The two movies portray a high fantasy world which is consistent and obeys its own laws of nature (Gunn, 2013, pp.106–107, 123; on the consistency of fantastic worldbuilding, see Wolf, 2012, pp. 43–47). They are high fantasy, since the world of these movies is not directly connected to the primary world, and is consistent with its culture and laws of nature. Magic is an inner-built part of the world, but so too is the fear of magic and the mundane everyday lives of its people. The "normal people" in the *Frozen* movies act pretty much the same as people from our own real world would act in the same kind of occasions. They fear the unknown and the supernatural, like the people of Arendelle fear Elsa's magical powers in *Frozen*, or King Runeard hates people who use magic in the sequel. The so-called normal people of Arendelle are prejudiced towards that what is different; for example, they are suspicious of the Northuldra people, who have different lifestyle to their own.

As such, the fantasy world of *Frozen* is a secondary one which has its own rules but which is still connected to our primary world in matters of behaviour, scenery, and language. As explained, people in the *Frozen* movies act similarly to the way the audience would in similar circumstances. The settings and milieus of the movies are plausible for us as viewers. Fjords, mountains, rivers, glaciers, forests, and cities are surroundings which are familiar to us, despite containing fantastical elements. As J.R.R. Tolkien wrote in his seminal essay, *On Fairy-stories* (1947), the flora and fauna of the fantasy world, or Faerie, as he named it, is also important to the worldbuilding (see Tolkien, 1964, p.9). It gives the world credibility and makes it approachable for us. But the fantasy world, or the Faerie, is created over many layers.

Next, I will discuss how the different surroundings of the *Frozen* movies represent their own independent fantastic milieus, but are also connected to our real world.

Arendelle

Arendelle is a beautiful, fantastic kingdom which is the central location or starting milieu for both *Frozen* and *Frozen II*. In *Frozen*, Arendelle is saved from the icy, eternal winter caused by Queen Elsa's powers. In the follow-up, Arendelle is saved by her sisters from angry elementals, spirits of nature, who almost destroy the city with a flood. The city had earlier been abandoned by its citizens because it had been attacked by the elemental spirits of Air, Fire, Water, and Earth.

As usual, even in fantastic worldbuilding, the milieus of the movies draw inspiration from the real world. As an aesthetic environment, Arendelle can easily be described as a Norwegian-influenced milieu, but it also has certain elements of late 18th century or 19th century German and Central European atmosphere to it; for example, the architecture, style of clothing, and also the social power system which is ruled over by nobility and the upper class. Also, Arendelle's geography, with its fjords and mountains, quite closely resembles Norway. Added to this, the selection of characters introduced in the movies are influenced by Nordic and Scandinavian people. The actual inspiration for the city of Arendelle was perhaps the city of Bergen in Norway. That is easily inferred, since Walt Disney Studios have officially organised tours for visitors to the city (see *Adventures by Disney*). Even though it is a fantasy movie, we even know the specific time when the movie *Frozen* would take place. Walt Disney Studio's official *The Art of Frozen* (Solomon 2013, p.65) states: "For a more classical fairy tale look, it was decided to place the narrative in the 1840s". That is an interesting date, since Hans Christian Andersen's "The Snow Queen" was published in the 1840s, in the year 1844 to be precise. So, there are actual inspirations for both the location and dates of the film which place it as a Nordic-style country: in particular Norway, on account of its geography and atmosphere, and Denmark, being the home country of Andersen and his story, "The Snow Queen".

The etymology of the name Arendelle is itself interesting. There are Internet pages, like the Disney Wiki, which claim the word to be of Norwegian origin, meaning "Eagle Valley". However, for example, the *Bokmålordsboka* and *Nynorskordboka* lexicons in Norway do not verify this assumption right away. Then again, "valley" is "dal" in modern Norwegian (nynorsk), and "eagle" is "ørn". So, the word might be a free translation—with applied artistic license—of "Ørndalen" into English as Arendal/Arendelle. There is in fact at least one place called Ørndalen in the city of Tromssa, in northern Norway. The word Arendelle itself could carry fantastic resonance to the ears of experienced viewers too, as it resembles Eärendil, a character name in *The Silmarillion* (Tolkien, 1977) or the old English word Earendel, which Tolkien used as the etymological background for it. It means "brightest of angels" and is a classical reference to Christ in an old English poem.

All of the names in the *Frozen* movies have connections to Nordic countries. Elsa and Anna are both names used in countries like Norway, Sweden, Denmark, Iceland, and Finland. Other character names, like Kristoff, Sven, or Hans, are all familiar names within a Nordic context. Prince Hans's name is, of course, also the first name of the godfather of the modern literary fairy tale, H. C. Andersen (on literary fairy tales, see Zipes, 1994, pp.17–20, 23).

Elsa and Anna

The fantastic worldbuilding in the *Frozen* movies is noticeable for the milieus and surroundings, but the characters and creatures of the movies have also been created with the same level of fantastic credibility, which strengthens it. Main characters have been created following the logic of classic fairy tales, Disney fantasies, and movies aimed at child audiences. The beginning of *Frozen* shows how Elsa, previously a princess, becomes the Queen of Arendelle. Her father and mother, King Agnarr and Queen Iduna, names revealed in *Frozen II*, die in a tragic shipping accident. Princesses Elsa and Anna become orphans and rulers of the kingdom. Having orphans as central characters in fairy tales or fantasy stories is archetypal (see e.g. Rothenberg 1983; Warner 2014). The classic fairy tale heroines Cinderella and Snow White are both orphans (or half-orphans), and Rapunzel is effectively abandoned by her parents. These have also all been adapted into animated movies by Disney Studios. Many heroes and heroines of fantasy, like Frodo Baggins in Tolkien's *The Lord of the Rings* (1954–55), Dorothy in L. Frank Baum's *The Wizard of Oz* (1900), Lyra in Philip Pullman's *His Dark Materials* (1995–2000), and Harry Potter in J. K. Rowling's *Harry Potter* series (1998–2008) are orphans. Orphanage is an archetypal motif even in classic adventurous books for children and young audiences, like in Robert Louis Stevenson's *Treasure Island* (1883), Rudyard Kipling's *The Jungle Book* (1893–1894), L. M. Montgomery's *Anne of Green Gables* (1908), Edgar Rice Burroughs's *Tarzan of the Apes* (1912), or Eleanor H. Porter's *Pollyanna* (1913). Interestingly, all of these have either been adapted for screen by Disney studios or premiered as television series or movies on the Disney Channel.

In *Frozen II*, a central revelation of the plot is that the people of Arendelle have been unfriendly towards their neighbours. In fact, they have been quite wicked when it comes to building a dam and ruining the beautiful homeland, the Enchanted Forest, of the peaceful neighbouring tribe of Northuldra. Incidentally, their natural way of living resembles that of the Sámi, indigenous people of the north, who inhabit the land area called Sápmi, which stretches across Finland, Sweden, Norway, and northern Russia. Both the fictional Northuldra tribe and the real-life Sámi people live in close connection to the surrounding nature, and herd reindeers. However, the singing of the Northuldra tribe in the movie more closely resembles that of the indigenous people of the northern Americas than the Sámi and their traditional *Joik* style.

Elsa and Anna's grandfather, King Runeard, the father of King Agnarr, is at last revealed to be behind the evil plot, in *Frozen II*. But Runeard's vicious plot also results in his death. In the movie, when the Northuldra folk realise what is happening, and how their homeland is being destroyed, a battle begins, resulting in King Runeard's death and enraging the elemental spirits guarding the peace and harmony of the land. The way the colonialist people of Arendelle come to the Enchanted Forest, build a dam, and destroy the land, quite clearly resembles what has happened to many indigenous people in our real world. So, even though the world is a fantastic one, it is concerned with real world problems. Of course, the answers that the movie gives us are quite peaceful: we should live in harmony with nature, provide space and freedom to indigenous people, and try to understand their lifestyle.

The fantastic worldbuilding is also evident when examining the creatures, such as the elementals, who are also important plot devices. In *Frozen II*, the main mission of the plot is to calm the elemental spirits of Air, Fire, Earth, and Water and return harmony and peace to the north. The spirits are represented as the tornado-like wind spirit Gale, the salamander-like fire spirit Bruni, the horse-shaped water spirit Nøkk (or Nokk), and the Earth Giants, who resemble large stone golems. Magical creatures and powers are active in the world of the *Frozen* movies. At the same time, while calming the spirits and searching for the truth, Elsa must realise the biggest secret, that she holds the decisive power. She is the peacemaker, the fifth element which brings tranquillity to the other elements. But she is also the one who frees the Northuldra from the imprisonment that King Runeard's actions have caused. In doing so, she also saves the city of Arendelle. In the end, Elsa becomes the fifth element and must live in the north. She leaves Arendelle and Anna, and her little sister becomes the new queen.

Elsa is the link between the elemental spirits and mortals. In *Frozen II*, it also states that "the river has two mouths and the mother had two daughters". This means that, while Elsa functions as the crucial interlink between the powerful forces of nature, her little sister Anna is the link between Elsa and the people of Arendelle. Elsa continues to live with the people of Northuldra, and Anna stays in Arendelle. That is basically because, in the second movie, it is revealed that Queen Iduna, Elsa and Anna's mother, was northern-born, a member of the Northuldra people who saved King Agnarr's life and left her tribe to go live in Arendelle. Elsa and Anna are in fact offspring of both the people of Arendelle—the "Westerners" —and the people of Northuldra, representing the North.

The Enchanted Forest

The Enchanted Forest is a fantastical milieu, being where the northern people of the Northuldra tribe live in *Frozen II*, and who are not present in the first movie. The Northuldra tribe call themselves "The People of the Sun", which closely resembles folk religions and myths of the pre-Christian Sámi people. The Sun, Beaivi, is one of the central (female) deities of the old beliefs (Pulkkinen 2011, p.228–229). It is also an ancient belief that the Sámi people are descendants of the Sun. This belief was further popularised outside of Sápmi, the area were Sámi people live, by the 19th century Sámi priest and poet Anders Fjellner's "Sons of the Sun" ("Biejjie-baernie", or "Beaivebártni soagŋomátki Jiehtasaid máilmmis", see Porsanger 2020).

In *Frozen II*, most events take place in the enclosed magical location of the Enchanted Forest. Here, the Northuldra tribe become captives within the forest, due to King Runeard's actions making the elemental spirits angry and turning Nature against all humans. As a result, the Enchanted Forest is overwhelmed by an impenetrable magic fog for decades. Elsa's magical powers are what allow the forest to at last be accessed.

The name Northuldra is a reference to Nordic folklore. Nort refers to actual orientation, "the north" (*nord* in Norwegian), and *huldra* (or *hulder*) to a seductive female forest (or swamp) spirit. The name has roots in the Old Norse (*norrønt*) words *hylja*, or *skjule*, meaning "to hide" (*Bokmålsordboka*, 2020). So, this is a perfect name for people who are "hiding" in a northern magical forest. Then again, the names of the Northuldra tribe are not as closely connected to Sámi names as those of the Arendelle people to Nordic countries. In *Frozen II*, Yelena,

Ryder, and Iduna are not typical Sámi names. Yelena, who is the leader of the Northuldra people, is clearly a Russian name, meaning "bright" or "shining", with roots in the Greek name, Helene (Ἑλένη).

In creating the Northuldra tribe, Disney Studios met with several "far north" people from Nordic countries, to give the film some realism and accuracy. Peter Vel Vecho, one the film's producers, confirmed that the production team visited Norway, Finland, and Iceland on research trips and met with many people, including members of the Sámi community (Hazelton, 2019). This was a process similarly used for the movie *Moana* (2016), with Disney consulting cultural experts from the Pacific islands. These examples show how Disney Studios decided to be culturally sensible in their fantastical depictions of real-world indigenous people. This was likely done to avoid the stigma of cultural appropriation, which Disney has previously been accused of (see e.g. Yin, 2014).

When making the movies, Disney consulted six Sámi experts: Anne Lajla Utsi from the International Sami Film Institute, writers Anne Buljo and Piia Nuorgam, Professor Veli-Pekka Lehtola from the University of Oulu, reindeer-herding expert Cecilia Persson, and Christina Hætta, head of the cultural unit for the Sámi Council, because they wanted the worldbuilding to be fantastic but also culturally aware (Hazelton, 2019). Alongside their Sámi collaborators, the movie-makers fine-tuned details of the Norhuldra characters' clothing and characteristics to ensure that they maintained their fantastical identity while still being culturally respectful (Ibid.). The Northuldra also incorporate a way of life that is important to Sámi culture: a deep connection and understanding of nature.

The Ahtohallan

> Where the north wind meets the sea
> There's a river full of memory
> Sleep, my darling, safe and sound
> For in this river all is found.
>
> ...
>
> Where the north wind meets the sea
> There's a mother full of memory
> Come, my darling, homeward bound
> When all is lost, then all is found.
> (*Frozen II*, 2019)

In *Frozen II*, the song "Ahtohallan", written by Kristen Anderson-Lopez and Robert Lopez, is a lullaby that Queen Iduna sings to her daughters, Elsa and Anna. It describes Ahtohallan, the farthest northern part of the world: "a river full of memory", and "a mother full of memory". The song is also a key to understanding the ending scenes of the movie. "For in this river all is found": the river explains all secrets to Elsa when she finally calms the spirits and is able to reach the far north region.

Like so many elements of the *Frozen* movies, the name Ahtohallan draws inspiration from the Nordic countries, since it is clearly inspired by the Finnish language. In Finnish, "ahto" means something that is packed or stuffed, and "halla" means frost or ice-covered material. A more typical word for "ahtohalla" in Finnish would have been "ahtojää", which means pack-ice, a large mass of drifting ice. In the second movie, the Ahtohallan, a frozen river, looks quite like large quantities of drifting ice. In Finnish, Ahto is also a male first name and a modification of Ahti, a deity of water in Finnish pagan mythology. So, Ahti or Ahto are suitable for naming an icy place (or entity) located in the north, in the middle of the Dark Sea.

The Ahtohallan—perhaps representing a strong goddess of nature—is a frozen river, now a glacier, which has strong magical powers. In the song, it is ascribed with the feminine pronoun "she" and also described as "a mother". It becomes evident that reaching the Ahtohallan will reveal the secret which Elsa is trying to uncover. That is, the truth of her grandfather's wrongdoings to the Northuldra people and the secret of the "fifth element", along with the truth about herself, her past and her future. The river is in fact full of "memory"; "The water has memory" is repeated throughout the movie. With her powers, Elsa can give light to the truth, bring justice for the Northuldra tribe, and at the same time save her own people. The ending of *Frozen II* is in this way much more philosophical and sophisticated than the first movie. In *Frozen*, the main task is to end the eternal winter, which has been caused by Elsa herself, and reveal the true nature of the antagonist, Prince Hans. In the sequel, the tasks are many: the protagonists have to reveal the family secret, correct the errors made by their grandfather, calm the spirits of nature, bring freedom to the Northuldra, and restore harmony between humans and nature. They finally achieve all this thanks to Ahtohallan.

The whole journey in *Frozen II* begins with Elsa hearing an unrecognised song which nobody else hears, coming from somewhere far away. In other verses of the song, it is said that "She [Ahtohallan] will sing to those who hear/And in her song, all magic flows." This verse is an invitation to adventure, since it asks "Can you brave what you most fear?/Can you face what the river knows?". Elsa's decision to dare to face this challenge is made easy in the movie, because the elemental spirits attack Arendelle and Elsa and Anna must save the citizens of the kingdom, who are being exiled by the forces of nature.

The song is also a warning of what will happen if Elsa fails in her task. It says, "Dive down deep into her sound/But not too far, or you'll be drowned". Elsa is almost destroyed when she "dives too deep" into the memories. She herself is frozen inside Ahtohallan but, once again, she is saved by her sister Anna, possibly with the unwitting help of the Stone Giants, who destroy the dam angering the spirits.

In the end, Elsa becomes the fifth element, and the link between nature and the kingdom of Arendelle is restored. What Elsa does after this is not revealed, though she perhaps becomes a kind of steward of the north, acting in cooperation with Ahtohallan, the mother of memory, and the Northuldra tribe, who continue living in the Enchanted Forest.

Conclusions

The *Frozen* movies portray a high fantasy world with connections to the traditions of fairy stories and fantasy and, interestingly, to real-world milieus and cultures, and the geography of the Nordic countries (particularly Norway, but also to the lifestyle of the Sámi people). The lands, fjords, cities, and forests of the movies are fantastical and unreal in their beauty, though they are at the same time linked to our real world. The fairy tale city of Arendelle, being the central starting location of both movies, or the magical spirit Enchanted Forest, filled with spirits and inhabited by the people of Northuldra, and the majestical ice masses of Ahtohallan, are all part of the fantastical worldbuilding. They are new and magical locations, but are also comfortably familiar to us.

This fantasy world is created with levels of language, visuals, and elements of myths and fairy tales. Names and milieus resemble our own world, while the fictional world still remains a coherent and functional fantasy land. Hugely successful at the box-office, and influential to millions of children, the movies truly brought animated fantasy and Disney blockbusters into the 21st century.

References

Adventure by Disney, 2020. *Europe: Norway*. [online] Available at: <https://www.adventuresbydisney.com/europe/norway-vacation> [Accessed 22 January 2021].

Beckett, S. ed., 1999. *Transcending Boundaries. Writing for a Dual Audience of Children and Adults*. New York & London: Garland Publishing, Inc.

University of Bergen, 2021. *Bokmålsordboka*. [online] Available at: <https://ordbok.uib.no/perl/ordbok.cgi?OPP=+hulder&ant_bokmaal=5&ant_nynorsk=5&begge=+&ordbok=begge> [Accessed 22 January 2021].

Disney Wiki, 2013. *Arendelle*. [online] Available at: <https://disney.fandom.com/wiki/Arendelle> [Accessed 22 January 2021].

Frozen. 2013. [film.] Directed by Buck, C. & Lee, J. USA: Walt Disney Animation Studios.

Frozen II. 2019. [film.] Directed by Buck, C. & Lee, J. USA: Walt Disney Animation Studios.

Gunn, J., 2013. *Paratexts. Introduction to Science Fiction and Fantasy*. Plymouth: Scarecrow Press, Inc.

Hazelton, J., 2019. *How the 'Frozen II' filmmakers dealt with the pressure: We built it very honestly from character out*. [online] Available at: <https://www.screendaily.com/features/how-the-frozen-ii-filmmakers-dealt-with-the-pressure-we-built-it-very-honestly-from-character-out/5145596.article> [Accessed 22 January 2021].

Kowalski C. & Bhalla, R., 2018. Viewing the Disney Movie Frozen through a Psychodynamic Lens. *Journal of Medical Humanities*, Volume 39, pp.145–150.

Lisma, L. & Arianto, T., 2018. Child Literature Genre Formulation in Walt Disney Animation Movie. *Jurnal Basis*, v. 5, n 2, pp.11–20.

Konnikova M., 2014. *How 'Frozen' Took Over the World*. [online] Available at: <https://www.newyorker.com/science/maria-konnikova/how-frozen-took-over-the-world> [Accessed 22 January 2021].

Pulkkinen, R., 2011. Saamelaisten etninen usko. In Seurujärvi-Kari, I., Halinen, P. & Pulkkinen, R. eds.. *Saamelaistutkimus tänään*. Helsinki: SKS.

Porsanger, J., 2020. Aurinko. In *Saamelaiskulttuurin ensyklopedia/Sámi Kultuvrra diehtosátnegirji/Encyclopedia of Saami Culture*. [online] Available at: <ttps://saamelaisensyklopedia.fi/wiki/Aurinko> [Accessed 22 January 2021].

Rothenberg, R-E., 1983. The Orphan Archetype. *A Quaterly Journal of Jungian Thought*, Volume 14, Issue 2, pp.181–194.

Rubin, R., 2020. *'Frozen 2' Is Now the Highest-Grossing Animated Movie Ever*. [online]. Available at: <https://variety.com/2020/film/box-office/frozen-2-biggest-animated-movie-ever-disney-box-office-1203456758/> [Accessed 22 January 2021].

Solomon, C., 2013. *The Art of Frozen*. San Francisco: Chronicle Books.

Zipes J., 1983. *Fairy Tales and the Art of Subversion: The Classical Genre for Children and Process of Civilization*. Reprint 1991. New York: Routledge.

Zipes, J., 1994. *Fairy Tale as Myth. Myth as Fairy Tale*. Reprint 2013. Lexington: The University Press of Kentucky.

Tolkien, J.R.R., 1964. On Fairy-Stories. In Tolkien, J.: *Tree and Leaf.* Reprint 2001. London: HarperCollinsPublishers, pp.1–82.

Yin, J., 2014. Popular Culture and Public Imaginary: Disney Vs. Chinese Stories of Mulan. *Javnost – The Public, Journal of the European Institute for Communication and Culture*, Volume 18, Issue 1, pp.53–74.

Warner, M., 2014. *Once Upon a Time. A Short History of Fairy Tale*. Oxford: Oxford University Press.

Wolf, M.J.P., 2012. *Building Imaginary Worlds: The Theory and History of Subcreation*. London: Routledge.

Criminal Cityscapes: Christopher Nolan's Gotham

Rachel Jones

Abstract

Gotham City has been home to the comic book hero Batman since 1940 (Batman #4, Boltinoff, et al. 1940). Through various incarnations, the city has been portrayed as a gloomy, crime-ridden city of rich and poor, with a murky underbelly driven by greed and corruption. The forces of good are often outnumbered or inept, creating an opening for a law-breaking vigilante – Batman.

This article examines the Gotham created by director Christopher Nolan in his trilogy of films – *Batman Begins*, *The Dark Knight*, and *The Dark Knight Rises*. The paper's intention is to explore worldbuilding in Nolan's combination of architecture, cityscaping and cinematography and how it creates a Gotham where organised crime not only thrives, but is the natural state. In addition, the surroundings and streetscapes take the viewer into a dark, surreal vortex where the justice systems – most notably Arkham Asylum – encourage the mind to warp. In Nolan's version of Gotham, this is seen through home-grown villains – Scarecrow, The Joker and Harvey Dent, in addition to Gotham's Mob – and through Batman himself.

Background

Batman was created in 1939 by Bob Kane and Bill Finger (DC Comics, 1939a). 'Batman' is the alter-ego of orphaned billionaire Bruce Wayne. Gotham City has been his home since 1940 (Boltinoff, et al. 1940). After watching his parents be killed by Joe Chill as a boy (Detective Comics, 1939b), Bruce leaves Gotham to find direction in life before returning to fight crime in his home city.

Traditionally, Gotham has been portrayed as a gloomy, crime-ridden city, sharply divided into rich and poor. Like many large cities, it has a murky underbelly of organised crime as well as individuals with their own reasons to break the law.

Christopher Nolan's Gotham consists of a trilogy of films. The first, *Batman Begins* was released in 2005 and was followed by *The Dark Knight* in 2008. The trilogy concluded with *The Dark Knight Rises* in 2012. These films will be dealt with sequentially in this article.

The definition of criminal is challenging in this instance. When using the dictionary definition[1], it is impossible to argue that Batman himself is not a criminal. Rather, here 'criminal' refers to the organised 'mob'-style groups and those committing acts of street violence towards persons unknown to themselves. A way to analyse criminality in cities is to explore the cityscape. Traditionally, the cityscape explores an aerial or portraiture view of the city. This aspect will be explored in this piece, alongside a more nuanced understanding of the streets themselves – how they shape the city's criminality and murky surroundings.

The aim of this paper is to demonstrate how Christopher Nolan's use of real-world cityscapes, combined with set building and cinematography, brings about the desired effect of a city synonymous with crime. Before discussing the individual films, it is necessary to understand the geographical features of Nolan's Gotham. Its location, on the Atlantic coast of the USA, is similar to that of New York City and like NYC it consists of conjoined islands. Wayne Manor is situated in the Palisades of the city, separated from Gotham's main islands. The house is

---

1. A person who has committed a crime.

large and has a major underground cave network. The Gothic, wooden style, and colourful greenhouse contrasts strongly to the blackness of Gotham city. It appears to be a stronghold, but despite its sheer size, the manor and grounds have very little security, with a large gate serving as the only protection from Gotham's criminality. In *The Dark Knight Rises* (2012) cat-burglar Selina Kyle, also known as Catwoman, is able to steal from Bruce's safe. Wayne Tower, the headquarters of Wayne Enterprises is located in Midtown Gotham. This area is affluent, and criminality centres around business fraud, and the Wayne Enterprises board is not exempt. The docks are Downtown, where gang leaders fight over smuggling rights and deprived areas are home to petty criminals. Arkham Asylum is located on The Narrows, a small islet located between Midtown and Downtown. This gives it a sense of geographical isolation, essentially a nexus of the city's 'worst' inhabitants. In *Batman Begins* (2005), the audience is provided with an aerial view of Gotham (41m25s). The city scenery is drawn from NYC, Chicago, Detroit, and Tokyo, but the overall impression is best described as 'Manhattan but Spiky'. The city is densely populated with many skyscrapers and islands dividing it up geographically.

This paper will first explore academic theory associating city structures with crime. Then, each film – *Batman Begins*, *The Dark Knight*, and *The Dark Knight Rises* – will be examined sequentially before a conclusion is drawn about Nolan's success in creating a criminal cityscape.

Academic Background

The Law of Crime Concentration (LCC) argues that much urban crime is concentrated into specific small areas of the city. This phenomenon has been reported across the US and in the Japanese cities of Osaka and Tokyo (Amemiya & Ohyama, 2019; Braga & Clarke, 2014). Indeed, Weisburd (2015, p.143) reported that 50% of crime concentrates into 4.2% of Sacramento's and 6% of Cincinnati's streets. This trend is common and consistent in larger US cities, a category which Nolan's Gotham undoubtedly fits into. Many studies ponder why this concentration occurs. There are two key types of crime prevention methods explored in such studies: physical and formal measures, such as jails and the city's structure; and informal social measures, such as community ties.

Eck & Weisburd's (1995) book chapter *Crime Places in Crime Theory* explored the physical structure of the City and how it impacted crime levels. They identified four key factors affecting crime rates: facilities; site features; offender mobility; and offender target selection. Facilities – such as schools, pubs, churches, apartment buildings etc., can act to increase or decrease crime. Studies have shown that the presence of hotels and public housing projects can increase the crime rates in areas (pp.8-12). Site features – the idea of organising space to 'defend' against crime – can also reduce crime rates. These features can include surveillance cameras, guards or attendants and electronic beepers in libraries and are often put in place to prevent thefts. However, the study warns that drug users may prefer buildings with controlled access, so crime is not necessarily reduced by these measures (pp.13-16). Offender mobility recognises that offenders move around cities, and that certain crimes are committed closer or further away from the offender's home (pp.16-18). Finally, offender target selection is based on how, for example, burglars choose where to rob. Interviews with offenders suggest that burglars often look for cues that a place is a soft target (pp.18-19).

Martin, *et al.* (2016) conducted a study into how arrests and incarceration impact crime rates. Their study found that higher incarceration rates reduced the robbery and aggravated assault rates in US cities, but that it did not affect homicide rates. Their study also showed that more segregated areas had a higher robbery and homicide rate than socially mixed areas. Informal social control also plays a key role in community crime rates. This encompasses social ties, community organisations and collective efficacy. These factors act to improve social cohesion and provide expectations for behaviour in a community (Sampson, *et al.*, 1997). It is important that all of these factors are considered in crime reduction programmes, but for the purposes of this article, the physical structure of the City itself will be predominantly considered.

Batman Begins

The central plot of *Batman Begins* (Nolan, 2005) revolves around Bruce Wayne developing his Batman persona. Early on in the film (11 minutes), we see Bruce and his parents, Thomas and Martha, on the city's monorail system. The train meanders through a high-rise city, centred around Wayne Tower. The following conversation highlights the importance of the Wayne family to the city of Gotham:

> Bruce Wayne: *"Did you build this train dad?"*
> Thomas Wayne: *nods*. *"Gotham's been good to our family, but the city's been suffering. People less fortunate than us have been enduring very hard times. So we built a new, cheap, public transportation system to unite the city. And at the centre... Wayne Tower."*
> (*Batman Begins*, 11m09s).

By placing this scene at the beginning of the story, Nolan intrinsically links the Wayne family with the city he has created. The quote from Thomas Wayne also conveys to the audience that a large portion of Gotham's citizens are struggling, in stark contrast to the Waynes' extreme wealth.

In his youth, Bruce had a terrifying experience where he fell down a disused shaft, which leads to a major natural underground cave system in his family's estate. Although rescued by his father, he developed a fear of bats. In Nolan's twisted universe, Bruce trying to escape his fear leads to the most traumatic moment in his life, as his parents are murdered. The scene begins with the Waynes inside a theatre viewing Arrigo Boito's Mefistofele (Salazar, 2018). The theatre is grand, with black tie attire, and contains bright colours, such as the red chairs. The opera contains dark and bat-like monsters which upset Bruce, causing him to ask his father if they can leave. Upon leaving the venue, the Waynes move outside to a juxtaposed back alley. The scene has overflowing bins, graffiti and steam coming up from the sewers. The milieu is dark and sombre and foreshadows the darkness that is about to enter Bruce's life. The family are alone and confronted by the petty crook Joe Chill demanding money. Thomas hands over his wallet, but Martha hesitates when asked for her pearls. Chill panics and fires his pistol, killing both Thomas and Martha before running off. These scenes all use contrast to create a scary view of Gotham: happy Bruce playing in his garden is suddenly frightened by a fall; a bright red theatre contrasts with black monsters on the stage; and a bright grand theatre setting immediately switches to a grimy back alley. Here, Nolan shows that any environment in Gotham can instantly turn to a fearful and dangerous one.

Fourteen years later, Chill is in court, wishing to be granted release in exchange for information about the Gotham mob[2]. Bruce is in the courtroom, armed with a handgun, but before he can use it, Chill is gunned down. The courtroom scene shows just how lax security is in Nolan's Gotham. Multiple people are able to get weapons into the building and have the opportunity to use them. Following these events, Bruce feels there is nothing more for him in Gotham and leaves to find his way in life. He travels to Bhutan, training with the League of Shadows[3] and Ra's Al Ghul, before returning to Gotham seven years later. Gotham has changed for the worse. The monorail is shown again during Bruce's adult life. The rail, based on Chicago's L train, is now run down with underbuilt stations consisting of nothing but metal pipes. The once hopeful and inspiring transport system has now become frightening, as illustrated by a scene where Rachel Dawes, Bruce's childhood friend and Gotham City prosecutor, is ambushed at a station and the later scene where Batman confronts his former mentor, and *Batman Begins*'s main villain, Ra's Al Ghul. Nolan uses the monorail's decline to show the audience how Gotham has declined since Bruce's youth. This is cleverly contrasted with the earlier scene where Thomas tells Bruce of his philanthropy in building the monorail. Gotham no longer has wealthy 'white knights' who want to help the city. Instead, the wealthy have turned to corruption and crime.

As a result of these events, the Gotham we see for the remainder of the film is 21 years after the death of Thomas

---

[2]. The Gotham mob is dominated by the Falcone Crime Family. The Family is led by Carmine Falcone and pours drugs and crime into Gotham City. Many high-ranking officials are on his payroll, making the mob almost immune from prosecution.

[3]. A secret organisation whose purpose was to restore balance to the world by intervening in what they perceive as the most corrupt and decadent places in society

and Martha Wayne. The city's financial muscle has gone and Gotham has entered an economic depression. Organised crime has risen and a high percentage of the police and law officers have been bribed into silence. These streets of Gotham are central to creating the atmosphere of criminality and fear.

> Rachel Dawes: *"You care about justice? Look beyond your own pain, Bruce. This city is rotting. They talk about the depression as if it's history, and it's not. Things are worse than ever down here. Falcone floods our streets with crime and drugs, preying on the desperate, creating new Joe Chills every day."*
> (*Batman Begins*, 25m30s)

It is very often night-time during scenes. In addition, it is also often raining and the lighting levels are low, despite the many neon lights on shop windows. Much like the scene depicting the deaths of Thomas and Martha Wayne, the bins around the city are often overflowing and steam rises from most streets. Laundry is hung out to dry, strung across the tops of streets, picking up the grime and smells from the poor sewage system. In addition, there is a lot of street furniture on the roofs of buildings, such as air cons, pipes, and stairs, these allow Batman to jump about to evade police and Gotham's various villains. Tunnels also add darkness and mystery to the city, and provide Batman with things to smash. Watersides also play a significant role in atmosphere creation. Down by the harbourside, the underclass reside and large containers restrict vision, allowing Batman to hide and launch surprise attacks, adding to his mysterious character. The meticulous detail Nolan and his team have given to street furniture in Gotham not only make it seem like a real-world city that the audience can relate to, but also creates a world which can be criminalised. The darkness provides a mask of cover for assailants, overflowing bins indicate a lack of care from Gotham authorities which no doubt provides a sense of confidence to criminals and disenchanted residents – if authorities don't care about the city, why should they obey the law?

Across the city, bridges can be raised and lowered, isolating certain parts of the city, notably The Narrows, where Arkham Asylum is located. Arkham Asylum is a hospital intended for criminals with psychological problems. However, Arkham is viewed in a poor light and there is a widely held belief among the residents, including those in authority, that all criminals should be in jail:

> Rachel Dawes: *"You really think a man who butchers people for the mob doesn't belong in jail?"*
> Dr. Crane: *"Well, I would hardly have testified to that otherwise, would I?"*
> Rachel Dawes: *"This is the third of Carmine Falcone's thugs you've had declared insane and moved into your asylum."*
> Dr. Crane: *"The work offered by organised crime must have an attraction to the insane."*
> Rachel Dawes: *"Or the corrupt!"*
> (*Batman Begins*, 41m44s)

The treatment of the patients in the Asylum is reminiscent of the worst of Victorian Britain (See Saunders, 1988), with little focus on rehabilitation. During the film, we see psychiatric doctor, and villain Scarecrow, drugging members of the mob to get them into his care at Arkham, rather than subject them to Gotham's prison system.

The overall message of the film is that Gotham has gone severely downhill since the death of the Waynes – the catalysts for change. The city's financial muscle has vanished and

Gotham has entered a depression. This leaves a gap for their son, Bruce, to 'save' the city. Bruce sees his mission as one of continuing his family's legacy of looking after the city. He can do this financially, by winning back control of Wayne Enterprises and utilising the Wayne Foundation to enhance the city, but to stem the tide of crime he feels he must fight violence with violence, taking on the role of Batman. Christopher Nolan predominantly used grimy and unkempt streets to indicate a lack of care or authority in Gotham, providing a world where criminality is likely to thrive.

The Dark Knight

Thanks to the appearance of Batman, Gotham City has undergone something of a revival by the time *The Dark Knight* (Nolan, 2008) rolls around. Batman is revered as a saviour and numerous would-be heroes try to copy him. With the mob having lost much of their power, there is less corruption among those in authority, allowing the new District Attorney, Harvey Dent, to implement his plans to 'clean up' the city. This is shown cinematographically at the beginning of the film by scenes of shiny, sunlit skyscrapers, a lack of litter on the streets, open spaces with parks and trees and no more of the smoke which blighted the streets during *Batman Begins*. There is a transport network of yellow school buses and people feel confident to participate in public parades. The bank is a grand, New York style building with large glass windows. There is little evidence of security although guns are kept in the office, showing that bank robbery rates must have reduced since *Batman Begins*. However, the mob has not disappeared and the Falcone family have a new head – Salvatore Maroni. He has become involved with a crooked businessman from Hong Kong, Lau, who is also trying to infiltrate Wayne Industries. The two sides of Gotham are compared, with the meeting of the mobsters in smoky clubs reminiscent of the 'old' Gotham and the clean modernity of Wayne Tower. The Gotham Nolan immediately shows appears different to the grimy Gotham the audience sees in the majority of *Batman Begins*. Indeed, it is reminiscent of the Gotham that existed when Thomas Wayne was alive. The brightness creates a more optimistic and pleasing world for the audience. Inevitably however, crime still haunts Gotham City. In this film's opening scenes, Nolan utilised the indoor environment to illustrate the city's criminality. Due to Batman, criminals have had to move indoors and are not as brazen as they were in *Batman Begins*.

Despite this, the city's residents are still on edge. A quote from Rachel Dawes, the assistant district attorney, sums the city up nicely:

> Rachel Dawes: *"My boss has been missing for two days which in this town means that I should probably start by looking at the bottom of the river."*
> (*The Dark Knight*, 1h18m)

Furthermore, the visiting prima ballerina from the Russian ballet doesn't believe Gotham is a good place for raising children. Harvey Dent is well aware of the situation. His assistant Rachel Dawes claims:

> *"If you're not being shot at, you're not doing your job right."*
> (*The Dark Knight*, 00h15m)

With the mob effectively in the shadows of a lightened city, there presents a unique opportunity for The Joker to emerge in his own flamboyant style. One thing the Joker never lacks is colour, from his purple and green sartorial style to his bright and smudged makeup. Amidst the revived Gotham backdrop, The Joker is able to rob a bank in broad daylight, utilising his own network of lackeys. His men wear clown masks when they rob the city bank. This is reminiscent of the group Anonymous, who were culturally significant when *The Dark Knight* was released. The group are known for culture disruption actions and wearing Guy Fawkes masks (see, for example, Knappenberger, 2012), something which clearly inspires Nolan's Joker. At the end of *Batman Begins*, The Joker's introduction is teased through the discovery of his calling card – a Joker. At no point prior to this is he mentioned.

Thus, it can be deduced that he has emerged in response to Batman's crusade. Nolan's Joker varies from previous iterations. A key element of this is his unkemptness. His hair is messy and his makeup is smudged, contrasting with The Joker's usual immaculate style. This is a real Joker for a real Gotham. Christopher Nolan made a bold decision to make this Gotham universe like a city which exists in the real world. The character of the Joker fits in with this – his roots clearly show under his green hair dye, he often has white paint on his hands. his makeup looks like a man who has been out all day, often further smudging or leaving gaps in its coverage, much like the degradation of a typical urbanite's makeup. The character both fits into the world and creates the world, as any person can replicate his look, but Nolan's Gotham gives him the unique opportunity to succeed with his outrageous plans.

As a result of new threats emerging, Dent is not a fan of Batman, believing he can clean up the city without the aid of a masked hero who acts outside of the law. Dent encourages the opinion that he is the city's 'White Knight' and blames the rise of unconventional criminals on Batman. In addition, when

Jim Gordon's wife believes her husband has been killed by The Joker's goons, she accuses Batman of being responsible:

Barbara Gordon: *"You brought this craziness on us"*
(*The Dark Knight*, 1h15m)

This indicates a turning against Batman in the city, with people now seeing him as a troublemaker, rather than a hero.

Unlike Batman, Catwoman and Two-Face, the Joker does not have a name and the viewer does not get to see 'behind the mask'. The Joker proves to be an unreliable narrator, giving varying accounts of his life story to different people, which may or may not be true. He has a deep knowledge of the city, giving reason to believe he was brought up there. He also has numerous resources and criminal connections. As the Joker gains ground, a surreal darker side of the city becomes more evident. The Joker's attacks become more erratic, most notably using a bazooka in a car chase and begging Batman to hit him with his motorbike. Alongside this, the darkness of Nolan's world intensifies. A pivotal scene in the film is when Harvey Dent and Rachel Dawes are kidnapped by the Joker's associates and tied to dynamite beside oil cylinders. The Joker gives the wrong address for where each is being held, fooling Batman, who arrives to save Rachel, but instead finds Dent, whose face is severely burnt during the rescue (Downey 2018). Police Commissioner Gordon is too late to rescue Rachel, who dies in a timed explosion. This scene is incredibly dark, both in terms of its emotional and physical value. Both Rachel and Harvey are left in complete darkness, not fully understanding their surroundings or what is going on.

After a visit by the Joker to where Dent is recovering in hospital, Dent blames Gordon for Rachel's death. His mind is as twisted as his features and he seeks revenge. With Harvey escaping, the Joker blows up the spotless, modern hospital, likely setting Gotham's development back years. Fear again reigns in the city. In a panic the citizens try to flee. Unfortunately for them, city leaders and planners haven't made any contingency plans for such a mass exodus and the streets are soon gridlocked. Most of the confusion is confined to the poorer area around the Narrows and two boats are used to evacuate the area: one with citizens and another with the inmates of Arkham Asylum. The boats have been sabotaged by the Joker and are primed to explode. The people on board have to choose to detonate the other boat and save themselves, or else both will be blown up after a set time. Typically these are both overloaded, with people in close proximity in confined spaces. Emotions are already high, but this compressing of characters elevates the tension. Hearteningly, neither of the boats decide to trigger the ignition, and the Joker's plan fails, as he is unable to blow both up.

The streets of Chicago were chosen for many of the chase and stunt scenes in the film. During these scenes, the city was again shown as being wet and smoky with low lighting when bad things happen. Continued police brutality is evident when The Joker is arrested and questioned in prison and the holding cells are overcrowded.

With the mob, Lau and the Joker taken care of, Batman has to confront Harvey Dent, who has taken on the alter-ego of Two-Face, deciding fates by the toss of a coin. Gotham's White Knight has become corrupt and instead of being a prominent figurehead of a clean, sunny city, he now moves in the darkness among the back streets and alleys. Dent threatens Gordon and his family and is killed when Batman comes to the rescue. Gordon and Batman fear what will happen if the citizens of Gotham find out that Dent was no longer a hero. Thus, they make up a story blaming Batman and he is forced to go into exile, allowing Dent's legacy of a cleaner, crime-free city to continue. Nolan's world shifted dramatically these events. Gotham's citizens no longer worship Batman, instead viewing him as the cause of the city's troubles. In this way, Nolan's world no longer needs Batman, rather ironically, since that is exactly what it was created for. This is a bold move for Nolan, as Gotham has always been synonymous with Batman. This move makes Nolan's Gotham different from any previous iteration.

The Dark Knight Rises

Nolan set the scene in the previous films, and in *The Dark Knight Rises* (Nolan, 2012) it is possible to analyse how criminals are able to abuse the city's facilities. The story picks up eight years after the death of Harvey Dent, who has been hailed as a hero and the Dent Act has been passed, allowing more criminals to be held, clearing Gotham of crime. The elite citizens of the city celebrate 'Harvey Dent Day' at Wayne Manor. A key person missing from these events is Bruce Wayne, who has become a recluse and moves with the aid of a walking stick. Outwardly the city has regenerated, with rebuilt buildings and more open spaces allowing sunlight to brighten the city, although there are still less pleasant industrial zones and homeless people living in tunnels. Minor criminals, such as the cat-burglar Catwoman, are still active.

Having explored much of the city in previous films, it would seem challenging to further expand the world in the third chapter of the trilogy. However, Nolan manages it, introducing the city's extensive sewer system as a new milieu. The sewer system consists of a complex labyrinth of tunnels and it is from there that the masked criminal Bane and his men plan an attack on the city. Bane has control of Wayne Enterprises' nuclear power head and he has kidnapped a nuclear physicist to transform it into a weapon to use on Gotham. It is underground, in the dark, where much of the action in the film takes place. Batman is lured to Bane's lair by Catwoman and Bane defeats him, breaking Batman's back and sending him to the dungeon where Bane was once a prisoner. During the fight, Bane utters:

> *"Peace has cost you your strength, victory has defeated you"*
> (*The Dark Knight Rises*, 1hr09m)

Essentially, Batman is a victim of his own success – having no-one to fight has weakened him and made him obsolete. This mirrors what the Joker said – that Batman created him and will not defeat his enemies because battling them is fun to him. Whilst the Waynes have a huge role in creating, and later contributing to the decline of, Gotham's cityscape, Bruce's alter-ego Batman creates and contributes to the eccentric criminals inhabiting Gotham. No matter what Bruce Wayne does, Gotham is affected, for better or worse.

During the film's climax, Gotham's numerous bridges take on a major role, trapping the residents, who are prevented from fleeing by the military, who are threatening to blow up the bridges. The city planners of Gotham clearly never envisioned a situation where the urban design would be used to attack the city. This is a clever use of the world by Nolan as its design is used as a weapon, meaning the entire world becomes dangerous and threatening.

The Dark Knight Rises also provides us with an insight into female criminals in Gotham. Selina Kyle and her roommate

Jen[4] are shown to be living in a run-down apartment, despite stealing high-value items. Bruce comments on this during a scene where he dances with Selina:

> *"You came here from your walk-up in Old Town. A modest place for a master jewel thief. Which means that either you're saving for retirement or you're in deep with the wrong people."* (*The Dark Knight Rises*, 32m04s)

Their apartment is accentuated with yellow lighting. Much like Gotham's nefarious streets, the apartment is cramped and full of clutter. Furthermore, Catwoman is able to assault a police officer whilst being interrogated in an airport, utilising her female charm and manipulating the officers' assumptions about women. When apprehended, Kyle is placed in a male prison, as she has repeatedly broken out of the female prison. We also see the rise of Talia Al Ghul, using the alias Miranda Tate, from Bruce's co-investor to holding a position on the Wayne Enterprises board. Throughout all of this, Talia is infiltrating the company with the aim of destroying Gotham. These characters add a different element to crime in Gotham. Their actions are completed inside, not on the streets where Batman traditionally fights crime.

Behind the Scenes

The UK DVD trilogy[5] is accompanied by seven hours of bonus footage. These provide a further insight into how the criminal cityscape was created. In the footage, Nolan explains that he wanted Gotham to be "an exaggerated contemporary New

---
4. Rumoured to be a version of Holly Robinson, Catwoman's comic book sidekick.
5. Barcode 5051892132411.

York", but he also wanted it to be recognisable as Gotham City. This exaggeration is mirrored by Paul Franklin, the Visual Effects Supervisor, who describes it as a "monstrously overwhelming place". This creates a distorted and disorienting atmosphere. To create these visions, photography of Chicago and a studio set for Gotham were used to create digital cityscapes. Nolan and his crew spent a great deal of time and effort building Gotham inside a massive warehouse, setting up the lighting, street scenes, etc.

Christopher Nolan is renowned as being a master of detail, crafting many side-notes which were not mentioned in the films. For example, he creates a Gotham City News channel with an item showing how Dent won the DA election with 68% of the vote and quoting Commissioner Loeb as saying how "Gotham surveillance cameras were a major reason for [the] drop in crime." In another episode, there is a profile of Bruce Wayne, the "Eternal Playboy". The report tells us about how Bruce's family helped construct Gotham's financial district, as well as the monorail. At the heart of Gotham's economic core is Wayne Enterprises, which specialises in technological developments. We also learn that Martha Wayne was a community activist and part-time teacher in a dangerous district of the city. These additions further flesh out the universe and show an immense attention to detail in its creation.

Reflection

Reflecting on LCC, it is possible that parts of Gotham are indeed pleasant to live in and we only properly explore the concentrated areas of crime. Such areas likely include the bright high-rise district of the city. However, Gotham appears to meander from one disaster to another. It lacks collective efficacy, requiring more of a community effort to reduce crime, rather than hiding inwardly, in fear. Gotham's law enforcement is formal in nature, but there is an argument that more local, informal control among groups of residents might be more effective. This is demonstrated when Commissioner Gordon, almost in the comic book tradition, commits his entire force to entering the sewage system, where they fall into Bane's trap. One local officer, Robin 'John' Blake, takes some initiative, trying to save the children of the city and ultimately helping Batman to save Gotham once again.

Eck & Weisburd's notion of offender mobility could well explain crime hotspots in Gotham. In *Batman Begins*, the monorail has clearly become rundown. The monorail would provide an easy route for offenders and, thus, there is likely a crime hotspot along it. The monorail itself is an excellent signifier for Gotham's decline. When the Waynes are alive, the monorail is new and smart, but following their deaths it becomes run-down and stations become hotspots for the mob.

Gotham has also synonymously come to be associated with Batman and conjures up images of dark, narrow streets with open access to sewers. Though Nolan's Gotham moved into the twenty-first century, the picture remains. The plot in all three movies revolves around 'saving' Gotham and its citizens, with Batman defending it, despite also abandoning it, first as a young man and later as a recluse. Batman not only wants to save the people of Gotham – in several cases he has pre-knowledge of plans to destroy the city, allowing for evacuation before these plans are set in motions – he wants to save the city itself.

The cityscape creates a sense of foreboding, with its 'spiky' appearance, dark, grimy and wet streets and isolating nature due to the high number of movable bridges. In creating a criminal world, Nolan has been successful. In essence, it screams of criminality. Nolan and his team created a fully realised urban space and fully utilised it across the trilogy. From the illicit trade at the harbour, to Bruce's manor on the Palisades and Bane's usage of the bridge system as a tool for attacking Gotham, all areas were effective in creating an atmosphere of darkness, criminality and, ultimately, heroism, as Batman emerges from the shadows to save his city.

References

Amemiya, M., & Ohyama, T., 2019. Toward a test of the "Law of Crime Concentration" in Japanese cities: a geographical crime analysis in Tokyo and Osaka. *Crime Science*, 8(11), pp.1–6.

Boltinoff, H., Finger, B., & Gordon, C., 1940. *Batman #4*, United States: DC Comics.

Braga, A.A., & Clarke, R.V., 2014. Explaining High-Risk Concentrations of Crime in the City: Social Disorganization, Crime Opportunities, and Important Next Steps. *Journal of Research in Crime and Delinquency*, 51(4), pp.480–498.

DC Comics, 1939a. *Detective Comics #27*, United States: DC Comics.
—, 1939b. *Detective Comics #33*, United States: DC Comics.

Downey, M., 2018. *The easy choice made impossible: Rachel Dawes should have survived The Dark Knight*. [online] Available at: <https://www.polygon.com/2018/7/18/17578680/the-dark-knight-batman-rachel-death-scene> [Accessed 15 November 2020]

Eck, J.E., & Weisburd, D.L., 1995. Crime Places in Crime Theory. In J.E. Eck & D.L. Weisburd, eds., *Crime and Place, Crime Prevention Studies*, 4th edition. Monsey: Criminal Justice Press, pp.1–33.

Knappenberger, B., 2012. *We Are Legion*. United States: FilmBuff.

Martin, A., Wright, E.M., & Steiner, B., 2016. Formal controls, neighborhood disadvantage, and violent crime in U.S. cities: Examining (un)intended consequences. *Journal of Criminal Justice*, 44, pp.58–65.

Nolan, C., 2005. *Batman Begins*. Warner Bros.
—, 2008. *The Dark Knight*. Warner Bros.
—, 2012. *The Dark Knight Rises*. Warner Bros.

Salazar, D., 2018. *Opera Meets Film: How 'Mefistofele' Scene Contextualizes Christopher Nolan's 'Dark Knight' Trilogy as Faustian Myth*. [online] Available at: <https://operawire.com/opera-meets-film-how-mefistofele-scene-contextualizes-christopher-nolans-dark-knight-trilogy-as-faustian-myth/> [Accessed 10 September 2020].

Sampson, R.J., Raudenbush, S.W., & Earls, F., 1997. Neighborhoods and Violent Crime: A Multilevel Study of Collective Efficacy. *Science*, 277(5328), pp.918–924.

Saunders, J.F., 1988. Criminal insanity in 19th century asylums. *The Royal Society of Medicine*, 81(February 1988), pp.73–75.

Weisburd, D., 2015. The Law of Crime Concentration and The Criminology of Place. *Criminology*, 53(2), pp.133–157.

Contributors by Paper

No elf is an island. Understanding worldbuilding through system thinking
Ricardo Victoria Uribe. Mexican writer, lives in Toluca, State of Mexico. Studied Industrial Design at the School of Architecture & Design of the Autonomous University of the State of Mexico, where he currently works as lecturer focused on sustainability. Holds a Ph.D. in Design from Loughborough University. He is one of the founding members of Inklings Press, an indie publisher of short stories anthologies of science fiction, fantasy, alternate history, and horror. His short story "Twilight of the Mesozoic Moon", co-written with author and fellow Inklings Press co-founder Brent A. Harris, was nominated for the 2016 Sidewise Awards for Alternate History. His horror story "Bone Peyote" was featured at The Wicked Library Podcast. Other short stories have been featured in anthologies by indie outfits such as Inklings Press, Rivenstone Press and Aradia Publishing.

In August of 2019 his debut science fantasy novel *Tempest Blades: the Withered King* was published by Shadow Dragon Press, an imprint of Artemesia Publishing, LLC. It was listed as finalist for the 2020 New Mexico-Arizona Book Awards. The sequel *Tempest Blades: The Cursed Titans* will be published in August of 2021.

Martha Elba González Alcaraz. Mexican writer, lives in Zapopan, Jalisco. Studied Pharmacobiologist Chemistry at the School of Chemistry of the Autonomous University of the State of Mexico. Holds an MBA from the University of the Valley of Mexico. She has published two stories with Inklings Press as one of the first authors featured in their anthologies. While she works in the medical device industry, she also works as freelancer proofreader and translator. She is currently working on a short story collection.

Fragmented Worlds: Glimpse Morsels for the Imagination
Allen Stroud (Ph.D) is a university lecturer and Science Fiction, Fantasy and Horror writer, best known for his work on the computer games *Elite Dangerous* by Frontier Developments and Phoenix Point by Snapshot Games. He was the 2017-2018 and chair of Fantasycon, the annual convention of the British Fantasy Society, which hosts the British Fantasy Awards.
He is also the current Chair of the British Science Fiction Association. His portal fantasy novel *The Forever Man* was published by Luna Press Publishing in 2017.
His military science fiction novel, *Fearless* is being published by Flame Tree Press in September 2020.

Relationships with the Land in Fantasy and Science Fiction: Landscape as Identity, Mentor, or Antagonist
Sarah McPherson is a Sheffield-based writer and poet who loves folk tales, speculative fiction, and finding the weird in the everyday. Her work has been published in Ellipsis Zine, Splonk, STORGY, Emerge Literary Journal, The Cabinet of Heed, and elsewhere, and she has been long/shortlisted in competitions including Writers' HQ, Reflex Fiction and Cranked Anvil. She has an MA in Landscape Archaeology from the University of Sheffield, and is fascinated by mythology, history, and the natural landscape, and how they impact us and our relationships.

Freedom Is Slavery: The sociopolitical implications of worldbuilding in speculative fiction
Sébastien Doubinsky is a bilingual French dystopian writer and academic. He is the author, among others, of *The Babylonian Trilogy*, *The Song Of Synth*, *White City* and *Missing Signal*. His latest novel, *Missing Signal*, published by Meerkat Press, won the Bronze Foreword Reviews Award in the sci-fi category. His new novel, *The Invisible*, a dystopian noir, was published in August 2020, also through Meerkat Press. He currently teaches French literature, culture and history at the university of Aarhus, in Denmark.

Worldbuilding with Sex and Gender
Cheryl Morgan is a writer, editor, publisher and critic. She owns Wizard's Tower Press and has written for a variety of outlets including *Locus*, *The SFWA Bulletin*, *SFX*, *Clarkesworld*, *Strange Horizons*, *Holdfast Magazine* and *SF Signal*. She is, to her knowledge, the first openly transgender person to have won a Hugo Award.
In addition to her science fiction interests she also co-hosts a women's interest show in Ujima Radio and lectures widely on transgender history.

Town Planning in Viriconium: M John Harrison and Worldbuilding
Peter Garrett is an independent writer and humanitarian physician, and a graduate of the Lancaster University School of Creative Writing. He has been shortlisted and longlisted, respectively, for the Fish Flash Fiction and Fish Short Story awards, and his novelette *Final Diagnosis* (Luna Press Publishing) was nominated for the 2017 BSFA awards. For most of the time he lives in the countryside of the northwest of Ireland in a big old house with his wife and far too many animals.

Worldbuilding in Ngũgĩ wa Thiong'o's *The Perfect Nine: The Epic of Gĩkũyũ and Mũmbi*
Dr Eugen Bacon is African Australian, a computer scientist mentally re-engineered into creative writing. She's the author of *Claiming T-Mo* (Meerkat Press), *Road to Woop Woop & Other Stories* (Meerkat Press), *Ivory's Story* (NewCon Press) and *Writing Speculative Fiction* (Red Globe Press, Macmillan). Her work has won, been shortlisted, longlisted or commended in national and international awards, including the BSFA Awards, Bridport Prize, Copyright Agency Prize, Australian Shadows Awards, Ditmar Awards and Nommo Award for Speculative Fiction by Africans. Eugen is a recipient of the Katharine Susannah Prichard (KSP) Emerging Writer-in-Residence 2020. Her newest collection *Danged Black Thing* is out with Transit Lounge Publishing in November 2021.

Environmental Change as Catalyst for Worldbuilding in Ursula K. Le Guin's *Always Coming Home*

Octavia Cade is a New Zealand writer. She's had over 40 short stories published, in venues such as *Clarkesworld*, *Asimov's*, and *Strange Horizons*. A non-fiction collection on food and horror was published in 2017, and several papers on speculative fiction have been published in *Scandinavica*, *Horror Studies*, and the *BFS Journal*. She's won three Sir Julius Vogel awards, and has been shortlisted for a BSFA award. She attended Clarion West 2016.

Tolkien: When worlds are built within dreams

Enrico Spadaro is an Italian researcher with a passion for J.R.R. Tolkien. He started studying foreign languages and literatures at university. In 2014 he obtained a master in Literary Translation at the University of Pisa, in Tuscany. In his final dissertation Tolkien's tale *The Lost Road* was translated into Italian. He continued his research on Tolkien in France at Aix-Marseille Université and he defended his Ph.D thesis in November 2018: the title of the thesis is *La Littérature-Monde de J.R.R. Tolkien: pertinence, discours et modernité d'une oeuvre originale*, under the supervision of Pr. Joanny Moulin. He worked as a teacher in French middle and high school, and he gave some lectures of English and Italian at the university.

In summer 2019, he applied for the postdoc Teach@Tübingen fellowship at the University of Tübingen in Germany,which started in October 2020, with a duration of six months.

He took part in congresses about literature and fiction: in May 2017, he communicated at the meeting *Chemins de Traverse en fiction*, held in Paris at *École Normale Supérieure*. In August 2019, he attended "Tolkien 2019" in Birmingham, where he presented a paper entitled *To the origins of Fairy-tales*.

He is currently a member of the Italian group "Tolkieniani Italiani", that analyses and comments Tolkien's themes and works.

Patrick McGrath's Ghastly New York: The Perfect Decaying Cityscape for Restless Minds

Tatiana Fajardo is a Ph.D candidate at the University of the Basque Country researching Patrick McGrath's Gothic fiction. She completed her MLitt in the Gothic Imagination at the University of Stirling (Scotland), writing her dissertation on the employment of art and science in Patrick McGrath's novels. She began a blog in which she discusses her literary, cinematic and artistic interests in 2017. Passionate about Gothic literature, her blog post on Dracula's "Bloofer Lady" was published by Sheffield University. Some of her essays have been translated into Swedish and published by Rickard Berghorn, both on his online *Weird Webzine* and in his printed books *Studier I vart* (2018) and *Två fantasistycken* (2018). These include her analyses of Ridley Scott's *Blade Runner* (1982) and Ingmar Bergman's *Hour of the Wolf* (1968). She presented her study of the employment of Romantic poets in the TV series *Penny Dreadful* (2014-2016) at the IGA conference in Manchester in August 2018. In 2019, her article "The Bloodlust of Elizabeth Báthory: From the Brothers Grimm to American Horror Story" was included in the book *A Shadow Within: Evil in Fantasy and Science Fiction* (Luna Press Publishing). In 2020, her article "Falling in Love with an Artificial Being: E. T. A Hoffmann's The Sandman in relation to Philip K. Dick's Do Androids Dream of Electric Sheep? and the Blade Runner film series" was included in *Ties that Bind: Love in Fantasy and Science Fiction* (Luna Press Publishing). Tatiana combines her work as a researcher with her job as an English teacher in Spain.

The Book of Copper and the Anvil of Death: William Blake's Gothic Creation Myth

Claire Burgess is a Californian currently living in Rome. She has a B.A. in Art History from U.C. Berkeley and an M.A. in English Literature from Ca' Foscari University in Venice, where she wrote her dissertation on Gothic worldbuilding in the art and poetry of William Blake. She is currently the managing editor for an online Classics magazine, though her presiding interests are all things dark and Romantic. She is currently working on a high fantasy novel with elements of both. When she's not reading or writing, she can be found exploring the Italian countryside with her dog, Willow.

Canada's Fantasy Worlds: Exploring Worldbuilding in Urban Fantasy
Ellen Forget is a PhD student at University of Toronto in the Faculty of Information and Book History and Print Culture program, and she is a graduate of the Master of Publishing program at Simon Fraser University. Her research interests include speculative fiction, digital readership, and small press publishing. She also works as a freelance fiction editor specializing in science fiction and fantasy.

Above the Level of the Everyday: The Estranging and Familiar Worlds of Simon Stålenhag
Kevin Cooney is an expert in human ecology and graduate of Harvard University. An independent scholar, freelance writer, and ecocritic, his interest in environmental issues and associated subjects embedded in uncanny and estrangement stories of horror and science fiction propels his work and analysis.

The Nordic Countries in Worldbuilding: *Frozen* and *Frozen II*
Dr. Jyrki Korpua, Ph.D in Literary studies. Lecturer and researcher at the University of Oulu, Finland. His research interests include fantasy and science fiction, worldbuilding, classical mythologies, J. R. R. Tolkien's fiction, Kalevala, Bible studies, utopian and dystopian fiction, graphic novels, and game studies. At the moment

he is working on the international Tove Jansson Companion project funded by Kone Foundation.

Criminal Cityscapes: Christopher Nolan's Gotham
Rachel Jones considers herself a global citizen. Brought up in South Wales, she completed an MA in Geography at the University of Aberdeen, before moving to Finland to complete a Master's degree in Urban Studies and Planning at Helsinki University. She is a sci-fi movie fanatic and in her spare time has acquired a Lego Star Wars Empire which she regularly likes to modify. Although she is generally on team Superman, Rachel has branched out to explore the world of Batman in her first Luna Press Call for Papers. Rachel also enjoys travelling, recently visiting Singapore, Estonia and Latvia and hopes to continue to do so in the future. She is currently studying Politics remotely at Brunel University London.

www.ingramcontent.com/pod-product-compliance
Lightning Source LLC
Chambersburg PA
CBHW071726080526
44588CB00013B/1918